Electoral Protest and Democracy in the Developing World

This book shows that the third wave of democracy has been accompanied by a worldwide wave of opposition-initiated, election-related protests. Such electoral protests result from a failure on the part of incumbent and opposition elites in the developing world to negotiate acceptable terms of electoral conduct, and their consequences for democracy depend on the context in which they occur. Where election boycotts receive international support, they increase the probability of democratic reform, but where support is primarily domestic, there is a higher probability of authoritarian backsliding. Based on an extensive new data set covering nearly 30 years of electoral protest and election-related reform in the developing world, this book explores the causes of different types of electoral protest and their consequences for democracy. Statistical analysis and case studies provide readers with a complete picture of the dynamics surrounding developing-world elections, protest, and democratization.

Emily Beaulieu is an Assistant Professor of Political Science at the University of Kentucky. She has published work on political economy and democracy in outlets such as *International Organization* and *Comparative Political Studies*. She is working on several projects on political violence and recently received a TESS grant to study the impact of partisanship and political polarization on perceptions of election fraud. She received her PhD from the University of California, San Diego.

D1610638

Electoral Protest and Democracy in the Developing World

EMILY BEAULIEU
University of Kentucky

CAMBRIDGE
UNIVERSITY PRESS

CAMBRIDGE
UNIVERSITY PRESS

32 Avenue of the Americas, New York, NY 10013-2473, USA

Cambridge University Press is part of the University of Cambridge.

It furthers the University's mission by disseminating knowledge in the pursuit of education, learning, and research at the highest international levels of excellence.

www.cambridge.org
Information on this title: www.cambridge.org/9781107612273

© Emily Beaulieu 2014

First published 2014

Printed in the United States of America

A catalog record for this publication is available from the British Library.

Library of Congress Cataloging in Publication Data
Beaulieu, Emily.
Electoral protest and democracy in the developing world / Emily Beaulieu.
  pages cm
Includes bibliographical references and index.
ISBN 978-1-107-03968-1 (hardback)
ISBN 978-1-107-61227-3 (paperback)
1. Elections – Developing countries. 2. Contested elections – Developing countries.
3. Democracy – Developing countries. I. Title.
JF60.B43 2014
324.9172′4–dc23   2013030371

ISBN 978-1-107-03968-1 Hardback
ISBN 978-1-107-61227-3 Paperback

For my mother, Ann Beaulieu, with love and gratitude

Contents

Tables and Figures

Tables

Figures

Acknowledgments

I am aware that most who write acknowledgments leave mention of loved ones until the end, but after the years that I have spent working on this project, I can scarcely imagine any people who are owed gratitude more immediately than those closest to me, who have endured the most.

My younger son, Layne Casimer Beaulieu, was born in the thick of this project and is now four years old. The time I took off after Layne Casey's birth allowed me the freedom to really think about my project, and it was then that the pieces finally fell into place. I used his first birthday as my deadline for finishing a draft of the manuscript and only missed it by a week (the deadline, not his birthday).

My first-born son, Herschleb Ewan, has pushed me beyond my limits since he was born six years ago. Becoming a parent woke me from years of uncritically accepting the life laid out before me and led me through an intense (and not always pleasant) period of working to craft a life that I could claim as my own. I have grown as a person because of Ewan, and this book is a reflection of the personal work that he inspired.

I owe an incredible debt of gratitude to my husband Matt who packed up four surfboards, moved to the middle of the country, changed careers, and took care of our children and home when I simply could not find the time to do it. His support through the process of writing this book and his support for my professional endeavors more generally have made it possible for me to have both a career and a family that I am proud of.

My parents have also supported me through this project in every conceivable way. My father was my first academic advisor. His example as a professor led me into academia, but his guidance and support allowed me to carve my own path in this profession. My mother's unflagging assistance has been absolutely invaluable. I dedicate this book to her because she was the first woman to show me, through her example, that I could follow my aspirations wherever in the world they might take me and still value home and hearth. In the past several years, she has been an integral part of that home and hearth, coming to help with kids and household for periods of time that really should have tested the bonds of family. When people ask how I have been able to "do it all," I have to confess that, for me at least, the secret to raising two small children while writing a book was to have my mother move in with me.

The friends and colleagues who provided support and guidance over the course of this project constitute an embarrassment of riches. Nicole Howell Neubert is my closest friend; from more than 3,000 miles away, she lived through the process of writing this book with me and always knew exactly what I needed to hear. Carew Boulding went through every aspect of this process with me – the manuscript writing, the child rearing, and the constant struggle to balance the two. Irfan Nooruddin provided support, guidance, and friendship beyond the call of duty. I am grateful to Susan Hyde for blazing this trail ahead of me and for being such a steadfast source of friendship and encouragement. Kathleen Cunningham has provided unflagging support for all adventures academic and personal since graduate school. For 12 years now, Gary Cox has been a source of profound intellectual inspiration for me, a wonderful mentor, collaborator, and friend. I gravitated toward Gary early in grad school, out of a desire to learn how to think about politics the way he did, and it was one of the smartest decisions I've ever made.

Thanks to those whose intellectual insights, professional influence, and assistance over the past 15 years contributed to this project directly and indirectly: Joel Migdal, Matthew Sparke, Liz Gerber, Neal Beck, Clark Gibson, Alan Houston, Mat McCubbins, Matt Shugart, Karen Feree, Peter Gourevitch, David Lake, Karre Strom, Michael Bratton, Melody Ellis-Valdini, David Fisk, Nathan Monroe, Kelly Wurtz, Laura Wimberley, Henry Kim, Nathan Batto, Royce Carroll, Nick Weller, Megan Reif, Sharon Lean, Alberto Simpser, Jacqueline Jimenz-Polanco, Manuel Sepulveda, Teofilo "Quico" Tabar, Hatuey DesCamps, Andre Blais, Ellen Lust, Paul Gronke, Jose Cheibub, Frederic Schaffer, Thad Hall, Fabrice Lehoucq, Robert Bates, Anne Edwards, Tracy Campbell, Karen Mingst, Mark Peffley, Steve Voss, Sophia Wallace, Trace Lasley, Whitney Turientine, Jonathan Powell, Ernie Yanerella, Judith Hanson Lasater, Jan Byrd, Denise Combs, Tiffany Barnes, Yu Ouyang, and Charles Dainoff.

Funding for dissertation improvement from the National Science Foundation (SES-0418519) allowed me to conduct dissertation fieldwork in Jamaica and the Dominican Republic. Some of that research appears in this book, and what I learned about electoral protest and democratic reform in those countries shaped my thinking about this topic, long before I knew the story I wanted to tell.

My thanks, also, to Lewis Bateman and two anonymous reviewers for Cambridge University Press, who saw the potential in this project and gave me invaluable suggestions for how to realize it.

Finally, I wish to acknowledge two people whom I have never met, but whose sage wisdom regarding the craft of writing saw me through the process. Margaret Levi wrote in the Acknowledgments of *Consent, Dissent, and Patriotism* that her colleague, Donald Mathews, had assured her most books take seven years to write. This acknowledgment gave me great comfort in the seventh year of this project, and I hope that reiterating it here might provide someone else comfort in the future. Anne Lamott's book *Bird by Bird* offered the fundamental truth that if you are writing just to get published you will never be successful. You must write because you have something to say. This book represents what I have to say. It would not have been possible without the support and assistance of everyone I have just mentioned here. Nevertheless, the work – mistakes and all – is mine alone.

1

Introduction

On June 15, 2009, a week after opposition candidate Mir Hussein Moussavi lost the Iranian presidential election, the streets of the capital city of Tehran were overflowing with hundreds of thousands of protesters. On losing, Moussavi characterized the victory of the incumbent, Mahmoud Ahmadinejad, as a "coup," made a public plea to the international community not to accept the results of the election (Borger and Black 2009), and called on his supporters to rally in protest (Worth and Fathi 2009). Iranian citizens responded with the largest public demonstrations in Iran since the Islamic Revolution in 1979 (Fathi 2009).

Not more than six months later, the main opposition candidate for president in Afghanistan, Abdollah Abdollah, boycotted that country's runoff election. When his opponent – the current Afghan president, Hamid Karzai – reluctantly consented to a runoff (after asserting he had won the first round of voting outright), Abdollah, who had finished second, demanded a number of administrative changes to prevent a recurrence of electoral malfeasance, which he alleged had occurred during the first round of the election. Formal talks ensued, with no small amount of U.S. diplomatic involvement, but ultimately this effort did not persuade Karzai to meet Abdollah's demands. The challenger subsequently boycotted the election, refusing to participate in the second round of voting (Filkins and Rubin 2009).

Although these examples unfolded within the distinctive contexts of Iranian and Afghan politics, they highlight patterns of electoral competition and protest that occur across much of the developing world. This book examines the increasingly common trend of opposition-initiated, election-related protest – henceforth termed "electoral protest." Figure 1.1 shows rates of electoral protest from the late 1970s to 2006. Most important to note in this graph is the dramatic increase in the rate of electoral protest since 1991. The total number of elections that have been followed by mass demonstrations has more

1

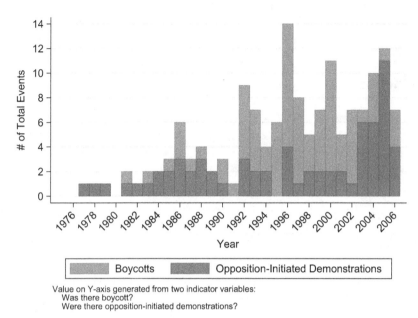

FIGURE 1.1. Annual Count of Electoral Protests (1975–2006).

than tripled since the end of the Cold War, and the rate of election boycotts has increased ninefold since the 1980s, with 74 boycotts occurring in 46 different developing countries from 1990 to 2006. Why are members of the political opposition who enjoy the legal right to participate in elections increasingly taking politics beyond the bounds of electoral competition to challenge incumbents with extra-institutional displays of protest? Moreover, what do these contentious choices mean for the future of democracy in the countries where they occur?

In this book, I argue that electoral protests occur when the process of ongoing negotiation between opposition and incumbent actors breaks down. What such protests ultimately mean for democracy will depend on the nature of the attention and support that they generate from either domestic or international actors. Characterizing electoral protest as a breakdown in negotiation is not meant to suggest that incumbent and opposition leaders are everywhere engaged in acts of explicit bargaining, as they were in Afghanistan, but it does capture the dynamics of politics in the developing world where political actors cannot rely on strong, stable institutions for purposes of coordination. In the absence of institutional constraints on behavior, the electoral process requires actors to engage in more strategic interactions over questions that have long been settled in wealthy democracies. For example, opposition parties boycotted the 1992 presidential election in Burkina Faso on the grounds that the incumbent president was misusing state funds to guarantee an electoral victory.[1] Although such occurrences are common in developing countries around the world, most wealthy countries have well-established rules regarding campaign spending and finance that candidates are not likely to spend their campaign period disputing. Not only do the political consequences of lower levels of economic development necessitate strategic negotiation between incumbent and opposition elites but they also introduce conditions that may cause these negotiations to break down in protest. Incumbent responses to these protests show evidence of further strategic considerations not only of domestic political competition but also of international pressure for democracy. Where the incumbent can enact reforms to appease international actors without the fear of certain electoral defeat, electoral protests can have positive consequences for democracy.

This book is about the dynamics of democratization in the developing world, and this introductory chapter explains what I mean by "dynamics," "democratization," and "developing world," in that order. The three sections covering these terms introduce key concepts for the book and identify this volume's contributions to existing debates in the literature. This study emphasizes an incremental approach to questions of democratic reform and democratization as a way to provide insight into the mechanisms by which full-fledged regime transitions occur. Furthermore, thinking about how elections work differently in developing countries offers an opportunity to gain insights that may be overlooked given the focus on the authoritarian regime type that has dominated the comparative literature recently. Finally, this book offers a new way to think about the causes and consequences of protest – one in which the strategic considerations of the object of protest are as important as the considerations of the protesters themselves.

DYNAMICS: ELITE NEGOTIATIONS, CAUSES, AND CONSEQUENCES OF ELECTORAL PROTEST

Electoral protest represents a breakdown in the process of ongoing negotiation between incumbent and opposition elites. In this way, it may have more in common with a strike, where negotiations between management and labor have failed, than with other coordinated demonstrations where protest is used to communicate demands to the government. As with strikes, the key actors involved in an electoral protest could find a way to resolve their dispute without fighting and, if they did so, would likely be better off compared with the expected outcome of a fight. Inefficient conflict in the form of electoral protest occurs when incumbent and opposition elites fail to resolve disputes about the conduct of the election in which they are competing. At its core, then, this is a

---

[1] Burkina Faso election victory hollow. Reuters. *The Globe and Mail* (Canada), December 2, 1991.

book about how political actors who are not technically on the same "team" still attempt to coordinate their behavior in the context of elections when they cannot rely on strong institutions.

Of particular importance in this theory is the substance of negotiations between incumbent and opposition elites. In the case of strikes, labor seeks higher wages and often more favorable rules, such as union shops, that will improve current working conditions and allow labor to continue to bargain successfully in the future. In the case of electoral protests, the opposition seeks improved access to high office and often more even-handed electoral rules, such as reform of the electoral administration, which will allow it to compete more successfully in the future. Given these goals, the immediate concern of the opposition is the extent to which the incumbent manipulates the election. The notion of electoral manipulation, based on Beaulieu and Hyde (2009), refers to any and all activities the incumbent could undertake to bias the election in his or her favor, encompassing both actions that are technically legal and those that meet the definition of fraud as an illegal and secret attempt to bias the elections in one's favor.[2] If the incumbent and the opposition are successful in reaching agreement, then the incumbent will only engage in an agreed-on level of manipulation and the opposition will participate in the election and accept the outcome. Over the course of the election, however, if the incumbent and the opposition cannot agree on an appropriate level of incumbent manipulation, the opposition may retaliate by staging an electoral protest.

The theory in this book considers two of the standard conditions that cause negotiation, or bargaining, to fail: (1) misrepresentation of private information and (2) commitment problems (cf. Fearon 1995). Actors can have problems reaching a satisfactory agreement if either side misrepresents private information relevant to the negotiations, such as their relative fighting power or the terms of agreement they would find acceptable. Here, the information the incumbent possesses, and may misrepresent, is the extent of manipulation he or she will commit. The opposition may also possess private information about how much manipulation it is willing to tolerate and how much trouble it will cause by waging a protest. If either side has private information and misrepresents it, the other actor may make an inefficient choice that can cause negotiations to break down and lead to protest. If the incumbent believes the opposition is misrepresenting how much manipulation it will tolerate, for example, the incumbent may miscalculate and engage in too much manipulation, causing the opposition to protest.

Even in situations with full information, credibility problems may cause negotiations to break down. Thus, electoral protest may also occur if one side or the other cannot credibly honor the understanding under which both sides are operating. The incumbent may promise a certain level of manipulation, for example, but ultimately may not be able to resist manipulating the elections

---

[2] This definition of fraud comes from Lehoucq (2003).

more than agreed. In other circumstances the opposition may not be able to resist protesting, even if the incumbent has held up his or her end of the bargain.

One needs nothing more than this basic assumption – electoral protests erupt when the government and opposition fail to agree about the acceptable conduct of the election – to conclude that electoral protests should be endemic features in the process of either creating or throttling electoral democracy in the developing world today. The question of whether such protest ultimately helps or hinders democratization can only be answered by considering the strategic choices made by the incumbent in response to protest. If electoral protest receives enough support from domestic or international actors, the incumbent should be motivated to respond, if only to avoid continued conflict and a possible violent removal from office. Because future electoral fortunes are at stake, domestic support for protest produces a dilemma for the incumbent: how to respond without implementing the type of genuine democratic reforms that may reduce his or her chances of winning future elections. Where there is domestic support for protest, the incumbent's preferred strategy is to try to appear responsive while making cosmetic changes that will allow for future electoral manipulation. International support for electoral protest, by contrast, can motivate the incumbent to reform the process without the same threat of electoral defeat and may induce him or her to enact reforms of a more genuinely democratic nature.

Causes of Protest

By considering the object of protest as a strategic actor and emphasizing the coordination (or lack thereof) between potential protesters and the state,[3] this theory of electoral protest represents a major departure from work to date on protest. Previous approaches to explaining protest have emphasized the ways in which protest can result from strategic considerations on the part of protesters. Theories of protest based on resource mobilization argue that certain actors facilitate coordination with the goal of encouraging individuals to protest (McCarthy and Zald 1977; Chong 1991). Inspired by the protest activities of the 1960s and '70s in the United States, much of this work focused on how professional movement organizations could overcome collective action problems and thereby induce individual participation. With informational theories, by contrast, the assumption is that individuals will want to protest when they know others are also likely to do so (Lohmann 1994; Tucker 2007). For both resource mobilization and informational theories, then, protest organizers and protesters themselves can be strategic actors who consider the actions of other potential protesters.

---

[3] Given the context of electoral competition, my theory characterizes the actor in control of the government as the "incumbent." In this section, however, I use the concept of the "state" to connect my work with the more common state–society dichotomy established in much of the work on protest and social movements.

In the political opportunity structure framework, protesters' strategic considerations are directed at the state. This approach claims that protesters are most interested in acting when they believe that the government is likely to be receptive to their demands (Eisinger 1973; McAdam 1982; Tarrow 1989). In a similar vein, the statist approach suggests that the regime itself can encourage or discourage protest simply by virtue of its own strength (Migdal 1974; Skocpol 1979). In contrast to the political opportunity structure orientation, in which certain institutional arrangements or types of leadership suggest a greater openness to protester demands, the statist approach focuses more on the coercive capabilities of the state: Strong states discourage protest, whereas weak states invite it by signaling vulnerability. What none of these theories emphasize, however, is how protest might result from the strategic interactions *between* protesters and the state.

My theory argues that electoral protest occurs when incumbent and opposition actors fail to coordinate on an agreement that would prevent protest by the opposition. Similar to the statist and political opportunity structure approaches, then, this theory emphasizes the role that the state plays in either encouraging or discouraging protest. Unlike these approaches, however, in my theory the state is not an exogenous structural force to contend with, but an incumbent actor pursuing specific goals in anticipation of opposition behavior. In Skocpol's seminal *States and Social Revolutions* (1979), for example, the state does not increase or decrease its coercive capacity with an eye to encouraging or discouraging rebellion. Instead, state strength is largely dependent on the fortunes of war, and ultimately these fortunes determine whether challenges to the state will succeed. By contrast, my theory argues that state actors are strategic, seeking to coordinate with would-be challengers in ways that will defuse their challenge. Protest results when those coordination efforts fail.[4]

The fact that my theory treats protest as a preventable occurrence rather than an inevitability underscores the centrality of elections to this theory. It may not make sense to think of protest as being preventable via bargaining between the state and would-be protesters on every conceivable issue, because the current regime cannot realistically identify and prevent all potential protest. Elections, however, come with formal organizational structures, easily identified actors, and scheduled public events. Thus, even where electoral institutions are arguably weak, as in most of the cases examined in this book, they still provide a focal point (some minimal organizational framework) and identified actors, such that the state could be expected to attempt to prevent protest in a way that might not be realistic in response to other groups considering protest.

---

[4] Works such as DeNardo (1985) recognize strategic interaction between protesters and the state, but only at the point where the state is responding to protest, not working to prevent it. Therefore I discuss this work in the next section, "Consequences of Protest."

After elite negotiations have broken down, my understanding of protest is consistent with the resource mobilization approach, which posits that professionalized entrepreneurs work to mobilize individual protesters. Electoral protests, however, engender the emergence of a different type of entrepreneur: the professional politician. In most work from the resource mobilization approach, entrepreneurs are committed activists whose focus is organizing and mobilizing to protest for a particular cause; however, in the cases of electoral protest I examine, protest is mobilized by individuals whose skills and objectives, first and foremost, are oriented toward competing in and winning elections. The most direct analog in my theory to the resource mobilization perspective would be those pro-democracy activists who organize protests against electoral manipulation. Instead, in the cases I examine, it is individuals who have invested time and resources competing for political office who turn their attention to protest activities. Thus, my work shows that politicians are capable of adopting the resource mobilization approach to encourage protest as a *strategy of electoral politics*, when attempts to avoid conflict through negotiation have failed.

Yet it may be easier for the politicians in question to mobilize protest because of their association with parties in the opposition, which means they often have a background as movement activists. Morgan Tsvangirai, for example, was prime minister of Zimbabwe from 2009 and is also a long-time political rival of President Robert Mugabe. He joined Mugabe's ZANU-PF party when Zimbabwe became independent from the United Kingdom in 1980, but was also very active in the Mine Workers' Unions, having been a miner since 1974. Tsvangirai became secretary general of Zimbabwe's umbrella trade union organization in 1989 and led the unions to form an opposition political party to the ruling ZANU-PF. Given his experience in union leadership, it is not surprising that, as leader of and candidate for the opposition Movement for Democratic Change, Tsvangirai would be capable of organizing electoral protest – a capacity that he demonstrated when he organized an election boycott in 2008.

Consequences of Protest

The specific consequence investigated in this study is whether electoral protest motivates incumbents to enact democratic reforms. A number of authors have addressed questions of democratic reform – considering either reforms *from* authoritarianism *to* democracy (Przeworski 1991, Bratton and van de Walle 1997, Acemoglu and Robinson 2006) or additional reforms of ostensibly democratic institutions (Cox 1987, Boix 1999, Lehoucq and Molina 2002, Przeworski 2009). If we take seriously Tilly's (2004) assertion that "(d)emocratization does not mean arrival at full definitive democratic functioning," (14) then we should consider all democratic reforms when thinking about the consequences of protest, whether they originate from authoritarian or democratic regimes. In fact, regardless of regime type, explanations of democratic reform share many common elements such as greater institutional constraints on political actors and expanded opportunities for participation in political processes.

In this book, I investigate the extent to which reforms undertaken by the incumbent in response to protest are actually democratic or might be attempts to appear responsive while continuing to secure incumbent advantage. Schaffer (2008, 2) claims that many governments in developing countries have enacted "clean election reform" in response to domestic and/or international pressure for more democratic elections; however, such reforms can actually end up having negative consequences for democracy (sometimes intentional, sometimes accidental). For example, clean election reforms can result in vote depression (which frequently affects one group of voters disproportionately), the proliferation of cheating, or general voter alienation (6–8). Particularly where a reform's partisan roots can be identified, Schaffer argues that some of these negative consequences may, in fact, be intentional (13). According to my theory, intentional attempts to use clean election reforms to partisan ends should be more likely when support for protest is largely domestic.

In my theory, incumbents respond to electoral protest based on the information that the protest reveals. Like Przeworski (1991), I characterize democratic reform as coming about through a process of elite negotiation (or "bargaining") and international pressure in the shadow of a violent recourse to protest. Election-related reforms are a way for incumbents to indicate responsiveness to electoral protests and may provide them a way to enhance the credibility of future commitments.

At the same time that incumbents are responding to threat, however, they are also trying to maintain as much of an advantage in the electoral arena as possible – in this way, the theory is also similar to those emphasizing that elites engage in reform to maintain or enhance an electoral advantage. For example, early theories of protest consequences argued that greater popular support makes the government more likely to reform (DeNardo 1985). By contrast, more recent theories emphasize the incumbent's strategic considerations when responding to protest. Bratton and van de Walle (1997) tell a story of incumbent elites instituting reforms in the face of mounting domestic pressure, when international and economic forces had constrained their range of viable responses, while still attempting to manipulate those reforms to their advantage. They show how leaders in Africa often turned to political concessions, such as amnesty for political opposition, relaxations on press restrictions, and reforms within the ruling party, with continued protest yielding constitutional reforms (108–11). Throughout their description and the explanation that follows, however, Bratton and van de Walle are careful to qualify these incumbent responses as representing an attempt on the part of the incumbent to "limit the extent of the power they would have to surrender" (163).

Acemoglu and Robinson (2006) formalize much of Bratton and van de Walle's account in a dynamic model of democratization. Here, as with previous explanations, incumbents respond to a threat of punishment by citizens by instituting immediate economic concessions, repression, or an institutional change (usually democratization). The authors argue that incumbent elites can find ways to stay in power through a mix of repression and side payments, but that they cannot improve their credibility without democratic reforms (203). Przeworski (2009) tests and finds support for Acemoglu and Robinson's model in the historical extension of male suffrage. Here again, incumbent reform efforts are characterized as responding to threat – specifically increased protest activity.

Other authors have found evidence of incumbents undertaking electoral reforms to enhance their credibility for future negotiations regarding elections while also attempting to maintain a competitive advantage. Lehoucq and Molina (2002) describe a situation of gradual reform in Costa Rica where political elites began to feel their electoral fortunes would be in jeopardy if they continued to engage in election manipulation; therefore they introduced meaningful reforms to reduce future manipulation. Building on the logic of reform outlined by Geddes (1994), they note that most reforms occurred when political forces were more or less balanced. In periods where one party dominated, that dominant party tended to kill reform legislation (11). In Renwick's (2010) work on electoral system reform, elites initiate reform when they anticipate electoral advantages from doing so or when they must respond to citizen pressure, which is mobilized by minority or opposition politicians who favor reform (211).

Finally, my theory has the potential to help us understand how some democratic improvements can emerge even in the absence of electoral protest. Lindberg (2006a) argues that electoral protests in Africa are futile because they do not produce democratization and that democratic improvements are actually more likely to occur when the opposition participates in the election. Based on the theory presented here, it might not be so much that these elections in which the opposition participates are leading to democratic improvements as much as they represent situations in which incumbent and opposition actors were able to successfully reach pre-election bargains that increased electoral fairness and resulted in opposition participation.

DEMOCRATIZATION

In addition to encouraging readers to think about protest in terms of elite negotiation, this study speaks to a specific debate within the comparative literature concerning elections and democratization. In 1991, Huntington heralded elections not only as hallmarks of democracy but also as the "death of dictatorship" (175). My book joins many other attempts to critically evaluate this claim that elections can be used as a tool to cultivate democracy, and not simply as an indicator of where democracy has taken root. Unlike those works that argue either for or against Huntington's claim, I assert that contextual factors will determine the ultimate, democratizing effect of elections: Where electoral protests receive domestic support, they are likely to push leaders toward reforms that are more cosmetic than actually effective, whereas international support for electoral protest can help make democratic reforms more likely. Because of my interest in these electoral dynamics, I emphasize a more incremental approach to democratization. Rather than focusing directly on regime transitions, I examine protest events before and after elections and subsequent incumbent responses for evidence of incremental democratic improvements.

In response to Huntington's (1991) assertion, some scholars have argued that undemocratic elections do not foster democratization, but instead function as a means for authoritarian regimes to maintain power (Posusney 2002, Gandhi and Przeworski 2007), distribute patronage (Lust-Okar 2005, Magaloni 2008, Blaydes 2010), or demonstrate the strength of the state (Wedeen 2008, Simpser 2013).[5] Others contend that even undemocratic elections provide real opportunities for liberalization (Howard and Roessler 2006, Pop-Eleches and Robertson 2009), leadership change (Marinov 2006, Tucker 2007, Greene 2007), and improved civil rights (Lindberg 2006a). One final possibility, offered by Brownlee (2007), is that elections in authoritarian regimes simply do not matter: They merely reflect underlying processes that generate cohesion or splits among elites within the regime that ultimately determine regime survival and prospects for democracy.

My argument is that even elections in which incumbents engage in excessive manipulation can have positive consequences for democratization, but that the specific consequences of a given election depend on two factors: (1) whether the opposition chooses to protest before or after the election and (2) what kind of support the protest receives. These factors determine whether elections are followed by democratic reforms or by authoritarian intransigence or backsliding. To understand these dynamics of electoral protest and reform, I argue that we must conceive of democratization as an incremental process and not one that is necessarily linear nor is always accompanied by full-fledged regime transition. I further argue that regime transition should not be assumed to be the endpoint of the democratization process. This approach of skeptical incrementalism follows from Tilly (2004) who, in his study of the history of contentious politics and democratization in Britain and France, describes democracy as "protected consultation" between state and society and counts as democratization "any substantial move toward higher levels of protected consultation" (14). Similarly, Acemoglu and Robinson (2006) argue that it may be more useful to consider "various shades of democracy" when thinking about democratization; they are interested in "all movements in the direction of increased democracy" (17).

---

[5] See Brownlee (2011) for a discussion of these explanations in the context of elections in the Arab world.

Examining the United States using this frame of reference illustrates what it means to consider democratization in terms of incremental change. There is general agreement that the United States, circa 2014, is a democracy; there is substantially less agreement about the point in history when it became a democracy. Did the United States become a democracy in 1783 with the conclusion of the Revolutionary War and independence from the British Crown? Was it with the emancipation of slaves and the end of the U.S. Civil War in the mid-1860s that the United States became democratic? Those who favor a narrower emphasis on free and fair elections might cite 1892, the first national election in which every state used the Australian ballot, as the start of democracy in the United States.[6] Still others would date the true birth of U.S. democracy to the ratification of the Nineteenth Amendment in 1920, which finally extended the right to vote to women, or perhaps to the conclusion of the civil rights movement in the 1960s, when the Voting Rights Act of 1965 addressed the de facto disenfranchisement of African Americans. Although claiming any one of these historical markers as the point in time when the United States "became" a democracy is likely to invite disagreement, it would be willfully perverse to dispute that each of these changes made politics in the United States *more democratic*.

This incremental, marginal approach to the question of democratization puts my work at odds with those who seek to make precise claims about countries' post-transition status; that is, to definitively answer the question, "Is this country a democracy or isn't it?" Many scholars have based their classifications on Huntington's (1991) metric of "competitive elections" (6).[7] Even when these regime classifications have come under criticism for their narrow emphasis on elections (Schmitter and Karl 1991; Carothers 2002), the proposed solution is typically a different definition of democracy, not a criticism of the attempt to parse democratic regimes from nondemocracies. And although my incremental approach to questions of democracy and democratization will not satisfy those who are interested in political revolution or regime survival, nor those who desire some means of identifying "true" democracies, it has the advantage of allowing us to understand better the dynamic processes associated with

---

[6] The term "Australian ballot" refers to ballots that are produced by the government and cast by individuals in secret, so named because the method was first used in Australia in the mid-1800s. This method of balloting has become the norm in electoral democracies today because it is thought to minimize opportunities for groups or individuals to exert undue influence compared to earlier methods such as oral ballot (voice vote) or parties printing their own ballots, both of which required voters to declare their preference publicly. The Australian ballot was first adopted in 1888 by the state of Massachusetts and the city of Louisville, but Kentucky was the final state to adopt the ballot in 1891.

[7] Bratton and van de Walle (1997), for example, designate African countries as "democracies" based on this criterion, and Przeworski et al. (2000) argue that one observable implication of competitive elections should be alternation in power, which is the primary indicator they use to classify regimes as democracies or autocracies.

electoral protest and democratization. For example, the incremental approach provides interesting contrasts with Howard and Roessler's (2006) work on "liberalizing electoral outcomes" (LEOs).

Liberalizing Electoral Outcomes

Howard and Roessler (2006) make important claims about the democratizing potential of elections, focusing on the circumstances under which elections lead to democratic improvements in regimes they label as "competitive authoritarian" (CA).[8] Although this book paints a similar picture of electoral events and democratic improvements to that of Howard and Roessler, I draw different conclusions. Whereas they find the participation of opposition coalitions to be key to effecting LEOs, and general protest in the population to be incidental to that process, I find opposition protest to be central to bringing about democratic reforms, which are highly correlated with their LEOs.

According to the original data I have collected for this project, rates of electoral protest and democratic reform in Howard and Roessler's sample of 50 elections are similar to rates of protest and reform in all developing-world elections in the same time period (1990–2002). Electoral protests occur in 15% of the 425 developing-world elections I observed during this time period compared with an incidence of 13% in the CA elections studied by Howard and Roessler. Furthermore, 17% of elections in both samples were followed by democratic reform. Comparing the list of LEO and non-LEO elections provided by Howard and Roessler to my own data on protest and reforms reveals a high rate of correlation between LEOs and subsequent democratic reform. Elections that experience LEOs are followed by democratic reforms at a rate of 40%, compared to just 7% of elections that do not experience LEOs.

Howard and Roessler's measure of protest does not directly identify strategic decisions on the part of the opposition to engage in electoral protest – they use the Banks data measure of antigovernment protest averaged for election year as compared to the previous year. Just as Howard and Roessler find a weak relationship between protest and LEOs, an initial analysis of my electoral protest data and LEOs reveals no relationship. Electoral protests occur in 13% of LEO elections and 13% of non-LEO elections. A closer inspection, however, reveal that 25% of LEO elections were preceded by electoral protest in a previous election occurring no longer than four years previously. By contrast only 5% of non-LEO elections were preceded by electoral protest in the previous four years. Taken together then, 38% of LEOs involved electoral protest, either in the election in question or in the previous election, compared to just 18% of non-LEO elections.

---

[8] Howard and Roessler classify regimes as "competitive authoritarian" based on Freedom House and Polity scores, excluding countries that receive the highest and lowest scores on each of these indices. Using these criteria, they identify 50 elections in CA regimes for the period 1990–2002.

Considered in light of other incremental approaches to democratization, this book provides clear evidence that strategic decisions on the part of the opposition can affect whether elections will help a country democratize. The 20% increase in the rate of electoral protest preceding LEO elections compared to non-LEO elections suggests that electoral protest must be taken seriously as another strategic opposition decision that can have a more positive impact on democratization than Howard and Roessler's conclusions regarding general protest and LEOs would suggest.

A final point of comparison returns to the book's theoretical underpinnings. Where Howard and Roessler see democratic (or liberalizing) outcomes as dependent only on the opposition's strategic decisions, I argue that the consequences of these elections for democracy depend not only on the opposition's strategic choices but also on the strategic responses of the incumbent. Given the small number of observations, the lack of consideration of conditional relationships in Howard and Roessler's article is understandable – but democratic consequences in my model are conditional on the incumbent's reactions, which we should expect to be strategic. Another factor that my theory has identified as critical for democratization is increasing international support for democratic elections. Thus this book provides a more nuanced picture of opposition and incumbent electoral strategies in the face of mounting international expectations and their ultimate consequences for democracy than previous work on the consequences of elections and protest.

THE DEVELOPING WORLD

A mix of empirical observation and theoretical insight informs my decision to focus on countries with lower levels of economic development. Observing electoral protests around the world from 1975 to 2006, the clearest pattern that emerged for me was that rich democracies did not, for the most part, experience electoral protest. With the exception of two minor boycotts by Basque parties in Spain, for example, no political parties in rich, established democracies staged election boycotts during this time period. Furthermore, my empirical observations revealed that elements of elite negotiation around elections and problems of information and credibility were prevalent in countries with lower levels of economic development. Finally, my attempts to match instances of electoral protest to any regime typology required either the exclusion of a number of instances of protest or the conceptual stretching of regime type, such that the concept of "electoral protest" itself became a defining characteristic of regime type rather than something to explain. As a result, I chose to focus this book on common conditions created by low levels of economic development, rather than emphasizing regime typology. Empirical regularities associated with electoral protest yield the first developing-world scope condition (international pressure to democratize); two more scope conditions (a resource imbalance between incumbent and opposition actors and low-information environments) provide further theoretical insights.

Empirical Regularities

This book focuses on elections that have occurred since the start of the third wave of democratization – from 1975 to 2006 – with particular attention paid to the impact of shifting foreign policy orientations among major world powers with the end of the Cold War.[9] Developing countries have been holding elections since the late 1980s/early 1990s in a global context of increased international pressure for democracy. Clearly, this global shift is not sufficient to explain electoral protest and democratization, because we see great variation across countries in this regard. But this increased international attention does help us understand why so many developing countries are holding elections and why electoral protest can sometimes lead to democratic reforms.

Consistent with much current scholarship on democratization, I posit that a shift in the international balance of pressure for democratization occurred as the European Union (EU) expanded and that this shift intensified when the Berlin Wall fell in 1989 and the Soviet Union dissolved in 1991.[10] The pressure toward freer and fairer elections, emanating from multiple sources in the West and amplified by the lack of antidemocratic counterbalance once provided by the Soviet Union, hit the developing world and was largely exogenous to the domestic politics of any single developing country. This book explores the domestic political dynamics that have resulted from this global shift.

Figure 1.2 shows both a global increase in the number of developing countries holding elections and a concurrent increase in the number of countries inviting international election observers to these elections for the period under study in this book, 1975–2006.[11] These coinciding trends highlight the international dimension of democratization since the end of the Cold War – indicated by the two vertical lines at 1989 and 1991. The vertical line at 1989 shows the year the Berlin Wall was brought down, and the vertical line at 1991 indicates the year that the Soviet Union officially dissolved – both events seen as central to the end of the Cold War (cf. Levitsky and Way 2010). The figure shows a marked proliferation in multiparty electoral activity after these temporal benchmarks.[12] Although no year prior to 1989 saw even 20 multiparty

---

[9] Samuel Huntington popularized the notion that countries do not democratize in isolation. Instead, we find "waves" of democratization. Huntington (1991) identified temporal groupings: a first, very long wave from 1828 to 1926; a shorter second wave following World War II; and the third wave beginning in Portugal in 1974. Some have characterized post–Cold War democratization as a "fourth wave" (Levitsky and Way 2010, 20).

[10] For examples of this approach see Hyde (2011), and Levitsky and Way (2010).

[11] Data on election observation are from Hyde (2011) and Hyde and Marinov (2012).

[12] In this book, the term "multiparty" refers to any election where parties in addition to the party of the incumbent government are legally permitted to compete.

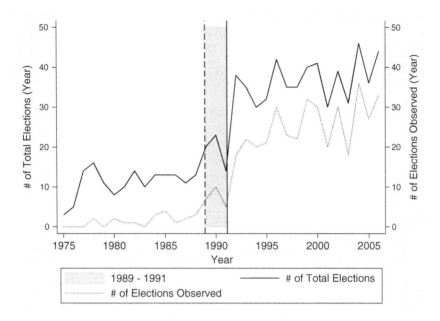

FIGURE 1.2. Multiparty Elections and International Election Observation (1975–2006).

elections in the developing world, only one year since 1989 has registered fewer than that number.

In addition to the notable spike in electoral activity since 1991, the regional clustering of electoral activity suggests an international dimension to contemporary electoral politics in the developing world. Whereas all of Latin America began holding elections before the end of the Cold War, most of sub-Saharan Africa and Central Asia have been slower to do so – adopting multiparty elections later or holding fewer elections overall. The timing of the first elections in the former communist countries of Eastern Europe clearly reflects the collapse of the former Soviet Union, and electoral activity in these countries since the early 1990s has been prolific. Recent research has suggested that these regional patterns are due to the proximity of influential western powers: the United States, in the case of Latin America, and the EU for Eastern Europe (Levitsky and Way 2010).[13]

Theoretical Relevance

The empirical patterns of elections and electoral protest described in the previous section suggest the current theoretical relevance of international pressure

---

[13] Levitsky and Way (2010) make an important argument about the positive role of international influences on democratization in a number of specific developing countries, which I address in greater detail later.

for democracy in the developing world. In explaining the role of contentious politics in British and French democratization, Tilly (2004, 9) stresses that "prevailing circumstances for democratization vary significantly from era to era and region to region as functions of previous histories, international environments, available models of political organization and predominant patterns of social relations." In the developing world today, two additional features are particularly relevant to questions of electoral protest and democratization: an imbalance of resources among political elites and low-information environments. It may be tempting to characterize these conditions as a consequence of regime type, such as competitive authoritarianism, but in later chapters I argue that both the imbalance of resources and the presence of low-information environments are better understood as consequences of low levels of economic development.

Low levels of economic development give the government disproportionate economic power and provide incumbent political actors who control the government disproportionate access to resources compared to the opposition. This resource imbalance helps us understand why the theory presented here allows the incumbent the option to manipulate elections while the opposition must resort to protest to challenge the regime. Because whoever wins elections controls the state, the disparity in resources between incumbent and the opposition can also make it difficult for either actor to credibly commit to an agreement regarding electoral manipulation and peaceful participation. Incumbents will have a harder time adhering to agreed-on manipulation where electoral defeat means the loss of access to state resources, and opposition actors will have a harder time accepting election outcomes as they come closer to gaining control of the state and its resources.

Examples of resource inequality abound in the developing world. Magaloni (2006) and Greene (2007) provide abundant evidence of extreme resource imbalance in Mexico during the reign of the Institutional Revolutionary Party (PRI) from 1929 to 2000. Much of the PRI's advantage came down to a simple ability to outspend opposition parties on campaign activities. Lust-Okar (2005) and Posusney (2005) show how another kind of resource imbalance – the ability to change formal institutions, particularly as they pertain to the legality of certain opposition parties or groups – allows incumbents in the Middle East to dominate the opposition. In the African context, Barkan (2000, 229) argues that a predominantly agrarian society with no independent, industry-based middle class provides those who control the state with an unfair advantage. In particular, though not necessarily unique to the African context, African incumbent politicians often enjoy: the ability to determine election dates, monopolize broadcast media, strengthen party organization, and employ more sophisticated campaign advisors/tactics (234).

Several authors offer a similar theoretical logic, in which resource inequality leads to difficulty making credible commitments. Flores and Nooruddin (2012) argue that in some electoral settings, such as postconflict environments, actors in the dominant majority will have problems credibly committing not to expropriate resources from the minority. In their stylized account of democratization, Acemoglu and Robinson (2006) articulate this precise dynamic in terms of economic inequality between elites and citizens: As inequality increases between elites and citizens, democratic revolution becomes more attractive to citizens and nondemocracy more attractive to elites (36). According to my theory, similar in this regard to Boix (2003), as resource inequality increases between incumbent and opposition elites, the opposition will be more desperate to gain control of the state and the incumbent more intent on maintaining control, which will make adherence to agreements about electoral conduct and peaceful participation more difficult to maintain.

Actors also require complete information to make decisions and achieve successful bargaining outcomes. When one party misrepresents information, it can lead to bargaining failure. The studies that are most relevant to bargaining failure and protest are those that focus on the importance of information for purposes of coordination or cooperation, which is often described as a need for "common knowledge" (Chwe 2001). For example, Chwe shows how cultural practices, ceremonies, art, and architecture can function to generate common knowledge. Cox (1997), in contrast, discusses the specific case of strategic voting and notes that, for voters to be able to coordinate on winning candidates (and, implicitly, agree on hopeless candidates), the probable winners and losers must be a matter of common knowledge (78). Where there is a lack of common knowledge, actors have increased opportunities to misrepresent information, and coordination may not be possible.

Although common knowledge is probably a reasonable assumption in the established democracies studied by Cox (1997), it is considerably more difficult to generate at the national level in the developing world. These countries typically lack reliable media and polling outlets, meaning that political actors have a more difficult time obtaining reliable information on which to base decisions. Lower literacy rates, another feature of lower levels of economic development, also compromise the information environment: Media are not under pressure to provide reliable information, because consumers who cannot read have fewer tools with which to verify the accuracy of the information they receive. In these lower information environments, opportunities to misrepresent private information increase, and as they do so, the probability that incumbent–opposition negotiations will fail also increases.

Developing Countries vs. Authoritarian Regimes

Empirically, this book's agnosticism with respect to regime type is the only way to provide a full accounting of the use of electoral protest, from which we can then consider the consequences of such tactics.[14] The decision to focus this study on developing countries rather than any particular regime type is also

---

[14] For example, less that one-fourth of the major election boycotts I record, and only one-half of the mass demonstrations I examine occurred in Levitsky and Way's (2010) sample of competitive authoritarian regimes.

an appropriate complement to the book's incremental approach to democratization. In addition, the previous section has suggested compelling theoretical reasons why the political context associated with lower levels of economic development must be considered to understand the causes and consequences of electoral protest.

Beginning with Carothers' (2002) criticism of earlier approaches to democratization and Schedler's (2002) article on electoral authoritarianism, much of the recent work challenging Huntington's observations about elections has developed classifications of nondemocratic regimes that hold elections (Schedler 2006; Howard and Roessler 2006; Levitsky and Way 2010). These scholars have provided several labels for this phenomenon, in addition to electoral authoritarianism and competitive authoritarianism: "hybrid regimes" (Diamond 2002; Ottoway 2003; Robertson 2011; Levitsky and Way 2010), "hegemonic regimes" (Magaloni 2006; Greene 2007), and "authoritarian regimes that hold elections" (Lust-Okar 2005, Brownlee 2007, Pop-Eleches and Robertson 2009). The underlying concern for all these works is what elections mean when they take place in circumstances that are not altogether democratic.

Beyond providing a caution as we assess the function of elections in a given country, it is not clear how knowing that a regime is "electoral authoritarian" or "competitive authoritarian" suggests more or different implications for democratization than could be arrived at with a simpler set of assumptions about how various actors are likely to behave in any electoral setting. Specifying that electoral authoritarian regimes are ones in which the incumbent has no intention of actually ceding power (Schedler 2002, 2006), or that the opposition uses electoral institutions to "contest seriously" for political power in competitive authoritarian regimes (Levitsky and Way 2010, 16), does not lead necessarily to any different conclusions about electoral dynamics from those based on the information that multiparty elections are being held in a developing country.

One possible rejoinder from those who favor regime typologies is that in certain regimes my assumptions about what the opposition is trying to accomplish with electoral competition and protest are simply incorrect. Where I assume the opposition wants to compete for and win political power, in Lust-Okar's (2005) study of regime dynamics in Jordan, Morocco, and Egypt, the opposition has no illusions of competing for power, but rather is competing for patronage. For Lust-Okar, legal opposition parties are only interested in being able to "express their demands and enjoy the benefits of participation (171)": They do not see themselves as competing for real power. When legal opposition parties initiate protest, it is for purposes of constructing an image as a legitimate opposition to the incumbent, not because they hope to challenge the structure of power (171). And if these challenges actually threaten the regime, then opposition leaders will face an authoritarian backlash (171).

In Blaydes' (2010) study of Egypt during the rule of Sadat and Mubarak's National Democratic Party (NDP), she also focuses on the function of elections as obtaining patronage distribution rather than as contests for power. For Blaydes, however, independent candidates and those loyal to the NDP sought opportunities for personal enrichment through the elections, but the opposition actors (primarily the Muslim Brotherhood) understood elections to be the route to obtain political power, even if they had a long time horizon and did not expect any single election to bring about the defeat of the NDP. Blaydes stresses that the Muslim Brotherhood had no ideological inclination to favor electoral democracy, but came to support electoral participation out of a kind of "tactical pragmatism" in the hopes of achieving a parliamentary majority and forming a government (151), something the party achieved in elections after the eventual fall of Mubarak.[15]

Although some may argue that certain regime types structure opposition preferences so that they see elections as means to gain patronage, not actual power, the more fundamental question raised by this perspective is as follows: Why would opposition elites who clearly prefer to receive patronage not also prefer more direct control over patronage? Clientelism and patronage politics are ubiquitous throughout the developing world, and although it may make sense to think of individual politicians as satisfied with gaining access to patronage, and not wanting to risk destroying the regime that provides that patronage, it probably makes less sense to think about opposition elites in this way. The leadership role of elite decision makers suggests more ambition, and having staked a political position as an identified "opposition" also suggests a dissatisfaction with simply receiving patronage from the current regime. If all opposition leaders wanted was patronage, they would have been better served joining the incumbent party and using their ambition to advance through the party ranks.

Thus it is not clear that an emphasis on regime typologies is more appropriate than a focus on economic development, and in terms of both empirical information and theoretical leverage, there may be compelling reasons to avoid regime classification. Diamond (2002, 27–9) notes difficulties in making clear distinctions among regime types, and Schedler (2002) acknowledges that categorical distinctions among regime types "tend to be blurry and controversial" (38). Elkins (2000) addresses the classification question with respect to issues of validity and reliability, concluding that continuous measures are more valid and reliable than categories. If what we are interested in observing is incremental movements toward (or away from) democracy, then the empirical usefulness of regime categories is also questionable.

Although my work explicitly avoids questions of regime type, anyone thinking about elections and democratization from the perspective of electoral or competitive authoritarianism (CA) should find a great deal of both empirical and theoretical overlap in these pages. For example, although they have less

---

[15] Even in Blaydes' account of the Muslim Brotherhood, however, she notes the care taken by the party not to pose too much of a threat to the incumbent regime.

of a direct focus on elections, Levitsky and Way (2010) examine both the international and domestic circumstances under which CA regimes become democracies. Although I do not make the definitive pronouncements about whether countries have attained democracy that Levitsky and Way do, many of my findings are consonant with their logic of international linkage and its consequences for democratization. Furthermore, when we examine my findings in the context of those cases considered by Levitsky and Way, we see that democratic reforms happen at a much higher rate following electoral protest.

The question of international influence and democratization is at the heart of Levitsky and Way's (2010) *Competitive Authoritarianism: Hybrid Regimes after the Cold War*. Although electoral dynamics are not central to their argument about the process of democratization, multiparty elections are a key component of the CA regimes that Levitsky and Way study. They define CA regimes as holding multiparty elections but violating some major aspect of democratic regimes, such as free and fair elections, civil liberties, or an "even playing field" between incumbent and opposition. Their "uneven playing field" shares many of the characteristics that I attribute to the developing world. In particular, they highlight situations where media access is biased in favor of the incumbent and the incumbent enjoys more favorable access to campaign resources.[16] Because Levitsky and Way construct historical case analyses of 35 CA regimes in their study, their argument is not concerned with the specific dynamics of particular elections, but instead focuses on the impact of international relations and state strength over time.

Nevertheless, electoral dynamics play a critical role in their assessments. Levitsky and Way consider states to have democratized once they have displayed "the establishment of free and fair elections, broad protection of civil liberties, and a level playing field" for a period of three electoral cycles (2010, 21). In their study, regimes with high linkage to the West – in terms of trade, communication, intergovernmental ties, and the like – tended to democratize. These regimes were found predominantly in Latin America and Eastern Europe. For CA regimes with low linkage to the West, democratization depended on the organizational strength of the incumbent regime: Where incumbents were strong, they could resist opposition challenges; where incumbents were weak, however, they were vulnerable to opposition pressure and leverage from the West (a second source of international influence) and, as such, were more likely to democratize.[17] Examples of democratization in situations where incumbents were weak and opposition organization high include Ukraine, Mali, and Benin.

---

[16] They consider as fully authoritarian those cases where electoral competition is accompanied by the routine exclusion of opposition candidates, severe repression that de facto excludes the opposition, or the widespread falsification of electoral results.

[17] Whereas linkage suggests connection to the West, leverage refers to countries that are economically and politically vulnerable to western pressure.

There is no systematic relationship between Levitsky and Way's conclusions and the dynamics of electoral politics investigated in this book. Rates of protest and democratic reform do not differ between those CA regimes that Levitsky and Way find to have democratized and those that remained CA or moved toward full authoritarianism. The only striking pattern that emerges is that, in the subset of my observations that correspond to Levitsky and Way's CA regimes, democratic reform follows protest at significantly higher rates: 30% of protested elections are followed by democratic reform compared to just 15% of those elections that are not protested.

Six cases of democratic reform occur in four countries that Levitsky and Way code as having democratized (Dominican Republic, Guyana, Mexico, and Peru) due to high linkage and/or leverage.[18] The remaining five cases of democratic reform following electoral protest occur in five countries that have not democratized according to Levitsky and Way. Three of these countries, however, are ones that I find making incremental, if unsteady, progress toward democracy: Haiti, Gabon, and Madagascar. Furthermore, both Haiti and Madagascar are characterized by lower levels of linkage (medium for Haiti, low for Madagascar), but high leverage and incumbent weakness.[19]

Thus, among the countries studied by Levitsky and Way, there are higher rates of democratic reform following protest compared to general rates of reform in the developing world. These reforms result either in the clear establishment of democracy or incremental shifts in the direction of greater democracy in all but two cases where protest and reform occur. Furthermore, all of the cases that I characterize as exhibiting democratic improvements had strong connections to international actors promoting democracy and/or were particularly vulnerable to international pressure, according to Levitsky and Way. Finally, the two cases where protest and reform occurred that do not appear to have made real progress toward democratization, Cambodia and Zambia, are both characterized by Levitsky and Way as countries with low international linkage, suggesting a lack of the kind of international support for protest that is a cornerstone of my theory.

To the seven cases of CA regimes studied by Levitsky and Way where contentious electoral processes have encouraged democratization, I can add six country cases that they did not study, either because the regimes were likely considered democratic or fully authoritarian or because the electoral dynamics in question occurred before the end of the Cold War: Lesotho, Jamaica, Bangladesh, Togo, Indonesia, and the Philippines. By and large, then, the argument and findings presented in this book are consistent with much of Levitsky and Way's argument and evidence. The differences that emerge are the result

---

[18] Peru is rated as having medium levels of linkage, but also a weak incumbent and high leverage.
[19] Given that Gabon's most recent rounds of electoral protest and democratic improvements happened after Levitsky and Way's 2008 cutoff, they might well re-characterize Gabon (particularly the issue of incumbent strength) in this time period.

of my incrementalist approach to measuring democratization and my focus on the developing world rather than a subset of authoritarian regimes. Although it does not offer any direct contradiction of their findings, this book provides a more general theoretical framework and empirical evidence within which to situate the specific cases considered by Levitsky and Way.

OUTLINE OF CHAPTERS

Chapter 2 presents the book's theory. Because the story here is about how conflict can result when political actors attempt to reach agreement in the absence of strong coordinating institutions, the theory takes its cues from Fearon's (1995) work on rationalist explanations for war. Using a simple decision tree, this chapter establishes the theory's key actors, their preferences and available actions, and the basic logic that electoral protest will result when actors fail to reach an agreement about how to conduct elections – specifically, the extent of pro-incumbent manipulation in the election – and that the consequences of protest for democracy will depend on how the incumbent chooses to respond. From the incumbent's decision to call an election to how the incumbent chooses to respond after the election, this theory identifies five points at which either the incumbent or opposition has decisions to make that will shape whether electoral protest occurs and its ultimate consequences for democracy. The incumbent decides to call the election, how much to manipulate the electoral system, and how to respond to instances of electoral protest; the opposition decides – before the election – whether to boycott or participate and, after the election, whether to accept the election outcome or engage in post-election protests.

Chapter 2 also elaborates on the developing-world focus of the book, discussing the three developing-world scope conditions in greater depth to explain why bargaining over electoral conduct is more likely to take place and, subsequently, why it is more likely to fail in the developing-world context. These three scope conditions are international pressure for democracy, the resource imbalance between incumbent and opposition, and low-information environments. The chapter makes the point that, although these conditions present a particular set of challenges for political actors in the developing world that actors in wealthy democracies do not typically face, they also vary from country to country in ways that will have important consequences for electoral protest.

The chapter ends with several real-world examples to demonstrate the plausibility of the theory's major assumptions. Examples from Kenya, Guyana, Gabon, and Zimbabwe show instances of explicit negotiation between incumbent and opposition actors, whereas examples from Equatorial Guinea, Bangladesh, and Venezuela offer evidence of these actors behaving as if they were engaged in explicit negotiations. Finally, examples from Guyana, Cote d'Ivoire, and Niger offer evidence of international pressure for democracy, resource imbalance, and a low-information environment, respectively.

Chapter 3 begins with Cameroon's 1997 election boycott as a touchstone for addressing the causes of electoral protest. The chapter discusses theoretical expectations regarding the causes of major election boycotts and post-election mass demonstrations in turn. For each type of protest, these expectations are analyzed using an original data set of more than five hundred multiparty elections in the developing world from 1975 to 2006. Findings from this chapter show that the decision to boycott is related to general conditions of low information and problems of incumbent credibility, whereas post-election mass demonstrations are most strongly associated with incumbent victory and the relative strength of the opposition, which might affect the credibility of either the incumbent or the opposition. Whether the incumbent was unable to credibly commit to restraint with respect to manipulation or the opposition commitment to accept the results of the election was not credible can be difficult to ascertain in any given case. This chapter draws other examples from Azerbaijan, Guinea, the Dominican Republic, the Philippines, Bolivia, Madagascar, and Mexico.

Chapter 4 examines the consequences of electoral protest with a focus on Election Day and its aftermath. Beginning with two elections in Cote d'Ivoire that took place a decade apart, the chapter considers the relationship of major boycotts and post-election demonstrations to such features of democracy as competition, participation, and violence. Electoral protests in Cote d'Ivoire have sparked civil conflict and instability, but are these events typical of what we observe during electoral protests across the developing world? The chapter finds that, although boycotts are nearly always associated with the return to power of the incumbent party, they are not systematically associated with reduced turnout or electoral violence. Post-election protests initiated by the opposition, by contrast, do not deprive voters of a meaningful choice at the polls and are associated with higher rates of regular, constitutional, turnover in office – but not with greater violence or instability – compared to other demonstrations that occur after elections. Other examples in this chapter come from the Comoros, Zimbabwe, Zambia, Kyrgyzstan, Cambodia, El Salvador, Mongolia, Poland, Macedonia, Ukraine, and Bangladesh.

Chapter 5 begins with a discussion of a major election boycott in Haiti and then tackles the final major question of the book: What do electoral protests mean for democratization in the countries where they occur? The analysis in this chapter helps elucidate the process by which electoral protest might have positive consequences for democracy. With respect to election-related reform, we observe different patterns after boycotts than after post-election mass demonstrations. Election boycotts are more likely than post-election demonstrations to elicit a reform response from the incumbent, but whether the incumbent undertakes democratic reform or more cosmetic, authoritarian "reform" depends on the nature of the support the boycott receives. Boycotts that receive domestic support encourage authoritarian reforms, whereas boycotts that receive international support are associated with a higher probability of democratic reform, which is associated with improved measures of future democratic performance. Post-election demonstrations, by contrast, seem to decrease the probability of authoritarian "reform," but do not have a clear, systematic relationship to democratic reform. The second half of this chapter is devoted to several cases that offer examples of (or exceptions to) the reported statistical patterns. Cases discussed in this chapter include Azerbaijan, Togo, Bangladesh, the Philippines, Equatorial Guinea, Chad, Jamaica, Gabon, Madagascar, and Panama.

Chapter 6, the concluding chapter, begins with a brief review of all the cases that motivated each of the preceding chapters. In addition to summarizing the book's main theoretical argument and findings, it offers two ways that the theory might help advance studies of protest and democratization. First, using evidence from China, I explore the possibility that my theory of protest-as-bargaining-failure may have applicability to instances of protest outside the electoral arena. I then take up the question of how my theory of electoral protest and democratization might also help us understand the dynamics in countries where prospects for democracy seem particularly dim. Here I return to the examples that began this introductory chapter – Iran and Afghanistan: I suggest that such cases hold out the possibility for international democracy promotion to exert some influence even if opposition actors are not necessarily fighting for more democratic elections, but that we must be careful to recognize the limits of international democracy promotion.

2

Elite Bargaining and Elections in the Developing World

After Guyana's president Cheddi Jagan died in 1997, his wife Janet assumed the office for the People's Progressive Party (PPP) and won reelection to the presidency in December of that same year. The opposition People's National Congress (PNC) began protest demonstrations on December 19, the day she was sworn into office, and those protests continued into January. In addition to near-daily street demonstrations, four separate bombing incidents were reported during this time.[1] In two cases the bomb attacks targeted public buildings – a hotel in the capital city of Georgetown and a TV station – and it was unclear who was responsible, though the president blamed opposition supporters in at least one case.[2] The other two incidents clearly targeted incumbent and opposition political actors. One homemade bomb was detonated outside of the home of an influential opposition supporter, and other bombs were found and defused outside of the home of President Jagan.[3]

In mid-January, amid continuing demonstrations, a delegation from the Caribbean Community (CARICOM) arrived to broker a resolution to the month-long political tension.[4] This intervention resulted in a negotiated agreement between the opposition PNC and incumbent PPP to establish a constitutional commission that would make recommendations to reduce political

---

[1] Guyana: CARICOM Peace Mission Brokers Agreement to Hold Fresh Elections. BBC Monitoring Latin America – Political Supplied by BBC Worldwide Monitoring, January 19, 1998, Monday.

[2] Bomb attack reported at Georgetown Hotel. 1998. *Miami Herald*, January 8; One injured by bomb outside TV station. 1998. Cana News Agency, Bridgetown, January 7.

[3] Guyanese bomb. 1998. *London Daily Telegraph*, January 12; Bombs defused near home of president. 1998. *Miami Herald*, January 22.

[4] CARICOM is an intergovernmental organization that promotes economic integration and cooperation among Caribbean nations.

conflict in the country.[5] As part of the agreement, new elections would be held within a year and a half, thereby allowing time to implement the commission's recommended reforms. In the meantime, both parties agreed to an audit process for the previous election, to address opposition concerns about manipulation.[6]

Electoral protest occurs when political elites controlling the state and elites representing the legal opposition cannot come to an agreement that allows the opposition to participate in the election and accept the results. More specifically, electoral protest occurs when elites cannot agree on the extent to which the incumbent will manipulate the election to her advantage.[7] Both the incumbent and the opposition would prefer an election where the opposition could participate instead of protesting, but they differ in the extent to which they would like the incumbent to manipulate the election. The incumbent would prefer to manipulate the election at least enough to secure victory, whereas the opposition would prefer incumbent manipulation so minimal that it would have no actual bearing on the election's outcome. As with many types of negotiations, incumbents and their opponents are often willing to make some concessions relative to these ideal positions. So, in theory, the incumbent should be able to adjust the manipulation she employs just enough to induce the opposition to participate without protesting. In practice, however, electoral protests do happen, as the case of Guyana demonstrates.

Drawing on the logic of bargaining and strategic interaction, as exemplified by Fearon (1995) in his article, "Rationalist Explanations for War," I argue that incumbent and opposition actors will fail to reach an agreement about electoral manipulation when problems of information or credibility arise. If either the incumbent or the opposition misrepresents private information, or if either actor's promises are not viewed by the other as credible, the two sides may fail to reach an agreement and electoral protest will result. These protests may or may not have positive consequences for democracy in the country in which they occur, depending on the strategic calculations of the incumbent. If the electoral protest attracts enough support that the incumbent feels pressured to respond, democratic reforms may result. If, however, the incumbent sees room to enact reforms that are not democratic, the end results may not be positive for democracy.

This theory of electoral protest and democratization finds a clear application in the contemporary developing world. Although the core insights in this chapter certainly could apply to politics in other places at other times, a unique confluence of circumstances came together in the developing world in

---

[5] Guyana: Opposition supporters defy ban on marches; Talks start to end crisis. BBC Monitoring Latin America – Political Supplied by BBC Worldwide Monitoring, January 16, 1998, Friday.

[6] Guyana: CARICOM peace mission brokers agreement to hold fresh elections. BBC Monitoring Latin America – Political Supplied by BBC Worldwide Monitoring, January 19, 1998, Monday.

[7] In light of the chapter's opening example and for clarity's sake, I apply feminine pronouns to describe "the incumbent" and masculine pronouns for reference to "the opposition" throughout the theoretical discussion in this book.

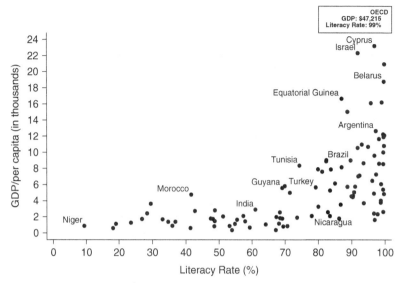

FIGURE 2.1. Literacy and GDP per Capita.

the late 20th century such that developing countries are both where electoral protests are happening and where they cause the most concern with respect to democracy. In addition to presenting a model of elite bargaining and bargaining failure to explain electoral protest and its consequences, this chapter highlights three scope conditions that help us understand why the dynamics described in the theory are playing out in developing countries today: (1) a post–Cold War international environment that promotes democracy, (2) the imbalance of resources between incumbent and opposition politicians, and (3) the quality and availability of information in a society. The extent to which any one of these features is relevant will vary from country to country, but less developed countries can be distinguished systematically from wealthy industrialized countries on the basis of these three features. In the course of elaborating on the book's theoretical logic, this chapter discusses how each of these three developing-world features is relevant to understanding where and why electoral protest occurs.

Before we turn to the theory, however, Figure 2.1 provides one striking example of how developing countries differ in terms of wealth and literacy from rich, developed countries. This chart reports data from the last election year for each country in the data set, and it shows a great deal of variation across the developing world in terms of wealth and literacy.[8] Despite the great deal of variation within the developing world, the text box in the upper right

[8] The only country in the data set not pictured in this graph is Kuwait, which meets the criteria to qualify as a developing country for this study, but had a GDP per capita in 2006 of $41,269.

corner of Figure 2.1 suggests why it is appropriate to consider developing countries distinct from wealthy democracies, which all report a literacy rate of 99% and (as of 2006) an average GDP per capita of $47,215.[9] The average literacy rate for developing countries, by contrast, is 72.5%, and the average GDP per capita is $6,130. I reported the OECD information in the text box so that the graph could retain a scale that would allow readers to observe the variation among developing countries – which would be difficult if the scale of the y-axis (GDP per capita) were reduced by half to accommodate the OECD average.

Although it is important to appreciate the gulf between developed and developing on the one hand, it is also important to appreciate the variation among developing countries – which explains why rates of electoral protest vary across the developing world. Selected country indicators also show how much variation can exist even within the same region. For example, Equatorial Guinea reported an adult literacy rate of nearly 87% and GDP per capita of $16,668 in 2004, whereas data from Niger taken just two years earlier reported an adult literacy rate of 9% and GDP per capita of $866.

The chapter continues with an overview of the theory of electoral protest as a result of elite bargaining failure. My theory assumes two actors – an incumbent and an opposition – engaged in ongoing negotiation throughout the electoral process. The incumbent currently controls the state and is assumed to want to retain control. The only thing the incumbent wants more than control of the state is to stay alive. The action available to the incumbent is to determine how much to manipulate the election in her favor. The opposition is legally permitted by the state to participate in elections and would like to gain control of the state via those elections. The actions available to the opposition, given the incumbent's chosen level of manipulation, are to participate in the election or to protest. Both actors face two different points at which they need to make decisions about manipulation (incumbent) and protest (opposition). The final decision addressed in the theory is how the incumbent will respond to opposition protests, if any have occurred during the electoral process.

Figure 2.2 offers a graphic representation of ongoing negotiations between incumbent and opposition actors before, during, and after an election. This illustration identifies five key decision points, which the chapter addresses in order. This discussion clarifies the strategic dynamics of the theory and highlights the relevance of the developing-world context. Examining each decision point in the negotiation process also provides the opportunity to unpack key concepts and address some of the complex issues that have been simplified in the theory, such as the assumption of unitary incumbent and opposition actors and the actions available to each. Decision Points 1 and 2 in the model

---

[9] Average of World Bank's GDP per capita for the EU, United States, Australia, Japan, and Singapore.

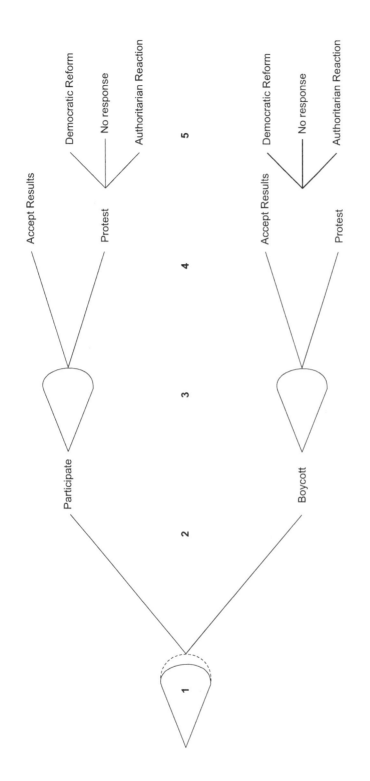

1. Incumbent calls for election and begins to implement some levels of manipulation m_1

2. Opposition anticipates $\hat{m}_1 + \hat{m}_2$, and decides whether to boycott or participate

3. Incumbent holds the election and produces some total level of manipulation $M = m_1 + m_2$

4. Opposition observes M and decides whether to accept results or protest after the election

5. Incumbent decides how to respond to instances of protest

FIGURE 2.2. Elite Negotiation Decision Tree.

receive the most emphasis because they provide opportunities to elaborate on concepts that reappear in various stages of the model. The chapter ends with several real-world examples of electoral protest to suggest that, despite its conceptual simplifications, this theory effectively captures the dynamics of electoral protest and democratization in the developing world.

DECISION POINT 1: INCUMBENT CALLS FOR ELECTION AND IMPLEMENTS SOME LEVEL OF MANIPULATION

The starting point for this theory is the incumbent government's decision to hold an election. In parliamentary systems, with their lack of a fixed timetable for elections, the need for incumbent decision is clear. Even in presidential systems, however, where the timetable for elections is fixed, the ability of leaders to delay elections, citing reasons of security or administrative logistics, means that an approaching election date can still be interpreted as the result of an incumbent's decision to allow the election to happen. But unlike in rich democracies, where the decision to hold an election sets a reliable, formal administration process into motion, an impending election in the developing world begins a process of negotiation between the incumbent and the opposition.

In the developing world, political actors cannot depend on the coordinating power of institutions. Electoral laws and administration processes in wealthy, established democracies – the result of earlier negotiated agreements – facilitate smooth electoral competition such that voters and political elites largely take it for granted that elections will be free and fair; elites focus on the competition for power within the extant framework of a mutually agreed-on set of rules.[10] Most developing countries, by contrast, have had a shorter history with electoral institutions for multiparty competition; only a handful of developing countries held multiparty elections before 1975, and many of the countries that began holding elections since the beginning of Huntington's (1991) third wave emerged from long periods of authoritarian rule. Political actors need time and repeated interaction with institutions to generate institutional legitimacy. Furthermore, because most developing countries in the world today were once European colonies, many inherited artificially imposed electoral institutions as colonizers transferred power. In Africa, for example, some countries' electoral institutions do not have the expected effects on party systems because of historical contingencies that override institutional incentives (Lindberg 2005, 55). Finally, the maintenance and administration of electoral institutions are typically underfunded in developing countries (Pastor 1999). Thus, a number

---

[10] Even though elites in established democracies can take electoral institutions for granted, they still attempt to challenge or renegotiate electoral rules, but they do so using existing institutional frameworks, such as legislation, rather than extra-institutional actions such as protest. Debates over campaign finance and gerrymandering of electoral districts are good examples of this behavior.

of factors can render electoral institutions relatively weak and unreliable in developing countries.

Given the strategic nature of electoral competition where there is a lack of institutional assurance, the incumbent and the opposition must agree on rules to play by. Electoral protests are usefully understood as part of a negotiation process – more specifically, as instances where negotiations have broken down. Here, the reader might wonder: If electoral institutions are so weak that political elites have to bargain over questions of electoral conduct, such as manipulation, why not simply skip the contest altogether and begin dividing up the spoils? To understand why incumbent and opposition are negotiating over issues of electoral conduct rather than negotiating direct transfers of power, we should consider the first of three developing-world scope conditions: international pressure for democratization. Put simply, incumbent elites hold elections and bargain with the opposition because they are under pressure from powerful international actors to demonstrate that their countries are electoral democracies.

International Pressure for Democracy and Elections

Developing countries rely heavily on foreign aid and assistance and, as such, are more likely to be vulnerable to shifts in international preferences regarding democracy.[11] Thus, although all countries might desire the kinds of international benefits suggested by Hyde (2011), developing countries are particularly sensitive to the costs and benefits associated with international relations. Given the benefit of more than two decades of hindsight from which to judge Huntington's identification of the start of third wave democratization in 1974, there is a strong case to be made for differentiating the democratization that preceded the demise of the Soviet Union from the democratization that followed.[12] As Hyde (2011) points out, democracy promotion was a priority for the United States and allied actors before the Cold War, but their democracy promotion efforts were typically overshadowed by Cold War politics (143–4). The end of the Soviet Union marked a sea change in international expectations for democracy; no longer would the specter of communism provide sufficient justification for developing countries to engage in undemocratic practices or for dictators to seek retrenchment behind the Iron Curtain.[13] With the end of the Cold War, donors began increasingly to attach democratic conditionality to foreign aid. U.S. funding for democracy assistance, for example, increased by orders of magnitude in the last two decades of the 20th century – from a rate near zero in the 1980s to more than US$ 700 million by the turn of the century – and

---

[11] What Levitsky and Way (2010) describe as "leverage."

[12] Levitsky and Way (2010, 20), for example, refer to the post–Cold War period as a "Fourth Wave" of regime transitions.

[13] See also Gleditsch and Ward (2006) and Kelly (2012) for similar arguments.

the United States, United Kingdom, and France all announced that they would begin to tie aid to democracy (Levitsky and Way 2010, 17–18).

Regional intergovernmental organizations also began to increase pressure for democracy among their member states and within their respective spheres of influence. In the early 1990s, the Organization of American States (OAS) for example, made "defending democracy" a priority (Farer 1993).[14] The organization has since demonstrated this commitment with its high-profile engagement in several elections in the region, such as Peru in 2000 (Cooper and Legler 2006). More recently the African Union (AU) has begun to move explicitly away from a doctrine of "non-interference" (Mwanasali 2008). Although this shift in Africa is more directly a response to armed conflict, it may provide an opening for the AU institutions to increase democracy promotion efforts in the region.

Levitsky and Way (2010, 87) identify the Americas and Eastern Europe as regions that have been particularly susceptible to post–Cold War pressure to democratize because of their geographic proximity to the United States and Western Europe, respectively. Developing countries in other parts of the world also find themselves vulnerable to pressures from powerful international actors, which are now displaying clear preferences for democracy. Barkan (2000, 230) notes that African countries are particularly vulnerable to pressures for political reform because of their dependence on the international donor community; even in regions such as the Middle East, where the pressure to democratize is arguably the weakest because of the region's geostrategic position and vast oil reserves, we see domestic leaders acknowledging international preferences for democracy. At the conference of Emerging Democracies in 1999, for example, the prime minister of Yemen, Abdal-Kareem al-Iryani, reminded the international community that Yemen required international financial support to "ensure the continuation of democracy" (Phillips 2008, 49).

The fact that powerful international actors expect to see evidence of democratic practices in the developing world helps us understand why incumbents are holding elections. Unlike elections in rich democracies, where procedural and administrative aspects of democratic competition are largely taken for granted, incumbent and opposition elites in developing-world countries still have to negotiate some fundamental procedural elements of the election process – namely how much manipulation the incumbent will be allowed to employ. In this first stage of the negotiation process, the incumbent begins to determine her total amount of manipulation for the election.

Incumbent Manipulation

In Figure 2.2 M represents the total amount of manipulation the incumbent will undertake throughout the course of the election – from any advance preparation until the final results are announced. We can think of $M \in [0, 1]$ where 0 would

---

[14] For a more detailed discussion of this process, see Hyde (2011, 150–7)

represent absolutely no manipulation on the part of the incumbent, and 1 would represent total control of the electoral process, what is commonly referred to as a "rigged" election that the opposition has no chance of winning. On the continuum of M from 0 to 1, legal activities that nonetheless confer an unfair advantage on the incumbent represent lower levels of manipulation (values of M closer to 0), whereas activities that meet the criteria for fraud constitute higher levels of manipulation (values of M closer to 1). Over the entire course of the election, $M = m_1 + m_2$. At this early point in the process, m_1 represents the incumbent's efforts to manipulate in advance of Election Day.

The incumbent has a wide range of manipulation tactics she might employ at the advance preparation stage (m_1). This is a stage when incumbent leaders often use the name recognition that comes with their office to raise funds for the upcoming election campaign. They find ways to increase their visibility among voters, for example, by dominating media coverage with reports of their civic-mindedness and good works. The pre-election period is also a time when incumbents can change electoral rules or manipulate electoral administration procedures.[15]

The administrative challenges associated with an election present numerous opportunities for manipulation. As Pastor (1999) points out, there are many opportunities for mistakes in electoral management, and questions often linger about whether such mistakes were honest or an intentional attempt to rig the election. For example, the pre-election phase presents opportunities to tamper with voter registers by deleting names of opposition supporters. Simpler yet, the incumbent's administration can neglect to update voter registers if the number of opposition supporters has grown. When problems of voter registration arise, the incumbent may claim that such problems are simply due to a lack of time and resources. Accusations of this type of manipulation were at the center of opposition protests in Cameroon in 1997, for example (see Chapter 3). The pre-election phase is also a time when incumbent party loyalists can be installed in administrative positions (as the PNC did in Guyana) and plans for Election Day manipulation of administration can be formulated.

In addition, although vote buying will not take place until much closer to the election itself, the pre-election period can be a time for establishing vote buying or brokerage networks. In Taiwan in 1993, nearly all major politicians engaged in vote buying using "brokers" who had a great deal of discretion in how to translate campaign money into votes (Wang and Kurzman 2007). Similarly, Lehoucq and Molina (2002) found that politicians in Costa Rica would buy voter identification cards from supporters of their opponents, ensuring that those individuals would not cast a vote.

The incumbent can also use violence or the threat of violence as a form of manipulation during the pre-election period. Violent repression of opposition campaigning and jailing (or otherwise harming) opposition candidates are

---

[15] Posusney (2005) provides examples of such early-stage manipulation in the Middle East.

common tactics at this stage. In the case of elections in the Comoros in 1992, for example, two of the three main opposition parties boycotted the elections, citing, among other complaints, the detention of several opposition activists.[16] In a more extreme example of violence, the protests that followed Ukraine's 2004 election were at least partly motivated by beliefs that the government had poisoned the main opposition candidate, Viktor Yushenko, in an attempt to eliminate him from the presidential competition.[17] Thus, repression constitutes another manipulation tactic available to the incumbent in this first stage of negotiations.

At this stage, as the incumbent takes steps toward implementing an overall level of manipulation (M), but also hopes to hold an election with opposition participation and acceptance of the results, two questions arise: How much manipulation can the incumbent commit and still hope to retain opposition participation and acceptance, and how can the incumbent know what level of manipulation the opposition will deem acceptable? I address both of these questions in the discussion of the next stage of negotiation and how information and credibility problems can lead to election boycotts.

DECISION POINT 2: OPPOSITION ANTICIPATES $\hat{m}_1 + \hat{m}_2$ AND
DECIDES WHETHER TO PARTICIPATE OR BOYCOTT

Once the election has been called, the opposition must decide whether to participate in the election or stage an election boycott based on his estimation of the total manipulation M. If the opposition finds his estimate of M to be acceptable, he will participate in the election. If the opposition finds M to be unacceptable, he will choose to boycott. Because at this point there is no way to observe incumbent manipulation that will occur on Election Day (m_2), the opposition will have to decide how confident he is in his own estimation of M (which can be based on how much he knows about m_1) and how much he believes he can trust the incumbent to adhere to a promised level of M. Thus, boycotts can result from either information problems or a lack of incumbent credibility.

The opposition may care about democracy, but need not do so for my theory to work. To understand why the opposition would stake its participation to levels of incumbent manipulation, all we need to assume is that the opposition wants to use the election to gain power. Given that the opposition has formed a political party (or parties) to compete in elections, it seems reasonable also to assume that he would like to win power in those elections. Accordingly, he should want the elections to be as free from incumbent manipulation as possible out of his own self-interest, because any reduction in incumbent manipulation increases the competitive chances of the opposition in the election. It may

---

[16] Keesings Record of World Events, Nov. 1992: Comoros – Legislative Elections.
[17] Poisoning Ukrainian opposition leader angers EU. Xinhua General News Service. December 13, 2004, Monday 6:00 PM EST.

be tempting to characterize the opposition in this model as a pro-democracy activist, and that may be an accurate description in some cases, but such characterizations are not necessary. Even an opposition who would use the same manipulation tactics as the incumbent if the roles were reversed should want to see incumbent manipulation reduced.

By asserting that the opposition would like to gain power via elections and restricting the options to "participation" or "protest," I am assuming that the opposition will not consider violent overthrow; admittedly this assertion restricts the opposition's available actions. Such a restriction, however, is tenable given my focus on legal opposition parties and the current international importance of democratic legitimacy. Even though the opposition does not have the option to violently overthrow the incumbent government in this model, support of opposition protests by either international or domestic actors might well lead the incumbent to fear imminent, violent removal from office.[18]

Resource Imbalance

The fact that the opposition does not have the option to manipulate the election in this model brings us to the second developing-world scope condition: the extreme imbalance in resources needed for political competition between the incumbent and opposition in developing countries. This resource imbalance is important because it greatly increases the stakes of competition for control of the state, shapes available actions, and creates problems of credible commitment. Political elites who control the state are going to be much more reticent to relinquish that control if a life in opposition means a life of relative poverty and political weakness.

In countries with weak political institutions and low levels of economic development, the state represents an unrivaled fount of resources to be exploited for political gain. In contrast, in more developed countries, political actors who control the state face formal constraints on their ability to use its power to their advantage. Clearly, control of the state still represents a political advantage in rich democracies, but opposition elites are not completely without recourse. In rich democracies, the private sector offers immense wealth that can be tapped and used as a political resource. Even if the Republican Party does not currently control the U.S. presidency, for example, the abundance of fund-raising opportunities in the private sector means that the party will still be competitive in future presidential elections. Although many decry an excess of money in American politics, the opposite situation is also highly problematic. Unlike the American setting, where resources exist outside the state and any political actor can, in theory, compete for these private resources,

---

[18] The opposition might also consider side payments instead of state control. See Powell (1999) for a discussion of side payments in bargaining. This model does not consider side payments explicitly, but we can think of side payments as making the opposition willing to tolerate higher levels of manipulation.

opposition actors in developing countries have little hope of competing with the incumbent's advantage by obtaining a matching level of resources.

Odds are good that whatever capacity the opposition has to manipulate the electoral system, he will be outdone by the incumbent. The notion that the incumbent can always "out-cheat" the opposition is most relevant at the national level. Clearly opposition parties that enjoy popularity or more coercive control over particular areas of the country may have a superior capacity for cheating in those localities. On a national scale, however, given the incumbent's access to government resources and administration, the incumbent should always be able to out-manipulate the opposition. In a fascinating and innovative study of election fraud, Ziblatt (2009) uses evidence from elections in late 19th-century Germany to argue that, when economic power is concentrated, it leaves would-be perpetrators of fraud "with the means and motives to undermine the quality of elections." Focusing on landholding inequalities in pre-industrial Germany and using disputed election cases filed with the German national parliament, Ziblatt finds that localities with greater inequality experienced more instances of election fraud.

Whereas the incumbent has the ability to decide whether and how much to manipulate elections, the opposition does not have access to the resources of the state and so cannot rely on similar manipulation tactics. He must instead turn to protest. In this pre-election stage, the opposition will decide whether or not to engage in an election boycott.

The Choice to Boycott

Boycotts are a coordinated, public refusal to participate in some activity, which is meant to challenge the status quo; for example, those that occurred in the Jim Crow South and during the Cold War when the United States boycotted the 1980 Olympics staged in the Soviet Union. Election boycotts occur when opposition leaders publicly withdraw their parties from participating as candidates in the election.[19] In most instances, opposition leaders not only refuse to participate themselves but also call on voters to refrain from participating.[20] For example, all but one opposition candidate publicly refused to participate in Mali's presidential elections in May 1997, objecting to the government's annulment of legislative elections in the previous month.[21] The major opposition parties also boycotted the rerun of legislative elections in July 1997

---

[19] The boycott of the bus system by African Americans to protest segregated transportation in Montgomery, Alabama, began with the arrest of Rosa Parks in 1955. The United States and 60 other countries boycotted the 1980 Olympics in Moscow to protest the Soviet invasion of Afghanistan. The USSR responded with a boycott of the 1984 Olympics in Los Angeles.

[20] On occasion leaders in exile will call for a boycott while living abroad – Juan Peron, for example, called on his supporters to spoil their ballots in Argentinean elections while he himself was living in exile in Spain. The analysis in this study considers only boycotts by eligible opposition parties and candidates.

[21] Keesings Record of World Events, April 1997: Mali, Presidential Election.

on the grounds that it would be as flawed as the previous contest, though some smaller opposition parties did compete.[22] More recently, opposition parties boycotted the parliamentary elections in Venezuela in December 2005 – accusing then President Hugo Chavez of attempting to rig the elections, claiming that new electronic voting technology violated the secrecy of the ballot, and noting that four of the country's five election judges had close ties to the president.[23]

Why would opposition elites ever choose to boycott, when by doing so they are effectively cutting off any immediate hopes of gaining power through elections? The assumption in this model follows from the general logic of boycotts: Actors undertake boycotts in the hopes of effecting policy change. Opposition leaders hope to force the incumbent into holding fairer elections in the future by engaging in this pre-election protest. Furthermore, if the kind of manipulation the incumbent is using contains elements of violent repression – or if the opposition suspects that Election Day manipulation will include violence on the part of the incumbent – a boycott may be an attractive option for reducing harm to opposition supporters.

My theory restricts the opposition's choice to "boycott" or "participate" assuming a unitary opposition actor. Were this assumption entirely accurate, the observable implication would be a unified opposition boycott. As the previous example from Mali suggests, however, boycotts are rarely unified. Incumbent manipulation is one cause of disunity. Often incumbents use some of their resources to cultivate loyalty among a small party or parties technically in the opposition, thereby splitting the opposition vote when opposition parties participate in elections. Even in cases where every major party that genuinely opposes the incumbent decides to boycott, these small parties will remain in the election, allowing the incumbent to claim some semblance of multiparty competition.

There are two types of election boycotts, which I term "major" and "minor." As in the example from Mali, major election boycotts occur when those parties representing a majority of opposition voters publicly refuse to participate in the election and encourage their supporters not to vote. In these cases, a substantial portion of the opposition coordinates efforts to behave *as if* it is a unitary actor. Minor election boycotts, by contrast, involve an opposition party (or parties) that represent a minority of opposition voters. Minor boycotts tend to focus less on issues related to general electoral fairness and more on issues relevant to the minority group represented by the boycotting party. Lebanon's minor boycott in 2000, for example, was mounted by several small, right-wing Christian political parties objecting to the Syrian occupation of Lebanon. The distinction between these two types of boycott is important to highlight because it shows how, in reality, the opposition's

---

[22] Keesings Record of World Events, August 1997: Mali, Re-run Legislative Elections.
[23] Deutsche Presse-Agentur. Two injured in blasts as boycott overshadows Venezuelan election. December 4, 2005, Sunday. 15:35:24 Central European Time.

decision to participate in a boycott (and, as a consequence, opposition–incumbent negotiations) might be complicated by the need for intra-opposition negotiation and coordination.

Even though oppositions are rarely completely unified, assuming opposition parties behave "as if" they are a unitary actor still provides a great deal of theoretical utility. Major boycotts are much more common than minor boycotts, and approximately two-thirds of major boycotts occur in elections where a single party dominates the opposition's share of legislative seats.[24] Although in many cases other opposition parties later become involved in the boycott, when a single party controls a dominant share of the opposition, the need for explicit coordination among parties is greatly reduced, because the actions of the dominant party alone would be sufficient to bring about a major boycott. Although intra-opposition dynamics may complicate negotiations between the incumbent and opposition in approximately one-third of major boycott cases, those cases do not show any statistically significant difference from other major boycotts in terms of causes or consequences. As such, the general classification of major boycott does a good job of capturing the theoretical logic presented here, and it receives the bulk of our attention in this study. The two factors that have the biggest impact on the opposition's protest decision in this pre-election phase are available information and incumbent credibility.

Information Problems and Negotiation Breakdown

In a situation where all actors have complete information, as in investment theory's efficient market hypothesis, the opposition would know the total size of M and make its decision to participate or boycott accordingly. With complete information, the incumbent would also know the exact level of manipulation that the opposition would be willing to accept. Under such circumstances, we would expect the incumbent to promise a level of manipulation that would induce the opposition to participate or at least would make the opposition indifferent between participating and boycotting. The incumbent wants to retain power and is thus motivated to manipulate elections, but she also wants international recognition for holding democratic elections – which is much easier to obtain with opposition participation. Unfortunately, when it comes to questions of how much manipulation the incumbent intends to commit and how much manipulation the opposition is willing to accept, both sides have incentives to misrepresent the truth. Where opportunities exist to produce and misrepresent private information, negotiations have the potential to fail. Failure to agree at this stage of the negotiation will produce a major election boycott.

---

[24] Based on cases where data are available, the proportion of major boycotts in which a single party dominates the opposition (69%) is actually lower than the proportion of all elections in which a single party dominates the opposition (77%), though this difference is not statistically significant.

How Much Manipulation Is the Incumbent Committing?

The incumbent would always benefit by being perceived as manipulating less than she actually is – because even though manipulation confers an electoral advantage, negative perceptions of manipulation (if detected) may be costly. Domestically, the cleaner that elites and voters perceive an election to be, the more likely they will interpret the results as a legitimate reflection of citizens' will. The more that any particular citizen believes the incumbent is genuinely popular, the less likely he or she should be to challenge the regime. Furthermore, because the incumbent is operating in the pro-democracy international climate described previously, perceptions that she is running a clean election should also result in increased international benefits.

The opposition typically has at least some idea about the size of m_I, but at the same time because he lacks the knowledge that actually comes with committing the manipulation in question, he cannot be absolutely certain of its size. Furthermore the incumbent should *always* try to misrepresent the extent to which she is manipulating the election, making a true assessment of m_I even more difficult. Essentially, even if the opposition is aware that the incumbent is engaged in manipulation at this stage, it will be very difficult for the opposition to be certain of the size of m_I.

How Much Manipulation Is the Opposition Willing to Accept?

The degree of opposition indifference to incumbent manipulation will depend on opposition strength, with a stronger opposition tolerating less manipulation. We can think of opposition strength as having two dimensions: (1) the proportion of support received in the electorate and (2) the extent to which the opposition is cohesive or fragmented. Clearly, as the opposition's popularity in the electorate increases, he becomes stronger vis-à-vis the incumbent. For a theory that assumes a unitary actor, as this one does, this measure would be sufficient to capture opposition strength. As previously mentioned, however, the extent to which oppositions are actually unified in reality differs. Even if the opposition enjoys a large proportion of support in the electorate, more fragmentation will reduce the opposition's strength.

Just as the opposition must estimate incumbent manipulation, so the incumbent will have to estimate opposition strength at this point – because the full extent of opposition strength will not be revealed until the election has occurred. What matters most, then, in this pre-election phase is the accuracy of the incumbent's information about the opposition's strength. Furthermore, just as the incumbent always has incentives to misrepresent the extent to which she is engaged in election manipulation, so the opposition actor always has the incentive to misrepresent the extent of his popular support and organizational unity. The extent to which the opposition even possesses private information in this regard is unclear – that is to say, it is likely but not certain that the opposition knows more about his own domestic support and organization than does the incumbent.[25] But even if he does not possess this private information, that should not deter the opposition from suggesting that he knows more about his support than the incumbent, if he believes doing so might result in a more favorable level of *M*.

Low-Information Environments

The potential for the misrepresentation of private information to cause bargaining failure brings us to the third and final scope condition of politics in the developing world. Low levels of economic development produce several structural barriers to obtaining reliable national-level information, such that political actors in the developing world are more likely to be operating in low-information environments. Both a lack of reliable, independent media and low literacy levels lead to a situation where reliable information is costly, in several senses of the word, for many political actors (elites included) to obtain. Much of the work to date on the political impact of limited information has focused on constraints – such as a lack of time, education, or other resources – on the individual's ability to make informed decisions and his or her subsequent use of information shortcuts.[26] By contrast, my argument is that structural barriers to information facilitate the creation – and misrepresentation of – private information, which then increases the probability of noncooperative outcomes such as electoral protest.

Three common factors contribute to creating low-information environments for elites in their negotiation over electoral conduct: the limited capacity of media outlets to generate accurate information, the limited capacity of individual citizens to act as critical consumers, and the extent to which the incumbent has engaged in manipulation in the past. First, national media in developing countries tend to be limited in scope and usually are not independent of the incumbent government. Barkan (2000) notes that in Africa, for example, the mainstream media are typically tightly controlled by the government. In accounts of the 2000 presidential elections in Kyrgyzstan, the media are described as having "devoted most [of their coverage] time to the pro-government candidates" (Abazov 2003, 550). In Cambodian elections in 1993, the ruling Cambodian People's Party (CPP) used state media to link its main competitor FUNCINPEC to the Khmer Rouge, going so far as to broadcast the 1984 American movie *The Killing Fields* on national television in the runup to the election (Roberts 1994, 158). Although some of the limits on the media's production of information could certainly be a consequence of regime type, governments of every type prefer favorable media coverage and try as best they can to control their image in the press. Furthermore, even in the most democratic regimes, low levels of economic development

---

[25] It is also possible that due to previous electoral manipulation the opposition, like the incumbent, may not have an accurate idea of its own support.

[26] For a comprehensive overview of the information shortcuts literature see Chandra (2004, 34).

leave the media lacking independent resources and, as such, weaker and more vulnerable to co-optation by the government, thereby reducing the prospects for a flourishing, independent media. A comparison of Freedom House's 2006 press freedom rankings to levels of economic development (measured by GDP per capita) and then to the competitive authoritarian regime type finds a much stronger correlation between press freedom and economic development than between press freedom and regime type.[27]

The second factor contributing to low-information environments is a population with relatively low literacy. A March 2009 online report from *The Guardian* found average literacy rates of 56.3% in the least developed countries compared to 99% in high-income OECD countries.[28] Literacy levels tell us something about individuals' capacities to consume information, and with the advent of radio and television literacy may seem less relevant to the creation of common knowledge in a society; however, literacy is critical to ensuring the overall accuracy of available information. News, whether delivered by television, radio, or print media, must contain accurate information if it is to generate useful common knowledge for elites, and literacy serves as an important check on the accuracy of available information. Media are under pressure to provide more accurate information when they report to a literate population that has other means to verify the information it is receiving. Media that report to an illiterate population are under fewer constraints.

Here it is important to remind the reader that we are discussing information environments in terms of information and media at the national level. I do not mean to suggest that individuals are completely uninformed even if they face information constraints from media or illiteracy. Clearly, as Chwe's (2001) work suggests, local institutions and social networks make local information plentiful and verifiable, even for those individuals who cannot read. The low-information environment becomes relevant, however, when we think about national-level elections because elite actors attempt to coordinate at the national level and must rely on information of a broader scope; at this level institutions that facilitate the creation of local, common knowledge are not likely to be sufficient.

Finally, the incumbent's earlier choices with respect to manipulation have consequences for the information environment. Electoral manipulation produces a kind of informational constraint for the elite actor who undertakes it, much like the "Dictator's Dilemma" described by Wintrobe (1998). To the extent that manipulation actually distorts the electoral outcome in favor of the manipulator, it gives her some advantage. Furthermore, because manipulation is typically attempted in secret, it may confer a bargaining advantage to the

---

[27] See http://www.freedomhouse.org/report/freedom-press/freedom-press-2007. CA Regimes are coded as in Levitsky and Way (2010).

[28] See http://www.guardian.co.uk/news/datablog/2009/mar/09/literacy. Accessed by author September 1, 2009.

perpetrator in the form of private information. At the same time, manipulation disadvantages all political elites equally (including the incumbent) because it reduces certainty about each actor's true support in the electorate. Although the manipulator knows what has been done to try to sway the election, once manipulation has occurred, she has no way of knowing for certain how the election would have turned out absent these efforts. The problem, then, is that manipulation today may impede successful bargaining tomorrow by constraining available common knowledge in the future. As such, even if the incumbent is genuinely trying to reduce manipulation at time t, previous manipulation at time t-1 may leave her with no accurate sense of the opposition's strength, which could cause her unwittingly to select a level of manipulation that the opposition will not accept.

Here, it is important to distinguish among electoral uncertainty, low information, and private information. Free and fair elections are inherently uncertain events: Until voters go to the polls and the votes are tallied, no candidate knows for certain who is going to win. However, increased information decreases the uncertainty inherent in free and fair elections. More information – from surveys, polls, and the like – makes electoral outcomes more predictable. Therefore the extent to which the society in question is a low- or high-information society will affect the degree of uncertainty surrounding even the most free and fair election. The absence of reliable media and regular polls, combined with a population lacking the literacy to critically consume such material, increases the uncertainty associated with elections. Voters may not have enough information on the candidates or the choices of their fellow voters to make meaningful choices themselves.[29]

In low-information environments actors operate under conditions of heightened uncertainty, but shouldn't that increased uncertainty be only a problem for individual citizens and not for political elites? It may be true that elites have access to more or better information than the average citizen, but this does not mean that they are unaffected by the low-information environment. Even though incumbent and opposition politicians are typically literate and clearly have incentives to gain more information about national-level events, a low-information environment is likely to pose problems for them as well. Even if elite actors are able to critically consume national-level information, the lack of a free and reliable press reduces information available for elite consumption. Furthermore, recall that prior manipulation also reduces the availability of accurate information for elite political actors. In low-information environments, political elites will have difficulty making accurate assessments of incumbent manipulation and opposition support.

Low-information environments not only increase general uncertainty but they also make it easier for actors to conceal or misrepresent information.

---

[29] Here the notion of a meaningful choice is meant to indicate that the voters are able to make decisions that accurately reflect their preferences, be those preferences sincere (policy-based) or strategic.

Information about the election that one actor has while the other actor does not constitutes private information, which is distinct from general uncertainty. Examples of private information are secret polling data that one political party keeps from the other. Such private information will give the actor who possesses it a better idea of the likely outcome of the election. Although there is no direct correlation between the level of available information in a society and the production of private information, a low-information environment makes it easier to create private information. We can think of there being an inverse relationship between the information environment and the possibilities for creating and misrepresenting private information. As the level of available information increases, opportunities to create and misrepresent information decrease. Thus, the available information in a society is important because it tells us something not only about the amount of electoral uncertainty under which political actors operate but also the probability that one or more actors possesses private information.

This ability to create and misrepresent private information has a direct impact on opposition choices and behavior in the pre-election phase. There are two scenarios in which a low-information environment might lead to a boycott. First, a lack of available information might lead the opposition to suspect that the incumbent is engaging in more manipulation than she claims. If the opposition finds that suspected level of manipulation to be unacceptable, he may boycott the election. Second, a lack of available information may lead the incumbent to believe the opposition has less support than the opposition claims. If the incumbent believes the opposition to be more tolerant of manipulation than he actually is, she may mistakenly choose a level of manipulation that is too high to be acceptable to the opposition. If the incumbent's chosen level of manipulation is unacceptable to the opposition, he will choose to boycott.

Credibility and Bargaining Failure

Thus far, the account given here is one of the role of private information and of incentives to misrepresent such information in causing bargaining failure over electoral conduct and leading to an election boycott. Another possibility in Decision Point 2, when the opposition needs to decide whether to boycott or participate, is that an inability to make credible commitments leads to bargaining failure. In cases where problems of credible commitment arise, the two parties might be able to reach an agreement, but at least one actor does not trust the other to adhere to the bargain, and so it fails (Fearon 1995, 401). At this stage in the negotiations, the incumbent's credibility is of the most concern. In determining whether to participate or boycott, the opposition must decide if he believes the incumbent's claims (either implicit or explicit) about the level of M in the election. If the opposition feels as if he can trust the incumbent to stick to a particular level of M (and finds M to be acceptable), then the opposition will participate. If the opposition does not trust the incumbent to adhere to M

(remember that at least some portion of $M - m_2$ – has yet to happen) then the opposition may boycott.

The opposition's credibility is less of a concern at this point because participation in the election is easier to verify than manipulation. Whereas the opposition may have real reason to be concerned about the extent to which the incumbent will adhere to an acceptable level of manipulation, the incumbent merely has to observe whether the opposition participates in the election as promised. Two factors in particular affect incumbent credibility: whether there are institutions that offer constraints on incumbent behavior and whether the incumbent has developed a reputation for being trustworthy (or not).

In sum, in this second stage of the model, the opposition decides whether to stage a major boycott or participate in the election. The imbalance of resources between incumbent and opposition help us understand why the opposition does not have the same options to manipulate as the incumbent does. Although a rational incumbent and opposition should be able to negotiate an agreement that would allow for opposition participation, two factors can cause bargaining to fail at this point. Low-information environments may create more opportunities for the misrepresentation of private information – on the part of either the incumbent or opposition – which will increase the probability of bargaining failure resulting in a boycott. The opposition may also boycott if problems of incumbent credibility make it difficult for the opposition to believe that the incumbent will adhere to a promised level of manipulation.

DECISION POINT 3: ELECTION OCCURS AND THE INCUMBENT PRODUCES SOME TOTAL LEVEL OF MANIPULATION $M = m_1 + m_2$

During the election itself, the incumbent will decide how much additional manipulation to commit (m_2). Among the options open to the incumbent for manipulation at this stage are to complete the process of vote buying, artificially inflate her vote totals by having her supporters "stuff" the ballot box, and engage in more violent repression in an attempt to keep opposition supporters away from the polls. A 2002 survey in Mexico found that 26.1% of respondents received gifts from parties or candidates in the 2000 election (Cornelius 2002, cited in Lehoucq 2007). Cox and Kousser (1981) detail the process by which politicians in rural New York – after the introduction of the Australian ballot – found it more efficient to pay supporters of their opponents *not* to vote, rather than trying to buy their vote. Campbell (2003, 275–6) provides another historical example: Democrats in Louisville, Kentucky, circa 1905, would target African American voters, who were typically Republican, with violent intimidation using "thugs" or police.

Another common tactic for m_2 is manipulating the vote count after polling stations have closed. Here again, examples abound from early American politics – exemplified by the Thomas Nast 1870 cartoon depicting William "Boss" Tweed, of the Tammany Hall political machine in New York, with the

"THAT'S WHAT'S THE MATTER."

Boss Tweed. "As long as I count the Votes, what are you going to do about it? say?"

FIGURE 2.3. American Electoral Manipulation under Boss Tweed. "That's What's the Matter. Boss Tweed: 'As long as I count the Votes, what are you going to do about it? Say?'" *Source:* Thomas Nast, 1871. Courtesy of University of Kentucky Special Collections Library.

caption, "As long as I count the votes, what are you going to do about it?" – indicating that those with political power were at liberty to manipulate vote counts to their advantage (Fig. 2.3).

Today, vote count manipulation can be a high-tech affair. For example, in the 1994 Dominican Republic election, the incumbent was found to have rigged computerized voter registers in each polling station to replace the names and affiliations of 20–40 opposition supporters with an equivalent number of fake supporters for the incumbent, thereby netting an additional 40–80 votes per station.[30] Vote count manipulation can also be a decidedly low-tech affair,

---

[30] Information from author interview, conducted May 2005, with Hatuey Des Camps, long time PRD politician and witness to the electoral events of 1994.

as in Nigeria where nonrandom patterns of last digits in vote tallies from recent elections were found to be consistent with individuals having altered the vote count by hand (Beber and Scacco 2012). Yet the incumbent must still take care with m_2, because the opposition's decision to accept the election results or engage in post-election mass demonstrations looms.

Regardless of the nature and amount of manipulation that the incumbent chooses to implement on Election Day, this third stage of the incumbent–opposition electoral negotiations is an information-generating event. As supporters from both sides turn out to participate in the election (or stay home) and the opposition has more opportunities to observe the incumbent's manipulation, the election generates information, which both the opposition and incumbent will take into account in the final stages of negotiation after the election. Violence is the most observable form of incumbent manipulation during the election – although there are often attempts to obscure the source of violence. Other forms of manipulation – vote buying, for example – may also be observed directly at this point, as may indicators of opposition support.

If the opposition chose to boycott the election, then the election results also provide information on the immediate consequences of the boycott. Because, by definition, major election boycotts require most opposition parties and candidates to withdraw from competition, we would expect boycotts to increase the probability that the incumbent wins the election. Furthermore, because boycott campaigns work to encourage voters to stay away from the polls on Election Day, then voter turnout also indicates whether election boycotts succeeded in reducing the number of voters. Finally, to the extent that election boycotts keep opposition supporters home on Election Day, they may also reduce election-related violence.

DECISION POINT 4: OPPOSITION OBSERVES M AND DECIDES WHETHER TO ACCEPT THE RESULTS OR PROTEST AFTER THE ELECTION

Based on more information on M and on his own electoral support, provided by Election Day, the opposition must decide whether to accept the results of the election or to call his supporters out in the street to protest. One possible outcome is that the opposition observes a level of M that is acceptable and so decides to accept the election results. Or the opposition may decide to protest – either because M exceeded a level the opposition found acceptable or because the election produced new information about opposition strength and the opposition no longer finds the previously agreed-on level of M to be acceptable. Put differently, either the incumbent's promise regarding manipulation or the opposition's promise to accept a certain level of manipulation proves not to be credible. Although it is difficult to determine whether problems of incumbent or opposition credibility ultimately lead to post-election mass demonstrations, opposition strength is central to the problem on either side. Nineteen percent of all elections (148) in the data set saw demonstrations after the election, of which 47% (69) were directly initiated by the opposition and 68% (100) saw some form of opposition involvement, either initiation or support of the protest.

When the opposition decides to protest after the election, opposition leaders make a public call for their supporters to take to the streets to demonstrate a rejection of the election. For example, opposition party candidates and their supporters staged rallies following the February 2003 presidential elections in Armenia. The incumbent, Robert Kocharyan, won a narrow victory in the first round of the election and ended up defeating the opposition candidate, Stepan Demirchyan, in the second round. Demirchyan then encouraged his supporters to turn out for protests, claiming that he was the actual winner of the presidential election and urging them to go to the president's residency and "take power by force."[31] This contentious tone of protest carried over into the actual demonstrations near the central election commission of Armenia, where protesters clashed with police.[32] However, some post-election demonstrations occur that are not initiated by opposition parties, such as after the 1986 elections in the Dominican Republic, where city workers protested vote counting in the municipal-level elections that were held concurrently with the national contest, or after the 2004 election in Guinea-Bissau where groups of voters protested the late opening of polling stations.

As with elections themselves, post-election demonstrations are information-generating events. Inherent to these protests are direct appeals to the public, which do more to generate information about the opposition's position and possibly to communicate opposition strength to the incumbent than would, say, simply holding a press conference (which mainstream media may or may not cover) and stepping aside. If opposition parties wish to generate common knowledge either about incumbent manipulation or their own support in the electorate, protest serves that function better than nonparticipation, rhetorical complaints, or formal institutional challenges to the incumbent.

Opposition Strength and Credibility

The information generated by the election makes it unlikely that negotiation breakdown (protest) will occur at this stage because of information problems. The issue of credibility, however, remains relevant to the opposition's decision whether to engage in protest demonstrations after the election. Whereas incumbent credibility is at the heart of the opposition's decision to boycott

---

[31] Armenian president threatens tough action over opposition unrest – BBC Monitoring Trans Caucasus Unit Supplied by BBC Worldwide Monitoring, February 22, 2003, Saturday.

[32] Armenian opposition protesters want Demirchyan declared poll winner – BBC Monitoring Trans Caucasus Unit Supplied by BBC Worldwide Monitoring, February 20, 2003, Thursday; Partakers in opposition rally clash with police in Yerevan – News Bulletin, February 20, 2003, Thursday.

before the election, in the post-election phase problems of both incumbent and opposition credibility may arise.

Recall that the opposition's tolerance for manipulation is going to depend on his strength: The weaker the opposition, the more manipulation the incumbent can employ while still expecting opposition participation and acceptance. As the opposition grows stronger, the amount of M he will tolerate shrinks, and the incumbent who wishes to avoid opposition protest will need to reduce the amount of manipulation she commits accordingly. At the same time as the incumbent may wish to avoid protest, however, she will feel a competing desire to maintain or even increase manipulation in the face of a strong opposition, because any reductions in manipulation efforts place her position of power in more jeopardy.

Whether the incumbent chooses to reduce manipulation or not, opposition strength increases the probability of post-election demonstrations. In a case where the incumbent cannot resist the temptation to manipulate to compete more effectively with a strong opposition, the opposition will protest on the grounds that M is unacceptable. Yet, even if the incumbent takes the risk of reducing manipulation, if the opposition is strong but does not win the election, he is likely to protest anyway. Supporters of Augusto Pinochet recognized this dilemma when the long time ruler subjected his presidency to a plebiscite, saying, "If the government's candidate wins everyone will say it was fraud. If he loses everyone will say it was a fair election."[33] Thus, a strong opposition may be unable to maintain the commitment to accept the outcome of the election if he loses, even if the incumbent did not exceed the agreed-on level of manipulation.

Just as we would expect to observe certain consequences from an election boycott, post-election mass demonstrations should have predictable elements and outcomes. Given the fact that these protests are more likely to happen when the opposition is stronger vis-à-vis the incumbent, we might expect such protests to be accompanied by higher levels of violence, compared to other types of protests. Furthermore, to the extent that these protests represent a departure from the peaceful transfer of power associated with the democratic ideal of electoral outcomes, they might have the potential to destabilize the country, producing more irregular transfers of power.

DECISION POINT 5: INCUMBENT DECIDES HOW TO RESPOND TO INSTANCES OF PROTEST

In this final stage, if electoral protest has occurred at any point during the election process and the incumbent retains power after the election, she will have to decide how to respond to the protest. It is the incumbent's response that

---

[33] Quoted in Huntington (1991, 84).

will determine the electoral protest's consequences for democracy in that country. Protested elections reveal information, and the information generated by the protest regarding support for the opposition should affect the incumbent's response. At their most informative, boycotts or post-election demonstrations may generate new public information about the nature and extent of incumbent electoral manipulation, as they did in the Dominican Republic electoral protests of 1994. Even if electoral protest does not reveal any new information about incumbent manipulation, however, it will reveal information about the nature and extent of opposition support. Opposition candidates publicly refuse to participate in the election or call their supporters into the streets after the fact, and these actions will either receive support from voters or not. Similarly, the protest will either generate international attention or it will not. The incumbent will use this information to decide how to respond.

Democratic Consequences: Incumbent Response

Faced with opposition protest, we expect the incumbent to make concessions relative to the extent that she feels threatened by the protest. The strength of the protest should determine whether the incumbent responds at all: If the protest yields little or no domestic or international support, the incumbent is likely to ignore it; if the incumbent feels substantial pressure as a result of the protest, however, she is likely to produce some reform or change to satisfy the protesters. If opposition support is so strong that the incumbent feels sufficiently threatened, she may choose to abdicate power, and often the individual who subsequently assumes power offers reforms to respond to the protests. This likely explains what happened following Indonesia's 1997 election: Long time President Suharto resigned several months after the election, in the face of mounting popular pressure, and his vice president, B. J. Habibie, assumed the presidency and instituted sweeping democratic reforms. Where opposition protest reveals enough strength that the incumbent does not necessarily fear for her life but fears for her capacity to stay in office in the long run if she does not respond, we should expect to see the incumbent respond with reform.

The kind of reform that the incumbent enacts when she chooses to respond will likely be determined by the nature of opposition support revealed by the protest. If support for the electoral protest is largely domestic, the incumbent faces a dilemma with respect to reform similar to the one she faced with manipulation in the election: Greater support for the protest makes the incumbent feel more pressure to reform, but greater domestic support for the opposition suggests that any democratic reforms the incumbent makes will hurt her own electoral fortunes in the future, because they will allow this domestic support for the opposition to more accurately translate into votes for the opposition. As such, we would expect incumbents who feel threatened by domestic actors to attempt to make reforms that will still leave them room to manipulate in the future. When the support for electoral protest is largely international, however, the incumbent is less threatened by the prospect of electoral defeat and more likely to enact democratic reforms that will increase her regime's international legitimacy and do not necessarily jeopardize the incumbent's future at the polls. Circumstances where the incumbent is faced with both domestic and international support for protest do not yield clear reform expectations, because the outcome may ultimately depend on whether the incumbent feels more pressure from domestic or international sources – with an authoritarian response signaling more concern about domestic support and a democratic response indicating more concern for international actors.

Reform and Credibility

In instances where the incumbent is motivated to enact democratic election-related reform, such reforms may represent an effort to increase her future credibility. Elites enhance their credibility when policy decisions are no longer made directly by individuals, but are transferred instead to institutions (Acemoglu and Robinson 2006, 26). This is why democratic election-related reform, particularly reforms that increase the independence of election administration and build in safeguards against manipulation, would work to enhance the credibility of the incumbent in the future. Specifically, these reforms would render more credible incumbent promises to hold a free and fair election.

International Pressure

Here the theory returns to its contextual starting point: international pressure for democracy. The theory does not suggest any direct impact of international pressure on the likelihood of bargaining success or failure; the opposition may feel emboldened to protest when it feels it has international support, but knowledge of such support should also motivate the incumbent to respond preemptively with less manipulation. We would expect international pressure to have consequences, however, for how the incumbent responds to electoral protest. Where the support for protest is largely domestic, it does not make sense to think that the incumbent would respond with democratic reform – given that more support for the opposition should translate into worse future electoral performance for the incumbent, particularly if she decides to curtail manipulation. But when electoral protests receive international support, incumbents should be motivated to respond with reform in the hopes of receiving international benefits and because they do not perceive the immediate threat to their electoral fortunes posed by domestic support for protest.

ELITE BARGAINING FAILURE

The theory outlined in this chapter provides a plausible explanation for electoral protests and their democratic consequences, but it raises the question of how realistic it is to think about incumbent and opposition elites as engaged in negotiations, particularly during elections, which we tend to characterize as a time when elites who are competing are not likely to cooperate. The anecdotal record provides several examples of elites formally bargaining over matters of electoral manipulation. For example, Barkan (2000, 234) describes bargaining in Kenya between the opposition and incumbent that resulted in a "minimum package of constitutional reforms – without which the opposition would have boycotted Kenya's second multi-party elections of 1997." At the behest of international donors, incumbent and opposition representatives met in the year before Guyana's March 2001 elections and managed to agree on a revised formula for the allocation of the country's 65 assembly seats.[34] After contentious elections in 1993, Gabon's incumbent and opposition parties negotiated a series of constitutional amendments, including a revised electoral code and the establishment of an independent electoral commission, all with the assistance of the Organization of African Unity (Fleischhacker 1999, 390). More recently, the March 2008 elections in Zimbabwe were preceded by a round of negotiations in January between the opposition and the incumbent over several election-related laws. Even though the government offered some concessions, negotiations broke down in late January and the opposition began to threaten a boycott.[35] The opposition ended up participating in the elections, but the main opposition candidate for the presidency, Morgan Tsvangirai, boycotted the second round of voting.[36]

Whereas the preceding examples describe circumstances where negotiation was explicit, in many other cases either the incumbent or the opposition acknowledges the issue of elite manipulation "as if" the two parties were formally negotiating. In Equatorial Guinea in 1996, the government decided to replace the voter registers that had been drawn up with the help of the UN after contentious elections in 1993, producing its own registers to be used in the 1996 election (Fleischhacker 1999, 353). Not consulted formally on this decision, the opposition voiced its disapproval publicly and ultimately boycotted the election.[37] In Bangladesh, the opposition Awami League accused the governing Nationalist Party (BNP) of fraud during a 1994 by-election and subsequently refused to take their seats in parliament. For the Awami League, the by-election was representative of a broader pattern of fraud, and therefore the opposition party demanded a law that would install a caretaker government before each future election (Ahmed 2001, 518). Though no formal talks

---

[34] Guyana: International electoral funding delayed pending accord between parties. BBC Monitoring Latin America – Political Supplied by BBC Worldwide Monitoring, June 4, 2000; Guyana: Commission reaches agreement on electoral reform. BBC Monitoring Latin America – Political Supplied by BBC Worldwide Monitoring, June 28, 2000.

[35] Clotty, Peter. Zimbabwe changes Media, Security laws. *Voice of America*. January, 21, 2008.; Latham, Brian. "Zimbabwe opposition MDC threatens poll boycott on constitution." Bloomberg.com, January 21, 2008.

[36] Zimbabwe: Tsvangirai officially withdraws but Mugabe to go ahead with run off. SW Radio Africa (allAfrica.com), June 24, 2008.

[37] Voting under way in Equatorial Guinea despite boycott. Agence France Presse. February 25.

between the parties were reported, the BNP publicly acknowledged Awami League demands and claimed to be amenable to them; however, the BNP claimed that it was constitutionally unable to meet those demands, because opposition parties had boycotted parliament in protest (518). The opposition in Venezuela announced a boycott one week before that country's 2005 election, accusing President Chavez of electoral manipulation. It claimed that new electronic voting technology violated the secrecy of the ballot and noted that four of the country's five election judges had close ties to the president.[38] Chavez publicly dismissed the opposition's accusations of fraud, saying, "What fraud? [The opposition] should accept the fact that they have no public. It's an attempt at political sabotage."[39]

In each of the three preceding examples, although the demands of the opposition and subsequent incumbent responses did not take place in a setting of formal bargaining, opposition actors did make demands for a certain level of electoral manipulation and incumbents did respond to those demands, as if formal negotiations were taking place.

International Pressure for Democracy in Guyana

With respect to the three developing-world scope conditions posited in this chapter, Guyana's history of elections provides a clear example of developing countries' vulnerability to international pressure and to the shift in western actors' preferences. Guyana's pre-independence elections in the 1950s and 1960s experienced interference from powerful western actors focused on combating communism. Early victories of the PPP (led by Jagan, a self-avowed Marxist) were typically followed by British intervention and installation of more explicitly anticommunist leadership (Trefs 2005, 354). Both the British and U.S. governments made it clear that they were not amenable to Guyanese independence under PPP leadership (355). When the conservative PNC narrowly lost the 1961 elections, the United States funded mass demonstrations and a general strike, and the British government declared a state of emergency (355). Under such international pressure Jagan agreed to electoral reforms, which ultimately made it possible for the PNC to win control of the government in 1964. Even though the PNC evinced a questionable commitment to democratic principles early on – quickly bringing election administration under the control of the government and staffing it with PNC loyalists – Guyana was granted independence from Great Britain in 1966.

Western interests in Guyanese politics began to shift as the end of the Cold War drew near. The United States tacitly accepted PNC domination, with its

[38] Deutsche Presse-Agentur. Two injured in blasts as boycott overshadows Venezuelan election. December 4, 2005, Sunday. 15:35:24 Central European Time.

[39] Toothaker, Christopher. 2005. Venezuela opposition parties pull out of congressional elections. *Associated Press, International* News, November 29.

rigged elections and suppression of dissent, throughout the 1970s and early 1980s. By the mid-1980s, however, "anticommunist" justifications for U.S. support of Guyana were growing thin, and the Reagan administration dramatically decreased Guyana's aid and access to capital (Levitsky and Way 2010, 148). The PNC government tried first to repair relations with the West through economic liberalization, but economic reforms failed to attract international support. As the global tide turned to favor democracy, the government found it necessary to implement a series of electoral reforms and invite international election observers to monitor the 1992 elections.

Resource Imbalance in Cote d'Ivoire

Events in Cote d'Ivoire's 2010 election highlight how an imbalance of resources can enable incumbents to out-manipulate the opposition, even when the opposition has some opportunities to engage in manipulation.[40] On December 1, when Yacouba Bamba, spokesman for the country's Independent Electoral Commission (IEC), attempted to announce the results of the country's November 28 presidential runoff election to the press, he was impeded from doing so by two members of the IEC who supported President Laurent Gbagbo. One of these individuals, Topaka Vehy Etienne, interrupted the announcement, stating that the IEC had not yet verified the results, and the other individual, Damana Pickass, eventually ripped the results from Bamba's hand and left the press conference.[41] These actions were justified later (by a representative of Gbagbo) on the grounds that suspicions of opposition fraud in some northern provinces of the country, where the opposition dominated, needed to be investigated.[42] Yet even if in this instance the opposition parties were responsible for Election Day fraud in the north, the government's blatant obstruction of the release of the election results highlight the kinds of manipulation opportunities still disproportionately available to incumbent elites.

Low-Information Environment in Niger

The boycott of Niger's November 1996 legislative elections is an example where a low-information environment contributed to the inability of the incumbent and opposition to reach an agreement to prevent a boycott. Although the number of private radio stations in Niger had increased since 1994, media freedoms had been suspended with the January 1996 coup d'état.[43] Thus, actors did not

---

[40] Electoral protest in Cote d'Ivoire is discussed in greater detail in Chapter 4.
[41] Video footage of this incident is available at http://www.unmultimedia.org/tv/unifeed/d/16496.html.
[42] See http://www.euronews.net/2010/12/02/results-farce-in-cote-d-ivoire-election/.
[43] Seminaire-Atelier de Formation et de Sensibilisation, "Mission de service public dans les entreprises de presse d'Etat et privée." Historical Introduction to Press Laws, in conference proceedings, Organized by FIJ/SAINFO/LO-TCO CCOG. NIAMEY (June 2002).

have the benefit of free media in the pre-election phase. General literacy rates in Niger were also very low; the World Bank's first recorded indicator in 2001 put the adult literacy rate at 9.39% of the population older than 15 years of age. This figure had only increased to 28% as of 2005. Finally, incumbent manipulation of presidential elections in July 1996 further compromised the information environment. In response, opposition parties staged demonstrations after the presidential election, alleging fraud; trade unions supported the opposition claims and called for general strikes across the country, which opposition representatives claimed were well supported.[44]

At issue in the presidential election was General Ibrahim Mainassara Bare's dissolving the IEC on the second day of voting and replacing it with a national commission controlled by the government. He then placed opposition candidates under house arrest and barred party representatives and independent observers from the vote-counting centers on the second day of voting. According to the U.S., State Department, "The government-appointed electoral commission subsequently announced provisional results showing voter participation and votes for Bare significantly greater on the second day than on the first. As a consequence, we do not believe the announced outcome of the elections is a true reflection of the wishes of the Nigerien people."[45] Opposition parties formed an alliance (Front for the Restoration and Defense of Democracy) for the November legislative contest, but ultimately chose to boycott those elections (Di Lorenzo and Sborgi (2001).

CONCLUSION

Thus, examples of both elite negotiations (and bargaining failure) and three developing-world scope conditions suggest that the simplified theory presented in this chapter offers a realistic picture of incumbent and elite behavior during the electoral process. Chapters 3–5 take up the theoretical logic presented in this chapter and subject it to empirical scrutiny using an original data set of electoral protest and election-related reform for all multiparty elections in the developing world from 1975 to 2006. Chapter 3 focuses on Decision Points 2 and 4 in the model – the causes of election boycott and post-election demonstrations. Chapter 4 focuses on Decision Points 3 and 4 – the consequences of boycotted elections and the aftermath of post-election demonstrations. Chapter 5 focuses on Decision Point 5 – the incumbent responses to protest – by addressing the democratic consequences of electoral protest in the countries where they occur.

---

[44] BBC Summary of World Broadcasts. July 15, 1996, Monday. NIGER. Offices of opposition parties closed down. Radio France Internationale, Paris, in French 1730 GMT, July 12.
[45] Ibid.

3

Causes of Electoral Protest

Every major opposition party boycotted Cameroon's presidential election in October 1997. Even though there were no reports of formal bargaining between incumbent and opposition prior to the boycott, the incumbent and opposition had begun to take action in response to each other's behavior much earlier that year. In January 1997, the opposition complained about problems with voter registration, and then President Biya postponed the legislative elections that had been scheduled for March to respond to opposition complaints. During this time the president also created a new election management body (*Cameroon: A Transition in Crisis, Article 19*, 10). After the delayed legislative elections were held in May, opposition parties complained about the president's manipulation of constituencies and voter registration, attributing the manipulation to the new, government-controlled electoral management body the president had created. In threatening to boycott the upcoming October presidential election, the opposition actors described the newly created system as "fraudulent" and reported their concerns to representatives of the French government. (Cameroon is a former French colony and still enjoys a particularly close relationship with that country.[1]) A representative of the French Foreign Ministry indicated that France would be paying close attention to the election and expressed a preference for opposition participation.[2] But despite opposition threats to boycott and the expressed preferences of powerful international actors, incumbent president Paul Biya refused to create an independent election management board, retaining instead the management body controlled

---

[1] Cameroon: Opposition Meeting banned. IRIN-WA Daily Media Update 59–97 of Events in West Africa, 7 October 1997. United Nations Department of Humanitarian Affairs.
[2] Ibid.

by the government.[3] The opposition, in response, refused to participate and boycotted the election.

According to the theory presented in Chapter 2, incumbent and opposition elites in developing countries bargain, or act as if they are bargaining, over the extent of pro-incumbent manipulation of the election because they feel international pressure to hold multiparty elections. Opposition parties initiate electoral protest when bargaining over the incumbent's electoral manipulation fails. Two general problems hinder the bargaining efforts of elites, even when both sides would likely prefer a bargained outcome to protest: information problems and credibility problems. The first problem, the misrepresentation of private information, can occur through the actions of either the incumbent or the opposition. Incumbent attempts to misrepresent the extent to which they are engaging in manipulation and/or opposition attempts to exaggerate the extent to which they enjoy support may cause bargaining over electoral manipulation to fail, triggering electoral protest. Furthermore, I argue in Chapter 2 that the low-information environment of many developing countries is likely to produce opportunities for the creation and misrepresentation of private information. However, even if misrepresentation of private information is not a problem, if neither the opposition nor the incumbent trusts one another to adhere to the terms of the bargain, problems of credibility might lead to a situation of electoral protest. In the pre-election phase, a lack of incumbent credibility is more likely to trigger electoral protest. Protest after the election can occur as a result of either the incumbent or the opposition lacking credibility.

This chapter focuses on Decision Points 2 and 4 of the model presented in Figure 2.1, presenting evidence consistent with the theory presented in Chapter 2. At Decision Point 2, the opposition must decide whether to participate in the election or boycott. Seven percent (or 57) of the 765 elections in this study experienced a major election boycott. At Decision Point 4, the opposition decides whether to accept the election outcome or to launch mass demonstrations in protest. Nine percent of elections (69) in this study were followed by an opposition-initiated demonstration. This chapter provides evidence that boycotts occur where problems of information or the incumbent's credibility are more likely to arise. By contrast, post-election demonstrations seem to stem from the credibility problems that the opposition's strength can create for either the incumbent or opposition. Whether such problems are ultimately the result of a credibility deficit on the part of the incumbent or the opposition is often difficult to discern in the post-election period.

The analyses presented in this chapter rely on an original set of data on multiparty, national-level elections in the developing world from 1975 to 2006, including presidential and legislative elections in presidential systems, as well as parliamentary or general elections in parliamentary systems. This data set

[3] Outcome of Cameroon Vote: Fear of the Future. *New York Times*, October 14, 1997, Tuesday, Late Edition – Final, Section A; Page 3; Column 1; Foreign Desk.

includes those countries receiving official development assistance (ODA) from the Organization for Economic Cooperation and Development (OECD) during the period 1975–2006. I established the universe of multiparty elections in these countries for this time period using the *Elections in . . .* volumes edited by Dieter Nohlen et al. and published by Oxford University Press, the Election Cycle listings published by the journal *Electoral Studies*, and the electionguide.org Web site.[4] Journalistic sources provided data on a number of measures described in this and subsequent chapters. This data collection effort enabled me to construct a comprehensive picture of electoral protest and related election events throughout the developing world for the 21-year period from 1975 to 2006.

MAJOR ELECTION BOYCOTTS

At Decision Point 2 in Figure 2.1, the opposition must decide whether to participate in the election or to boycott it. The incumbent has already called for the election and begun to engage in some level of pre-election manipulation. The full extent of the incumbent's electoral manipulation, however, is not observable at this point in time, and it may never be completely known if implemented with enough secrecy. For her part, the incumbent should agree to a level of manipulation that will make the opposition willing to participate in the election.[5] Whether the incumbent will succeed in convincing the opposition to participate, however, will depend on available information and how credible the opposition finds the incumbent's promises regarding manipulation.

The election boycotts under study here are those organized by a political opposition that has the legal right to compete in the election. A boycott is considered to have occurred in this study if any eligible political party or candidate publicly refused to compete in the election and followed through with that refusal on Election Day. Encouraging voters to stay away from the polls is typically another component of an opposition-initiated election boycott, but such activity is not an essential element of the boycotts in this study. First and foremost, the election boycotts studied here involve the public refusal to participate on the part of opposition parties or candidates. To collect systematic evidence of this refusal to participate, I gathered reports from newspapers of record around the world and newswire articles in Lexis Nexis, using, most commonly, a search of "[country] election" for the period of time before and after the date of each election in the data set.[6] I chose to rely on international news

---

[4] See Appendix A for more information on data collection and coding decisions.

[5] Recall from Chapter 2 that I assigned the female gender to the incumbent, and the male gender to the opposition in the discussion of the theory.

[6] For each election, searches were conducted for the period six months before the election and three months after. For each case, I used the preliminary search term "[country] election boycott" and "[country] election protest." Where these preliminary searches did not yield sufficient information, I then used the more general "[country] election" search.

sources as opposed to more local news reports, given that one of the central issues in my theory is the quality of available information within each country.[7]

Once I determined that a particular election was boycotted using these methods, I analyzed information from each boycott case to determine whether the boycott in question was a "major" or "minor" boycott, as these categories are mutually exclusive.[8] Although previous work on boycotts characterizes them as either "total" or "partial," I prefer the major/minor distinction, because total boycotts are exceedingly rare and major boycotts provide an appropriate representation of the construct of a boycott developed in Chapter 2.[9] The boycott of the 2003 presidential election in Guinea, for example, was a near-total boycott on the part of the opposition, with the leader of only one small opposition party standing in the election, and general speculation held that this particular party was bankrolled by the incumbent to give an illusion of competition.[10] This example typifies major election boycotts; recall from Chapter 2 that when minor parties or candidates remain in the race it is usually because they are receiving some incentive from the incumbent, typically financial, to do so. In the Dominican Republic in the early 1990s, President Balaguer was notorious for using import tax exemptions as a common side payment to support small political parties. Such support, again, was understood as a way to fragment the opposition and guarantee that some small portion of the opposition would remain "friendly" to the regime.

Drawing a distinction between major and minor boycotts allows me to capture the dynamics outlined in the theory and to identify those opposition actors most likely to be engaged in bargaining with the incumbent, while avoiding the difficult judgment involved in deciding whether a boycott was truly "total." In my model, *Major Boycott* is a dichotomous variable, equal to 1 in those instances where a party or parties representing 50% or more of opposition voters take part in the boycott. Major election boycotts can be undertaken by a single main opposition party, or they can be a coordinated effort among several prominent opposition parties. The Cameroon boycott described in the beginning of this chapter is an example of a major boycott. The boycott of Azerbaijan's presidential election in 1998, in which five prominent opposition candidates refused to participate, is an emblematic example of a major boycott[11]: Most of the legal opposition candidates publicly refused to participate in the election well in advance of Election Day, citing specific issues that they felt gave the incumbent an unfair advantage in the election, and after bargaining with the incumbent broke down. Reports were not clear about the specific provisions of the electoral law that the opposition was protesting in 1998, but two features

---

[7] Similar techniques were used to code measures of post-election mass demonstrations, election-related reform, and violence and international reactions.

[8] See Appendix A for detailed information about each boycott.

[9] See Bratton (1998) and Lindberg (2006a) for examples of this approach to election boycotts.

[10] Rory Caroll. 2003. News roundup: Africa: Guinea's ill ruler clings to power. *The Guardian* (London), December 22.

[11] "Presidential Elections." Keesings Record of World Events. October 1998 – Azerbaijan.

of Azerbaijan's electoral law at that time – the registration requirements and the configuration of the Central Election Commission – could be seen as particularly disadvantageous to the opposition. The registration requirements then required 50,000 signatures from at least 75 single-member constituencies and monetary deposits equal to 25 times the minimum salary for an assembly member for each nominee on a political party's basic list of 25 candidates and reserve list of up to 5 additional candidates (Grotz and Raoul Motika 2001, 351–2). The Central Election Commission then consisted of 14 members selected by the incumbent-dominated parliament and a chairperson selected by the president.

In instances of a *Minor Boycott*, one or more small parties (representing less than 50% of the opposition) join a boycott. For example, the Mohajir Qaumi Mahaz (MQM) party in Pakistan represents the Urdu-speaking Mohajir population – Muslims who emigrated from India after the 1947 partition of India and Pakistan. According to the Minorities at Risk database, Mohajirs report that they are excessively taxed relative to their political representation and that their political organizations have been consistently targeted by the government for repression.[12] In fact, MQM attributed its 1993 election boycott (coded as "minor" in this project) to military discrimination against its candidates. This instance is fairly typical, in that minor boycotts are often undertaken by small opposition parties representing a minority religious or ethnic group in the population and do not primarily address the general conduct of the incumbent, so much as the treatment their party or group has received.

This qualitative difference between the substance of major and minor boycotts is important to keep in mind. Minor boycotts should not be thought of as instances where major boycotts failed to materialize, because most often they are undertaken in the specific interests of a minority party or group, whereas major boycotts address more general electoral manipulation on the part of the incumbent. Thus, this study focuses on major election boycotts, both because they more closely resemble the dynamics described in Chapter 2 and because they are nearly twice as common as minor boycotts. Whereas 57 major election boycotts occurred in the developing world from 1975 to 2006, only 26 minor election boycotts occurred during the same time period.

The major/minor distinction used here captures both the largest source of variation across election boycotts in this study and the theoretical logic described in Chapter 2. Nevertheless, the examples offered thus far should show readers that, even within the major boycott category, we are likely to find interesting differences from case to case. Some boycotts are undertaken by a single large opposition party (Jamaica 1983), whereas others involve formal or informal coalitions of opposition parties (Niger 1996, Democratic Republic of Congo 2006); some major boycotts are relatively peaceful (Zimbabwe 1995), whereas others are accompanied by violence (Egypt 1990). Given the relatively rare nature of these events, more fine-grained distinctions among boycott cases would make it difficult to draw any general inferences about their occurrence,

---

[12] See http://www.cidcm.umd.edu/inscr/mar/data/pakmohaj.htm.

but the analysis in this chapter as well as in Chapter 4 considers many of these differences. Readers are encouraged to use the case information provided in the book's chapters, along with the information included in Appendix B, to gain a more nuanced understanding of major election boycotts.

To consider the causes of major election boycotts, this chapter returns to key insights from the previous chapter's discussion of Decision Point 2: that the information environment and incumbent credibility will affect the ability of incumbent and opposition actors to reach an agreement that would allow them to avoid a major election boycott. The next two sections develop empirical hypotheses based on those theoretical insights.

Information Environment

The theory in Chapter 2 posits that incumbent and opposition actors should be able to reach a negotiated agreement to avoid electoral protests such as election boycotts. The theory also suggests that one reason why these actors might fail to reach such an agreement has to do with private information and incentives to misrepresent private information. The incumbent likely has incentives to misrepresent the extent to which she is engaging in electoral manipulation, thereby enhancing her chances of electoral success while minimizing perceptions of cheating. The opposition may also have incentives to misrepresent the amount of manipulation he is actually willing to tolerate, in the hopes of lowering incumbent manipulation and enhancing his chances of electoral success accordingly. Because incumbent and opposition actors probably always have these incentives, what becomes important then is the extent to which either actor has the *opportunity* to misrepresent private information. Low-information environments are relevant then, because they increase opportunities for individuals to misrepresent private information. As such, we would expect that lower information environments will increase the probability of a boycott occurring.

H_1: As Adult Literacy Rates Decrease, the Probability of a Major Election Boycott Increases

Although the specific causal mechanisms regarding the impact of information on bargaining failure – the presence and misrepresentation of private information – are very difficult to observe in any systematic way, there are a number of observable indicators that suggest where private information is more likely to be generated. I used adult literacy rates in this study to approximate a country's information environment.[13] Even though Chapter 2 provides a theoretical argument for the relevance of literacy rates as an indicator of the overall information

---

[13] The World Bank World Development Indicators provide information on literacy rates for adults 15 years and older in countries around the world. The measure used here reflects adult literacy for a given year or for the most recent year previously recorded. Election years for which no previous literacy rate was recorded are coded as missing for this measure.

environment, it is worth reiterating that this measure is meant to capture the overall availability and accuracy of information in a given society, not to represent the actual literacy level of any individuals involved in the political process.

Adult literacy is only one way of measuring a country's information environment, but for purposes of empirical analysis, using literacy rates has two advantages. First, this measure generates a larger number of useable observations than do available data on press freedom or the number of media outlets, for example. Second, literacy provides a measure of the information environment that is arguably more exogenous to the political regime than indicators of press freedom are likely to be. Clearly, policy choices have an impact on education over the long term. Such effects, however, are relatively diffuse, and other factors beyond the political regime – factors related to economic development, such as school attendance – will also affect literacy rates. Measures such as media freedom or number of media outlets, by contrast, are a direct reflection of the incumbent government's current attitude toward the dissemination of information. Thus, it would be difficult to discern whether such measures were capturing the information environment as a consequence of economic development or of further manipulation on the part of the incumbent.

Incumbent Credibility

Problems making credible commitments are the second major source of bargaining failure when elites negotiate levels of pro-incumbent manipulation in the pre-election phase. Even in situations of full information, a lack of credibility on the part of either the incumbent or the opposition may result in bargaining failure. In the pre-election phase, the incumbent's credibility will be at issue. If opposition parties do not trust the incumbent to adhere to the terms of an agreement, they may decide to protest. Thus, the incumbent must convince the opposition that she will adhere to an acceptable level of manipulation.

Opposition credibility is not as important here because opposition participation is more easily observable than incumbent manipulation. Furthermore, although the opposition may be tempted to misrepresent private information, there is less a sense, in the pre-election period, that the opposition will commit to participation but will have a hard time resisting the impulse to boycott. Opposition parties, and the individual candidates associated with those parties, should want the opportunity to win seats in the election. Finally, it is not clear that the incumbent would behave differently, in terms of manipulation, if the opposition's promise to participate were not credible. True, a boycott would reduce the incumbent's need to manipulate because it would naturally reduce competition during the election. In the pre-election period, however, the prudent incumbent will plan for manipulation under the assumption that she will actually have to compete with the opposition.

H$_2$: As Levels of Incumbent Constraint Decrease, the Probability of a Major Election Boycott Increases

In the pre-election period, then, the issue becomes the extent to which the opposition perceives the incumbent's promised level of manipulation to be credible. As with private information, it is quite difficult to observe the credibility of commitments. The actual commitments associated with pre-election bargaining are only observable when explicit bargaining is occurring, as it did in Azerbaijan in 1998; it may not be possible to observe those commitments when elites are simply making strategic decisions as if explicit bargaining was occurring, as in Cameroon in 1997 or Guyana in 1985. Furthermore, even if explicit bargaining is taking place, it often occurs in private meetings between elites that go unreported, making any kind of systematic observation of commitments – and subsequent assessments of their credibility – an incredibly difficult task. Therefore I used an indicator of executive constraint to capture incumbent credibility.[14] Recall from Chapter 2 that imposing institutional constraints on themselves is one way in which incumbent leaders enhance their credibility to attract investment (North and Weingast 1989) or make themselves more credible to their opposition (Acemoglu and Robinson 2006). Thus, where incumbents are less constrained, their commitments to acceptable levels of manipulation should be less credible, which may trigger a major boycott.

Opposition Strength

The strength of the opposition relative to the incumbent has important consequences for the probability of post-election demonstrations and is discussed later in the chapter. However, opposition strength does not have a clear impact on the opposition's decision to boycott, because it produces conflicting incentives for both the incumbent and the opposition in the pre-election phase. A stronger opposition candidate will be in a position to demand lower levels of manipulation from the incumbent, because he can threaten to use that strength against the incumbent if she manipulates excessively. Thus, the incumbent should be motivated to reduce manipulation. At the same time, a stronger opposition means tougher electoral competition, and so the incumbent is going to feel more pressure to manipulate to maintain her advantage. For the incumbent, then, opposition strength will trigger competing desires to decrease and increase manipulation.

[14] The Polity IV data set (Marshall, Jagers, and Gurr 2010) provides an annual measure of executive constraint. This indicator is a 7-point scale, where higher values indicate greater constraints on the executive. An *Executive Constraint* score of 1 represents executive incumbents who are not constrained in their decision making by any other government institutions. A score of 7, by contrast, indicates a situation of parity between the incumbent and some other institution (typically legislative).

For the opposition candidate, as his strength reduces his tolerance for manipulation, the chances increase that the incumbent will manipulate more than the opposition can accept, which should trigger a boycott. Furthermore, as the opposition grows stronger, the boycott may have more of an impact on domestic and international audiences. Yet, here again, is a conflicting motivation – as the opposition candidate becomes stronger, he is also more competitive if he participates in the election. Thus, a stronger opposition will simultaneously have more motivation to boycott and more motivation to participate in the election. Because of these conflicting motivations on the part of both the incumbent and the opposition, we should not expect opposition strength to have any clear relationship to the probability of an election boycott.

H₃: Opposition Strength Should Be Unrelated to the Probability of a Major Election Boycott

Opposition strength depends on both the relative size and cohesion of the opposition. For example, opposition parties that enjoy little support from the electorate or are very fragmented will have a harder time competing with the incumbent. For this study I measured opposition strength as an interaction of two quantities meant to capture the level of support enjoyed by the opposition in the electorate and the extent to which the opposition is unified or fragmented. *Opposition Support* measures the proportion of legislative seats controlled by the opposition prior to the election; it is meant to be a proxy for domestic support for the opposition. *Opposition Cohesion* is a dichotomous variable that indicates whether a single party controls the majority of those opposition seats. Where a single party controls more than 50% of the opposition's legislative seats, the opposition is considered to be cohesive. The logic behind this interaction is that the political opposition's strength will be a function both of its support in the electorate and its ability to coordinate among various parties – an ability that will be enhanced if a single party dominates. By interacting these two variables, then, *Opposition Strength* equals zero where the opposition is fragmented and equals the percentage of legislative seats held by the opposition where the opposition is dominated by a single party.

A Model of Major Election Boycotts

The unit of analysis in this study is one election in one country. I selected elections from 1975 to 2006 both to focus on the period since the third wave of democratization and to enable an investigation of differences between the Cold War and post–Cold War period. From the known population of elections over this time period, I chose the elections to be included in this study based on the following criteria: (1) Did the country receive ODA from the OECD during the time period 1975–2006? (2) Was the election for a national-level office – the president, legislature, or both? (3) Were parties, groups, or candidates outside

TABLE 3.1. *Logistic Regression: Major Election Boycott*

DV: Major Election Boycott	Model 1	Model 2
Literacy	−0.021*	−0.031**
	(0.009)	(0.009)
Executive Constraint	−0.467**	−0.388**
	(0.099)	(0.114)
Opposition Cohesion		−0.469
		(0.804)
Opposition Support		−2.688
		(2.139)
Opposition Strength		0.189
(Cohesion*Support)		(2.839)
Cold War	−0.736	−1.490[+]
	(0.506)	(0.767)
International Observers	−0.738	−1.120[+]
	(0.502)	(0.638)
GDP *per capita*	−0.000	−0.000
	(0.000)	(0.000)
Executive Election	−0.213	−0.119
	(0.345)	(0.470)
Sub-Saharan Africa	0.286	0.638
	(0.545)	(0.559)
Constant	1.478[+]	2.795**
	(0.836)	(1.014)
N	500	384
Wald chi^2	(7) 89.99	(10) 106.55
Prob > chi^2	0.000	0.000
Pseudo R^2	0.200	0.288

* Significant at the level $p > .05$, two-tailed z-test.
** Significant at the level $p > .01$, two-tailed z-test.
[+] Significant at the level $p > .05$, one-tailed z-test.
Note: Robust standard errors clustered by country.

the ruling party allowed to compete in the election? Every election for which the answer to those three questions was "yes" was included in the study. In all, 765 elections satisfied those criteria. The coding of all election events was done by hand to ensure that every coding of electoral protest reflected an instance of protest that was, in fact, election related.

Table 3.1 presents the results of two logistic regression models used to test Hypotheses 1–3. The dependent variable in these models is dichotomous and records instances where major election boycotts occurred. The logistic regression uses these observations to estimate the probability of a boycott occurring. Positive coefficients suggest variables that are associated with an increased probability of a boycott, whereas negative coefficients suggest variables that are associated with a decreased probability of a boycott. Based on the preceding hypotheses, Model 1 is constrained and estimates the probability of major boycotts where the opposition strength variables are assumed to be unrelated to the decision to boycott; as such, the values of their estimated coefficients are forced to be equal to zero. Model 2, in contrast to Model 1, is unconstrained, allowing the estimated coefficients for the opposition strength variables to vary in order to evaluate H_3. The number of observations in each model represents all observations with available measures on all variables in the models. Both models provide consistent results that allow for an evaluation of H_1 and H_2.

Both models in Table 3.1 include a series of control variables, which are discussed later in conjunction with the main results. In terms of geographic patterns of boycotts, however, it is important now to note two features of these models. First, both models are estimated with the standard errors clustered by country to account for the fact that election events in a given country will not be independent of other elections in that country. Second, all models include a control variable for sub-Saharan Africa, because the comparison of regional patterns of electoral protest revealed this region to consistently display relatively high rates of protest. The positive estimated coefficients associated with *Sub-Saharan Africa* in Models 1 and 2 suggest that elections in this region are associated with an increased probability of boycott; however, the relatively large standard errors associated with these estimates indicate that, in the context of multiple regression, the regional difference associated with sub-Saharan Africa is not statistically significant.

Model 1 provides support for H_1 and H_2. The negative coefficient associated with *Literacy* suggests that as literacy rates increase, the probability of a major boycott decreases. The relatively small standard error associated with this coefficient indicates a relationship that attains conventional levels of statistical significance. Holding the value of all other variables in the model at their mean and modal values, moving from countries with the literacy rates hovering around 10% (Burkina Faso in the 1970s, Mali in the 1990s, Niger in the early 2000s) to the highest literacy rates in the sample, which are on par with the 99% rates found in developed countries (Former Soviet States) decreases the probability of boycott by 14%. The validity of the relationship is strengthened by the fact that both models include a control for wealth (*GDP per capita*). Although the estimated coefficients for *GDP per capita* do not suggest a statistically significant impact on the probability of boycott, by including this measure in the model we have more confidence that the *Literacy* measure is not merely reflecting poverty, but is actually capturing some feature of the country's information environment.

The Cameroon boycott described at the beginning of this chapter provides an example of how a low-information environment can increase the probability of a major election boycott. All available indicators and information suggest that Cameroon constitutes a low-information environment. Freedom House ranked the country as "not free" with respect to civil rights and press status for 1997, and the World Bank recorded an adult literacy rate of 41%. Further compromising the information environment was the issue of media ownership. Although the government monopoly over television and radio station ownership officially ended in 1990, as of 1997 the government had still not devised any system for licensing private media outlets (*Article 19*, 13). Before the 1997 elections, the government was planning to establish some rural radio stations, but with an explicitly apolitical purpose to promote local development initiatives and "improve the standing of traditional knowledge" (*Article 19*, 17). The only regularly published newspaper at this time was government owned, and a 1996 law (no. 96/04) had provided the government with sweeping powers to seize and ban privately owned papers (*Article 19*, 17). After the October 1997 presidential election, official reports of voter turnout differed from those of the opposition, with the government claiming higher turnout and the opposition claiming a successful boycott campaign.[15] The inability of the incumbent and opposition to agree on turnout figures after the election, with each advancing claims to indicate its own relative strength, suggests that the pre-election bargaining environment was also characterized by a dearth of common knowledge and attempts to misrepresent private information. All told, Cameroon's information environment at the time of the 1997 election was ripe for the creation and misrepresentation of private information, which may well have contributed to the inability of the opposition and incumbent to reach an agreement that would have avoided a boycott.

The negative coefficient associated with *Executive Constraint* suggests that, as the incumbent leader is more constrained, the probability of a major boycott decreases. This coefficient also obtains conventional levels of statistical significance. Moving from the lowest levels of executive constraint (*Executive Constraint* =1) to the highest level of executive constraint (*Executive Constraint* = 7) decreases the probability of boycott by 10%. Examples of the lowest levels of executive constraint can be found in Brazil and Ecuador in the late 1970s, Guyana in the early 1980s, Nigeria in the early 1990s, and Uzbekistan since the late 1990s. High levels of executive constraint are seen in Nigeria in the late 1970s and early 1980s; South Africa since the 1970s; and Uruguay, Poland, and Thailand for the entire period under study. Returning to the case of Cameroon, it received the second-lowest rating (*Executive Constraint* = 2), suggesting very little meaningful constraint on the incumbent. No doubt, Biya's refusal to create an independent election administration made his promises of fair elections seem less credible, particularly in light of opposition suspicions that he had used the executive-controlled election administration to manipulate the previous legislative elections.

---

[15] Observer group leader says no major problems in elections. BBC Summary of World Broadcasts, October 16, 1997, Thursday, Part 5 Africa, Latin America, and the Caribbean; WEST AFRICA; Ghana; AL/D3051/A; Voter turnout in presidential poll estimated at 62 per cent. BBC Summary of World Broadcasts, October 16, 1997, Thursday, Part 5 Africa, Latin America, and the Caribbean; WEST AFRICA; CAMEROON; AL/D3051/A.

Inclusion of a control for the type of election suggests that the incumbent's credibility is important regardless of the type of election. *Executive Election* is a dichotomous variable indicating whether the election will determine control of the executive – presidential and parliamentary elections are given a value of 1, and legislative elections in a presidential system receive a value of 0. We might expect elections where the position of the executive is in play to further compromise the incumbent's credibility where manipulation is concerned. Unlike a parliamentary election, which will just affect legislative support for the executive in presidential systems, presidential elections *always* put the incumbent's position of power at risk. The relatively large standard errors associated with the estimated coefficients for this control variable, however, suggest that election type has no statistically significant impact on the probability of boycott.

The relationships of *Literacy* and *Executive Constraint* to the probability of major boycott retain their significance in Model 2, which includes additional variables to test H_3. The positive coefficient associated with *Opposition Strength* suggests that a cohesive opposition with more support in the electorate would be more likely to boycott, but the large standard errors associated with this coefficient and with the coefficients of the constituent terms (*Opposition Cohesion*, *Opposition Support*) indicate these relationships do not attain conventional levels of statistical significance. The opposition's strength appears to be unrelated to the probability of opposition boycott. The lack of relationship is important to note, because it suggests that those factors conditioning when an incumbent will respond to protest with reform are not driving opposition decisions to boycott.

Both Models 1 and 2 include two important variables meant to control for international pressures for democracy – one of the three scope conditions associated with electoral protest in the developing world, but the one that is hypothesized to matter less with respect to the causes of electoral protest and more where the consequences of protest are concerned. *Cold War* is a dichotomous variable indicating whether an election took place during the Cold War or not, receiving a value of 1 if the election took place before 1991 and a zero if the election was held after 1991. The negative coefficient associated with *Cold War* in both models suggests that elections held during the Cold War had a lower probability of election boycott. The relationship, however, is weak – lacking statistical significance in Model 1 and only approaching conventional levels of statistical significance in Model 2.

International Observers is another dichotomous variable, indicating whether international observers were present at a given election.[16] There is some debate regarding the relationship between electoral protest and the presence of international election observers. Beaulieu and Hyde (2009) found that election boycotts were associated with an increased probability of electoral protest, specifically election boycotts in new democracies in the period 1990–2002, and reasoned that observer presence made incumbents more likely

---

[16] Information for this variable is from Hyde (2011) and Hyde and Marinov (2012).

to engage in "strategic manipulation" and opposition parties more likely to respond with an election boycott. More recently, Kelly (2011) has argued that it is poor election quality, rather than the monitors themselves, that motivates opposition parties to boycott in the presence of international observers. As with *Cold War*, the estimated coefficients for *International Observers* in this model are inconclusive. The negative coefficients suggest a reduced probability of boycott in the presence of international observers, but the fact that this coefficient lacks statistical significance in Model 1 and only approaches significance in Model 2 makes it difficult to draw any conclusions about the relationship between observers and the probability of election boycotts.[17]

Elections in the Dominican Republic in the early 1990s provide examples of internationally observed elections that did not produce major election boycotts. These elections were observed by respected groups such as the Carter Center and the Organization of American States, and though the 1990 and 1994 elections were contentious, with the opposition charging incumbent president Joaquin Balaguer with excessive electoral manipulation, major opposition parties participated in both elections. The country's high-information environment may explain why boycotts did not occur. Although low levels of economic development kept the press somewhat dependent on the government for funding, and several incidents of press intimidation have been reported over the years, the media in the Dominican Republic are generally understood to be relatively free and vibrant.[18] As of 1990, approximately 80% of the adult population was literate.[19] Since 1978, political elites have relied on modern, American-style opinion polls (Hartlyn 1998, 122). Although neither of these elections produced a major boycott, both were followed by post-election mass demonstrations. This next section, which takes up the question of post-election demonstrations initiated by the opposition, revisits the issue of international election observer impact in the post-election period.

POST-ELECTION MASS DEMONSTRATIONS

At Decision Point 4 in Figure 2.1, the opposition must decide whether to accept the election or call its supporters into the street to protest. At this point, the opposition has already decided whether to participate in or boycott the election. Election Day has come and gone, and the full extent of incumbent manipulation has been realized. The election itself has generated a great deal of information, so it is less likely that information problems will lead to bargaining failure between the incumbent and the opposition at this point. For the decision

[17] As with opposition strength, the lack of a systematic relationship between international observer presence and boycott suggests that opposition parties are not simply responding to the possibility of attracting international attention when they boycott.

[18] Attacks on the Press 2000: Dominican Republic. http://cpj.org/2001/03/attacks-on-the-press-2000-dominican-republic.php; Freedom House. Freedom in the World 2002.

[19] UNESCO Institute for Statistics.

whether to call for post-election demonstrations, credibility becomes the central issue. At this point, both the incumbent's or the opposition's credibility may be at issue, likely depending on how much strength the opposition was able to display in the course of participating in the election. Faced with a strong opposition, the incumbent may not have been able to resist increasing manipulation beyond a level acceptable to the opposition. At the same time, even if the incumbent exercised restraint with respect to manipulation, a stronger opposition that lost fair and square may find it difficult to resist crying foul.

As a complement to pre-election protest, this study focuses on the organization and initiation of public mass demonstrations, although opposition parties have several tactics at their disposal to express their public rejection of the results after the election. Sometimes opposition leaders publicly denounce the election, as in Kazakhstan following the 2004 elections, when opposition party leaders announced at a news conference that the second round of voting "exceeded any thinkable boundaries as far as vote-rigging, falsifications, and voter bribing are concerned."[20] Other times opposition leaders file legal challenges to protest elections. In January 2000, for example, Sri Lanka's main opposition party appealed to that country's Supreme Court to cancel the country's 1999 elections.[21] Although verbal rejections are common and may be construed as cheap talk, legal challenges, by contrast, can be costly and time consuming, but demonstrate a willingness to work within existing institutions. A third option for opposition parties is to call their supporters out into the streets in protest. Like the boycotts that precede them, post-election mass demonstrations initiated by opposition parties indicate that the political opposition is engaging in contentious politics beyond the bounds of political institutions. I consider post-election mass demonstrations to have occurred when citizens take to the streets after an election to protest some aspect of the election's results and/or conduct. In contrast to boycotts, the involvement of citizens is an essential element of opposition-initiated post-election protest.[22]

The *Protest* measure is a dichotomous variable, equal to 1 if any post-election mass demonstrations were reported for reasons related to the election. In addition to a basic coding for whether mass demonstrations occurred after a given election, a ruling was made regarding opposition initiation of mass demonstrations. *Opposition Demonstration* refers to cases where reports indicated the opposition was instrumental in coordinating the mass demonstrations. Most often, reports of a public call to protest or public announcements

[20] BBC Monitoring Central Asia Unit. Kazakh opposition party claims violations in runoff elections. Supplied by BBC Worldwide Monitoring October 4, 2004, Monday.

[21] Associated Press. Sri Lanka's opposition seeks dismissal of presidential election. January 12, 2000, Wednesday, BC cycle.

[22] See Appendix C for detailed descriptions of post-election mass demonstrations. This appendix includes both cases of post-election demonstrations where the opposition initiated the protest and where the opposition was not reported to have initiated it, but was implicated as participating in or otherwise supporting the protest.

of plans for protest from opposition leaders – followed by mass demonstrations that news reports linked to the original pronouncements – signaled opposition initiation. Such linkages could be made by describing the protesters as "opposition supporters" while referencing calls for protest by opposition leadership in describing the actual protests themselves. In other cases, news reports that placed major opposition candidates or leaders at the site of the demonstrations (often addressing the crowd), even if they did not describe the initial calls to protest, were also coded as opposition initiation of protest.

Information Problems

Although information problems can lead to bargaining failure in the pre-election phase, the information-generating function of the election itself makes it less likely that problems of information will account for post-election mass demonstrations. Before the election, particularly in low-information societies, there is much more opportunity for the incumbent to misrepresent information about how much she will manipulate the election and for the opposition to misrepresent information about how much manipulation he is willing to tolerate. Once the election has occurred, however, much of the information that was previously private has become public. As such, the overall information environment will matter far less than the conduct of the election itself.

H_4: Adult Literacy Rates Should Be Unrelated to the Probability of Post-Election Mass Demonstrations

Credibility Problems

According to the theory of ongoing elite negotiations developed in Chapter 2, if bargaining failure does not result from information problems, then it must stem from credibility problems. As with the information environment, however, once an election has occurred, general indicators of credibility (such as executive constraint) are less likely to be relevant than are observable indicators of credibility that can be inferred from the election events themselves.

H_5: Executive Constraint Should Be Unrelated to the Probability of Post-Election Mass Demonstrations

The first observable indicator of credibility during the election is who wins. Incumbent loss is a clear indicator that the incumbent's promise to reduce manipulation was credible. Although incumbent victory does not necessarily mean that incumbent manipulation beyond the level acceptable to the opposition occurred, it certainly allows for that possibility. Furthermore, incumbent victory opens up the opportunity for the opposition to claim excessive manipulation, even if it did not occur. Thus, in the post-election period, post-election demonstrations may reflect the incumbent's inability to maintain a commitment to curtail manipulation, or it may reflect an opposition that cannot credibly commit to accepting the results of the election – it may not be able to resist the opportunity to accuse the incumbent of manipulation.

Here, incumbent victory is measured by whether the incumbent party retained power, thereby avoiding the complications stemming from the variation in term limits across countries, For presidential elections, then, cases where the incumbent party retains the presidency are coded as *Incumbent Victory* = 1.[23] For parliamentary elections, *Incumbent Victory* is coded as 1 if the party that controlled government before the election wins enough seats to form a government after the election. Cases where a party that previously controlled government does not win enough seats to control the government and is forced into coalition negotiations after the election are not counted as an incumbent victory (*Incumbent Victory* = 0).[24] If presidential and legislative elections are held simultaneously and incumbent control is returned for the presidency but not for the legislature (or vice versa), my coding rule privileges control of the executive in determining the value for *Incumbent Victory*. There are several cases of extremely unstable party systems where judgments had to be made based on available information about the candidates and parties and their relationships to previous party organizations.[25] Finally, it bears noting that cases where the incumbent was initially declared the winner, and then stepped down under pressure from post-election protest, such as the Philippines in 1986 or the Ukraine in 2004, are still coded as incumbent victories, because the original results of the election determined them to be the winner, even if those results were subsequently overturned.

H$_6$: Incumbent Victory Should Be Associated with an Increased Probability of Post-Election Mass Demonstrations

Much like incumbent victory, a stronger opposition suggests potential credibility problems for both the incumbent and the opposition. Protest associated with a stronger opposition may reflect its reaction to an incumbent's inability to resist additional manipulation in the face of stiffer electoral competition. Yet, as the opposition grows stronger, it will be less willing to accept defeat, even if the incumbent did not exceed acceptable levels of manipulation. Thus, it is unclear whether opposition strength relative to the incumbent will compromise the credibility of the incumbent's promise to limit manipulation

[23] The Philippines presents one of the only challenges to this coding decision. Since 1984 when direct election of the vice president was reinstated and it is possible for vice presidents to be elected from a different party from the president, it is not clear whether the election of an individual from the incumbent president's same party or an election of a former vice president to the position of president is the better representation of the incumbent retaining power. See Appendix A, pg. 147 for more on this case.

[24] I coded Mongolia's parliamentary elections of 2004, for example. as not representing an incumbent victory because, although the government did not necessarily lose the election, it was forced into a coalition government with the opposition.

[25] Haiti during the era of Duvalier and his protégé-turned-competitor Rene Preval is one such example where judgments about associations with the incumbent were particularly challenging.

or the credibility of the opposition's promise to accept the results of the election. What is clear, however, is that, as the opposition's strength grows, the credibility of both sides becomes questionable in the post-election period, and we should expect to see more post-election mass demonstrations as a result.

H7: Increased Opposition Strength Should Be Associated with an Increased Probability of Post-Election Demonstrations

A Model of Post-Election Mass Demonstrations

Table 3.2 reports the results of two logistic regressions similar to the models presented in Table 3.1. In these models, however, the dependent variable is a dichotomous measure indicating whether an election was followed by post-election mass demonstrations. Here again, positive estimated coefficients indicate variables associated with an increased probability of post-election protest, whereas negative coefficients indicate a decreased probability of protest. In addition to the key explanatory and control variables used in Table 3.1, these models also include measures indicating whether a major boycott occurred (*Major Boycott*) and whether the incumbent party was returned to power (*Incumbent Victory*). As with the previous models, these regressions used all observations where measures were available for all variables in the models.

Based on the preceding hypotheses, Model 1 in Table 3.2 is constrained, estimating the probability of post-election protest where the values of the estimated coefficients associated with *Literacy* and *Executive Constraint* are forced to equal zero, which allows us to evaluate H6 regarding the impact of opposition strength on the probability of protest. In the unconstrained Model 2, the values of the coefficients associated with *Literacy* and *Executive Constraint* are allowed to vary, which gives us the opportunity to evaluate H4 and H5 regarding the impact of these variables on the probability of post-election mass demonstrations. The results of these models are supportive of the preceding hypotheses, suggesting that post-election demonstrations are not affected by information problems or general indicators of incumbent credibility. Rather, they depend on aspects of the election itself, in which problems of either incumbent or opposition credibility may arise.

Model 2 provides support for H4: Literacy rates should be unrelated to post-election demonstrations. The coefficient associated with the *Literacy* variable is positive, but the relative size of the standard error means this relationship does not attain conventional levels of statistical significance. Thus, the probability of post-election mass demonstrations seems to be unrelated to the general information environment. Likely the information generated by the election itself means that if bargaining between incumbent and opposition is going to fail at this point, it will not be because one side has misrepresented private information. Instead bargaining failure in the form of post-election mass demonstrations is more likely to result from credibility problems. Similar to the models in Table 3.1, controls for *GDP per capita* appear to have no impact on

TABLE 3.2. *Logistic Regression: Post-Election Mass Demonstrations*

DV: Post-Election Demonstration	Model 1	Model 2
Literacy		0.018
		(0.012)
Executive Constraint		−0.056
		(0.124)
Opposition Cohesion	−2.379**	−2.209*
	(0.898)	(0.894)
Opposition Support	−7.781**	−6.984*
	(2.786)	(2.770)
Opposition Strength (Cohesion*Support)	8.029**	7.263*
	(3.008)	(2.886)
Major Boycott	0.731	0.854
	(0.614)	(0.6010)
Incumbent Victory	1.330**	1.176*
	(0.458)	(0.592)
Cold War	0.887+	0.967
	(0.486)	(0.631)
International Observers	2.263**	1.919**
	(0.607)	(0.679)
GDP per capita	−0.000	−0.000
	(0.000)	(0.000)
Executive Election	−0.263	−0.072
	(0.371)	(0.436)
Sub-Saharan Africa	−0.553	−0.170
	(0.560)	(0.709)
Constant	−2.242*	−3.078*
	(1.007)	(1.571)
N	514	383
Wald chi^2	(10) 38.74	(12) 35.71
Prob > chi^2	0.000	0.000
Pseudo R^2	0.185	0.174

* Significant at the level $p > .05$, two-tailed z-test.
** Significant at the level $p > .01$, two-tailed z-test.
\+ Significant at the level $p > .05$, one-tailed z-test.
Note: Robust standard errors clustered by country.

the probability of post-election demonstrations. In both Models 1 and 2 the estimated coefficients do not attain conventional levels of statistical significance.

Model 2 also provides support for H$_5$ – that executive constraint should be unrelated to the probability of post-election mass demonstrations. The estimated coefficient associated with *Executive Constraint* is negative, suggesting higher levels of executive constraint should be associated with a lower probability of post-election demonstrations, but the relatively large standard error means this relationship does not attain conventional levels of statistical significance. Thus, the probability of post-election demonstrations appears to be unrelated to general indicators of incumbent credibility. As with the models in Table 3.1, both of these models also show a lack of a statistically significant relationship between election type (*Executive Election*) and the probability of post-election mass demonstrations.

As we turn to those variables associated with election-specific indicators of credibility, statistically significant relationships to the probability of post-election mass demonstrations emerge. With respect to *Incumbent Victory*, the positive estimated coefficient in both Models 1 and 2 suggests that the probability of post-election mass demonstrations increases when the incumbent party retains control of the government as a result of the election. The size of the associated standard error in each model means that this estimated relationship attains conventional levels of statistical significance. These results provide support for H₆: Incumbent victory should be associated with an increased probability of post-election protest. For example, mass protests followed the re-election of President Gloria Macapagal-Arroyo in the Philippines in 2004. After the election, reports of President Arroyo's attempts to secure votes in the Mindanao region of the country surfaced.[26] At that point Fernando Poe Jr., the losing opposition candidate and a popular actor, accused the government of fraud and responded with post-election mass demonstrations.[27]

In the overwhelming majority of cases, the opposition initiates post-election protests when the incumbent has won the election. However, 8 of the 69 cases of opposition-initiated, post-election mass demonstrations occurred when the incumbent did not win. Of these eight cases that do not fit the standard pattern of post-election protest and incumbent victory, two are idiosyncratic enough to warrant further in-depth discussion here, but the six remaining cases can be described quickly. In three of those six cases, the opposition party launched protests before knowing the results of the election were known, and in the end the incumbent did not win.[28] In three other cases, smaller opposition parties protested when larger opposition parties won.[29]

The two cases of note, where post-election mass demonstrations occurred even though the incumbent lost, are Bolivia in 1979 and Madagascar in 2001. In both cases, presidential election rules required an absolute majority to win the election in the first round of voting. In Bolivia, Hernan Siles Zuazo, presidential candidate for the opposition Democratic and Popular Union (UDP), won the most votes in the first round of voting, but did not secure a majority; according to Bolivia's constitution, the legislature was then responsible for choosing the president. The legislature did not select the incumbent David Padilla (who, as

---

[26] From a conversation with Frederic Schaffer, June 7, 2010.

[27] XINHUA GENERAL NEWS SERVICE. June 24, 2004, Thursday. Philippine opposition supporters stage protest rallies; Deutsche Presse-Agentur. Actor's supporters protest alleged fraud in Philippine polls. May 11, 2004, Tuesday.

[28] El Salvador 1988, Mongolia 2004, Afghanistan 2005.

[29] Guinea Bissau 2005, Poland 2005, Macedonia 2006.

it happened, was not the president but the chairman of a military junta who had assumed power the previous November) – hence, there was no incumbent victory in this case – but neither did it select Siles, who subsequently staged a hunger strike and called for mass demonstrations.[30] A general strike occurred four days later, throwing Bolivia into chaos as three more presidents assumed the country's top position before another military junta took control in July 1980.[31]

Post-election protests in Madagascar in 2001 came about in an atmosphere of confusion that followed the first round of voting in the presidential election. The government election commission declared that the opposition challenger, Marc Ravalomanana of the I Love Madagascar party, had won a plurality at 46.6% of the vote and thus a runoff would be required. An independent observer group (comprised of international observers and members of Malagasy civil society) maintained that their independent count gave Ravalomanana 52.2% of the vote, an absolute majority (Marcus and Razafindrakoto 2003, 28). The Supreme Court ruled that a recount should occur, but without any government oversight this amounted to a pro-incumbent decision as far as the opposition was concerned. It was in this atmosphere that Ravalomanana's supporters began weeks of demonstration (28). International actors including the UN and the OAU, as well as the United States and Russia, all expressed concern over the situation and urged a peaceful resolution.[32] Consistently the main criticism expressed by international actors was of Ravalomanana's declaration that he was president; there was no discussion of electoral malfeasance on the part of the incumbent, Didier Ratsiraka. This crisis escalated until Ratsiraka fled the country and Ravalomanana, true to his boasts, assumed the presidency.

With a handful of exceptions, incumbent victory nearly always precedes opposition initiation of post-election mass demonstrations. The other indicator in the model hypothesized to be relevant to cases of post-election demonstration – *Opposition Strength* – provides an indicator of how competitive the opposition was likely to be in the election. In both models, the positive coefficient associated with *Opposition Strength* attains statistical significance. Because *Opposition Strength* is an interaction term, however, we cannot interpret the positive coefficient as a linear relationship between this variable and the probability of post-election demonstration; we must instead consider the conditional relationship between the cohesiveness of the opposition (*Opposition Cohesion*) and how much support the opposition has in the

[30] Bolivian candidate protests. *Washington Post*. August 5, 1979, Sunday, Final Edition.
[31] *New York Times*, August 1, 1979, Wednesday; *New York Times*, August 5, 1979, Sunday
[32] Annan calls for peaceful resolution to political crisis in Madagascar. Xinhua. February 8, 2002 Friday.; Madagascar: US objects to opposition candidate's self-proclamation as president. Television Malagasy. BBC Monitoring Africa. February 23, 2002, Saturday; Zambia; Malagasy political impasse worries Mwanawasa. *The Times of Zambia*. Africa News. February 23, 2002 Saturday; Russia Calls for Normalization of Situation in Madagascar. Xinhua. February 25, 2002 Monday.

electorate (*Opposition Support*). At very low levels of *Opposition Support*, having a cohesive opposition (*Opposition Cohesion* = 1) nearly doubles the probability of post-election demonstration from 39% to 79%.[33] As the amount of *Opposition Support* increases beyond 10% of the legislative seat share, however, the probability of protest declines precipitously, for both cohesive and fragmented oppositions. Because we have controlled for instances where the opposition loses (*Incumbent Victory*), we might interpret the decreased probability of protest associated with *Opposition Support* as evidence that, as the opposition performs better in the election, it is more likely to accept the results of the election without protest.

Even within a particular post-election mass demonstration sparked by an incumbent's victory over a competitive opposition, it can be difficult to know whether the incumbent or the opposition had difficulty making credible commitments. Following Mexico's 2006 elections the second-place candidate Lopez-Obrador, accused the incumbent PAN party of rigging the election.[34] Preliminary vote counts showed Lopez-Obrador with a slight lead over the incumbent candidate, Calderón Hinojosa (37% and 34.4%, respectively), a trend that held with more than 50% of the votes counted: however, by the time 98% of the votes were in, the two candidates were tied, and the final vote count reported by the Federal Electoral Institute showed Calderón Hinojosa with just under 36% of the vote and Lopez-Obrador with just over 35%. In response to this outcome, Lopez-Obrador organized mass demonstrations in his electoral stronghold of Mexico City and brought everyday life in the capital to a standstill for months after the election. Despite these charges, EU observers declared the elections largely fair, and the United States, Spain, and Canada all congratulated the president-elect.[35] Whether this case of post-election demonstration is indicative of a manipulating incumbent fearing defeat or of a strong challenger unwilling to accept defeat remains an open question.

As in the boycott models, controls for international factors were included in these models, but with no theoretical expectations of a relationship to protest. In the presence of observers, the opposition may be more motivated to call attention to manipulation, but the incumbent should also feel more motivation to secure opposition participation and acceptance of the election results. Nevertheless, some interesting empirical regularities emerge from Models 1 and 2 in Table 3.2. The estimated coefficient for the presence of international observers (*International Observers*), however, is positive and attains conventional levels of statistical significance in both models. This suggests that the presence of international election observers increases the probability that the opposition will protest after the election. The estimated coefficient for *Cold War* is positive but only approaches conventional levels of statistical significance in Model 1,

---

[33] These values calculated holding all other variables at their mean and modal values.

[34] Associated Press Online. July 10, 2006 Monday 5:30 AM GMT. Mexico candidate claiming election fraud.

[35] Ibid.

offering a weak indication that post-election demonstrations might have been more likely in the Cold War period.

Thus, the results in this chapter do not produce consistent findings regarding the role of international election observers, but do provide some indication that observers are associated with an increased probability of some types of electoral protest. I used international observer presence in these models as an indicator of international pressure to democratize, which, I argue, should neither encourage or discourage electoral protest, but rather should help us understand why elections are happening and why incumbent manipulation is at the center of incumbent–opposition negotiations around elections. It may be the case, however, that international observers do more than remind the respective actors of international pressure to democratize; they may also affect these actors' credibility. We might think of observers as enhancing the credibility of both actors. Much like a referee, this external actor may be perceived as keeping both sides honest. In actuality, however, observers might hamper the abilities of both actors to make credible commitments. Previous research has demonstrated the strategic considerations for incumbent leaders associated with inviting election observers (Beaulieu and Hyde 2009, Hyde 2011). Observers may make it more difficult for incumbents to adhere to an agreed-on level of manipulation, even if manipulating more requires more work to conceal those activities in the presence of observers. Such a finding may be consistent with Kelly's (2011) argument that observers go to those elections that have more problems. Another possibility, following the logic of Beaulieu and Hyde (2009), is that opposition parties may find it harder to resist the temptation to challenge the outcome of the election through protest when they have attentive international actors involved in the electoral process.

CONCLUSION

This chapter has provided systematic evidence consistent with the theory in Chapter 2 that electoral protests are the consequence of elite failure to strike a bargain about electoral conduct, either because of problems with information or with credibility. Election boycotts are more likely to occur in low-information environments. In the pre-election period, the incumbent and opposition have to make decisions without the information that will ultimately be provided by the electoral contest itself. Given that both sides have incentives to misrepresent any private information they hold at this point, the extent to which the information environment allows for the creation and misrepresentation of private information becomes incredibly important.

Literacy rates provide an aggregate indicator of the information environment and should not be interpreted as reflecting the capabilities of individual political actors. Rather, a society with lower literacy rates presents more opportunities for the creation and misrepresentation of private information, which will affect even highly literate elites. When individuals can read they have a means of verifying the information they hear on radio or television or in conversations with friends. As the percentage of individuals who can read increases, media should be under more pressure to present accurate information – or run the risk of having their inaccuracies uncovered. In contrast, low-information societies provide more opportunities for private information to be generated and misrepresented, increasing the probability that the incumbent and opposition will not be able to reach an agreement that will allow the opposition to participate in the election.

Election boycotts are also more likely to occur as incumbent credibility declines. Again, in the pre-election period, with the electoral process yet to unfold, the opposition will have to decide if it trusts the incumbent to adhere to an agreed-on level of manipulation. Where incumbents are more constrained by institutions, their promises are likely to be viewed as more credible. As the incumbent faces fewer constraints, the probability of a boycott increases.

Post-election protest, by contrast, is unrelated to the problems of information and incumbent credibility that are likely to arise in the pre-election period. The election itself provides a large amount of information, so the general availability of information is no longer relevant for opposition decisions. Furthermore, the incumbent has, by the end of the election, established some overall level of manipulation. Thus, more general impressions of the incumbent's credibility can be replaced by what was observed in the election. Hence, post-election mass demonstrations are related to those factors more likely to be relevant during the election event itself – (1) incumbent victory and the (2) strength of the opposition – which might motivate either the incumbent or opposition to deviate from the original agreement.

Another interesting finding in this chapter has to do with the relationship of international observer presence to the probability of electoral protest. Although observers do not appear to have a systematic impact on the probability that a major boycott will occur during the pre-election period, observer presence does increase the probability of opposition protest after the election. The lack of relationship between observer presence and boycott initiation is consistent with the idea that international pressure for democracy structures the circumstances under which incumbent and opposition are bargaining, but should not necessarily lead to more or less bargaining failure. In the post-election period, by contrast, observer presence may have an amplifying effect on the credibility problems that both incumbent and opposition are likely to encounter. If the incumbent has been unable to resist increased manipulation, international observers may be able to uncover and publicize this activity – provoking protest from the opposition. On the other hand, an opposition that is already considering rejecting the election results in protest may perceive observer presence as providing the additional benefit of an attentive, pro-democracy audience.

4

Election Day and Its Aftermath

The major election boycott during the October 2000 presidential elections in Cote d'Ivoire sparked a wave of domestic unrest and international pressure that ultimately prevented the incumbent, General Robert Guei, who had been brought out of retirement by the junta that took control of the country during a coup the previous December, from taking office. The two main opposition parties, the Rally of the Republicans (RDR) and the Democratic Party of the Cote d'Ivoire-African Democratic Party (PDCI-RCA), boycotted the presidential elections after prominent candidates were disqualified on the basis of hastily passed pre-election legislation requiring candidates' parents to have been born in Cote d'Ivoire.[1] Opposition supporters followed the boycott with post-election demonstrations, in which acts of violence occurred, though the bulk of that violence seemed to come from police forces firing on demonstrators.[2] International reaction among democracy promoters including the United States, France, and the EU was decidedly negative.[3] The United States went so far as to declare the elections illegitimate, and France – Cote d'Ivoire's former colonial master – threatened to impose sanctions.[4] Although Guei initially declared himself the winner of the election, international pressure

---

[1] Mawusi Afele. PREVIEW: Boycott threat, disqualifications mar Ivory Coast elections Deutsche Presse-Agentur, October 20, 2000, Friday, International News.

[2] Ann M. Simmons. Celebration turns violent in Ivory Coast: Political forces clash in election rift. *The Gazette* (Montreal, Quebec), October 27, 2000; Demonstrators shot in election aftermath. *The Globe and Mail*, October 25, 2000.

[3] EU, US, OAU call for I Coast to continue the return to democracy. Agence France Presse, October 28, 2000; US favors new election in Ivory Coast. Agence France Presse, October 26, 2000.

[4] Washington strongly condemns "illegitimate" Ivory Coast elections. Agence France Presse. October 25, 2000; Ivory Coast; France threatens to impose sanctions against Cote d'Ivoire. *Africa News*, October 25, 2000; NEWS, DOCUMENTS & COMMENTARY, Panafrican News Agency.

and domestic protests caused him to flee before the results were official, and the sole opposition candidate who was allowed to remain in the race, Laurent Gbagbo of the Ivoirain Popular Front (FPI), was sworn in as president.[5]

This was the last presidential election Cote d'Ivoire held until ten years later, when Gbagbo found himself the object of post-election mass demonstrations that erupted in the wake of blatant pro-incumbent manipulation; these protests eventually led the country to the brink of civil war in Spring 2011. Problems began when pro-Gbagbo members of the electoral commission physically prevented release of the results of the December 2010 presidential runoff election to the general public.[6] Despite the incumbent's claims of opposition fraud, the United States, EU, African Union, and UN all endorsed the results – declaring victory for the opposition candidate, ex-IMF economist Alassane Ouattara of the RDR (Clayton 2010). In mid-December Ouattara called on his supporters to protest, urging them to take control of state television and radio.[7] These protests resulted in government retaliation that left at least 12 protesters dead; by the end of March 2011, at least 400 were reported dead in the post-election violence (Clayton 2010; Dixon 2011). On April 11, military forces loyal to Ouattara, with the support of UN peacekeepers, captured Gbagbo and removed him from office, extraditing him to the International Criminal Court in the Hague, Netherlands.[8] As of this publication date, instability has persisted as the Ouattara government has struggled to conduct government business and calm army infighting.[9]

Whereas Chapter 3 explored the causes of electoral protest, this chapter investigates the circumstances surrounding those protests and whether they contribute to electoral violence. With respect to election boycotts, this chapter examines how boycotted elections differ from those in which the opposition participates. For post-election demonstrations, this chapter explores whether those protests have a destabilizing effect. Although boycotts are not associated with an increased probability of post-election demonstrations, as shown in Chapter 3, this chapter further investigates some cases where elections began with a major boycott and were followed by opposition-initiated demonstrations.

---

[5] Ivory Coast; Laurent Gbagbo wworn in. *Africa News*, October 27, 2000; NEWS, DOCUMENTS & COMMENTARY, allAfrica.com.

[6] Press footage of these events can be found at http://www.unmultimedia.org/tv/unifeed/d/16496.html.

[7] Ouattara urges supporters to take charge of State TV and Top Office. *The Nation* (Nairobi), December 14, 2010; Violence feared as Ouattara calls for street protests. Radio France Internationale, December 15, 2010.

[8] See   http://www.voanews.com/english/news/africa/UN-Ivory-Coast-Crisis-Not-Over-Yet-119617614.html.

[9] Ivorian government pledges to pay salaries "next week." ONUCI FM. April 23, 2011; President Ouattara calls for reunification of Cote d'Ivoire's army. Radio France International. April 23, 2011.

This chapter represents a preliminary step in assessing the consequences of electoral protest for democracy by investigating how electoral protests affect the democratic quality of the elections and the overall stability of the political system in which they occur. When the opposition has decided to protest, either on Election Day or immediately afterward, consequences may vary greatly. For example, electoral protests in Cote d'Ivoire have a history of producing violence and political instability. It does not seem to matter whether the opposition chooses to boycott in advance of the election or competes and protests afterward (though post-election protest also followed the 2000 boycott): These electoral protests clearly make it difficult for elections to function as a peaceful means of allowing citizens a say in who governs. On systematic investigation, however, the case of Cote d'Ivoire proves to be exceptional with respect to the level of turmoil and chaos that accompanies electoral protest.

The chapter first focuses on Decision Point 3 of the theoretical model presented in Chapter 2, considering what we should expect to observe on Election Day if the opposition chooses to boycott. Next, the chapter discusses post-election demonstrations at Decision Point 4 and considers those instances of protest that span both the pre- and post-election periods. First, however, a few words about endogeneity.

THE QUESTION OF ENDOGENEITY

Concerns about endogeneity arise when we use observational, as opposed to experimental, data to help us understand complex phenomena where actors behave strategically and allow their expectations to inform their decisions. Does the high rate of incumbent victory in the United States suggest a real "incumbency advantage," or is it merely a reflection of the fact that incumbents who have reason to believe they will do well in the next election run again, and those who would probably lose choose not to run?[10] Are sanctions really ineffective, or is their apparent lack of efficacy merely a byproduct of the fact that sanctions are almost exclusively applied to the most "difficult" countries?[11] What is the true nature of the relationship between electoral protest and election-related reform? Could some of the consequences of electoral protest actually be causes of the phenomenon?

For the regression models presented in Chapter 3, endogeneity was not a concern because all measures representing the causal factors associated with electoral protest were taken prior to the occurrence of the protest events.[12] Furthermore, it seems implausible that anticipation of electoral protest could affect those measures in advance. It is unlikely, for example, that knowledge of an impending election boycott would cause those coding *Executive Constraint*

---

[10] Cox and Katz (2002) argue it is the latter.
[11] See Nooruddin (2002) for a treatment of selection bias and sanction efficacy.
[12] For a review of the importance of temporal sequence for causal inference, see Miller (1999).

for the Polity index to change their evaluation. At the same time, unmeasured indicators of protest success may be driving occurrences of electoral protest. What if opposition parties only come together to engage in a major boycott when they see the opportunity for success?

In this chapter and the next I present interesting correlations that are consistent with this book's theory about the conditional consequences of electoral protest for democracy. The findings presented here certainly suggest that my story of protest, reform, and democratization is plausible, but they do not obviate the possibility that something else might be going on. To be more specific, that "something else" amounts to two other possibilities: (1) that the causality is actually reversed or (2) that the relationship between protest and reform is spurious.

The first concern regarding the endogenous nature of the relationship depicted here with observational data is that the direction of causality may be actually the reverse of the one I portray. Given that reforms are enacted after the protests purported to motivate them, and given what we know about temporal sequencing in causality, it cannot be the case that the actual events of reform caused the protests that pre-dated them. However, if we think of the event of actual reform as merely the observable indicator of something that everyone knew was going to happen, then one could argue that perhaps opposition parties launch protests when they know reforms are more likely, in the hopes of being able to take credit for the reforms. Yet given the substantial proportion of electoral protests that fail to motivate reform, this claim seems like a stretch at best.

A less extreme, and more plausible, variation of this argument – the one suggested in response to Chapter 3's results – is that opposition parties only protest in those circumstances where they feel they have a better chance of the incumbent actually responding with reform. This argument brings us to the second, more serious alternative explanation for the patterns we observe regarding protest and reform: the possibility that their relationship is spurious. This possibility, suggested by Brownlee (2007), is that election-related protest and reform are only related because some other processes are driving both phenomena: "Accounts of elections or protest movements thereby describe the climax of a longer drama, one in which institutional variations shape the opening acts" (13).

It is possible that some underlying factor – let us call it "incumbent weakness" – is actually at work causing both electoral protest and the subsequent consequences for democracy that we observe. However, as described earlier, major boycotts are qualitatively different from their minor counterparts and are not systematically related to either indicators of opposition strength or international observation – both of which suggest they are not systematically related to those factors that will ultimately condition an incumbent reform response. Furthermore, if this alternative hypothesis were actually the case, we might expect stronger correlations between protest and the various indicators of democracy and political stability used in this chapter and the next, not the patterns of conditional relationships we observe in Chapter 5.

Even if there is some heretofore unmeasured factor that influences an incumbent's propensity for reform and subsequently motivates the opposition to protest, this does not obviate the possibility that it is the act of protest that actually motivates the incumbent to reform. The fact that opposition parties might protest when they expect that protest to be successful does not negate the possible causal relationship between protest and the desired outcome of the protesters. Consider a very simple analogy: tooth brushing. I brush my teeth because I believe that doing so will prevent tooth decay. I brush my teeth and observe that I tend not to have much of a problem with tooth decay, with the exception of a couple of small cavities that I attribute to a genetic predisposition for tightly spaced teeth. It would not make sense to suggest that, because the expectation of reducing tooth decay motivates my decision to brush, the tooth brushing itself had no causal impact on the current state of my teeth. The mere fact that I took a particular action (tooth brushing) with expectations about the results of this action (reduced tooth decay) does not obviate the causal relationship of tooth brushing and tooth decay prevention.

Similarly, then, even if opposition parties are initiating electoral protest because they have reason to expect it to result in reform for reasons I have not adequately captured here, this does not necessarily mean that the protest itself has no causal impact on reform. Ultimately, then, the plausibility of protest consequences will rest on the story that I have told in this book and the evidence I have brought to bear in the matter.

BOYCOTTED ELECTIONS

In Decision Point 2 of the model presented in Chapter 2, the opposition decides either to participate in the election or to boycott. If the opposition chooses to boycott, there will be no participation from major opposition parties in the following period – the period in which the election takes place. Recall from Chapter 3 that boycotts are more likely to occur in low-information environments and where the incumbent faces fewer institutional constraints. This section investigates how election boycotts change the character of elections. With respect to the democratic function of elections, three issues become relevant: competition, participation, and violence.

Competition

Since Schattschneider's classic (1960) definition, competition has been seen as a key component of representative democracy. Although much of this book has focused on the need for coordination among elites to agree to terms acceptable to both incumbent and opposition, the fact remains that, once the rules of conduct have been established, elections are a competitive exercise. Just as monopolies distort market efficiencies, so too can uncompetitive elections limit the electoral process's functions of democratic representation and account-ability. Because major election boycotts require the public withdrawal of the majority of opposition candidates from the election, they should facilitate incumbent victory by removing the incumbent's toughest competition. In fact, using the measure of incumbent victory developed in Chapter 3, incumbents were reelected in all but two instances of major election boycotts, compared to winning only about 60% of elections that were not boycotted.[13]

The election in Cote d'Ivoire presented at the start of this chapter is one case where a major election boycott did not produce incumbent victory; the other instance occurred in the Comoros where two of the three main opposition parties boycotted legislative elections in 1992. In the latter case, the opposi-tion Comorian Union for Progress (UDIZMA) and the National Union for Democracy in the Comoros called the boycott to protest the government's fail-ure to update voter registers and its detention of several opposition activists.[14] Although the election did not result in an automatic victory for the incumbent, neither did it produce a clear transfer of power to the opposition. Essentially, the boycott was largely incidental to the fact that the party system was highly fragmented and that the personalistic party that had brought the incumbent president Said Mohammed Djohar to power in 1990 was not cohesive or orga-nized enough to compete successfully in another election. The Comoros had only begun its transition to multiparty elections in that year with a presidential contest that saw the former president of the Supreme Court – Djohar – elected as the country's interim president. Furthermore, the party that supported the new incumbent – the Rally for Democracy and Renewal (RDR) – was newly formed as well, and the country also had a new constitution (approved just four months before the October 1990 elections) that encouraged a proliferation of parties. The combination of the opposition boycott, the young presidential party, and general party proliferation produced a legislature with six parties, none of which represented the main opposition or the incumbent.[15] This par-liament proved so unstable that President Djohar dissolved it in June 1993, and in the election that followed the RDR won an absolute majority of seats.[16]

As with Cote d'Ivoire, however, the aftermath of the 1992 election boycott in the Comoros was not typical of what follows most election boycotts – the unambiguous return to power of the incumbent. Furthermore, in the case of the Comoros, the instability that followed appeared to be temporary, because the incumbent was able to solidify power in fresh elections held less than a year later, and President Djohar remained in power until he was deposed in a coup in 1995. We expect, then, that most cases of major election boycotts are associated with a guarantee of reelection for the incumbent, though whether the

---

[13] The incumbent lost in 8 of the 26 elections experiencing minor election boycotts.
[14] Keesings Record of World Events, Nov. 1992: Comoros – Legislative elections.
[15] See Thibaut (1999), p. 254.
[16] Ibid.

boycotts themselves cause this outcome or merely reflect a set of circumstances where incumbent reelection is a foregone conclusion is an open question.

Participation

If competition is one major dimension of democratic politics, participation is the other.[17] For democratic government to be representative of or accountable to the people, then the people must have the opportunity to participate in the political process. Although the centrality of elections to democracy has been called into question, many still see voting in elections as the sine qua non of democratic politics.[18] Recall that in election boycotts, opposition parties or candidates withdraw from the election and call on their supporters to stay away from the polls on Election Day. Thus, questions about participation in the wake of an election boycott naturally center on the issue of voter turnout.[19] The average turnout across developing countries from 1975 to 2006 was approximately 67%. For elections experiencing a major election boycott, average turnout dropped to 57%. Certainly a 10% reduction in turnout suggests that boycotts might be effective in their efforts at voter demobilization, but does this difference in means reflect a statistically significant relationship between boycotts and turnout once we control for election and country-specific turnout patterns?

H_1: Major Election Boycotts Should Be Associated with Reduced Voter Turnout

Table 4.1 shows the results of an ordinary least squares regression where voter turnout is the dependent variable. Explanatory variables in this model include whether a major boycott occurred; turnout in the previous election, regardless of the previous election type (*Previous Turnout (unmatched)*); whether the election determined control of the executive branch of government (*Executive Election*); and the level of economic development (*GDP per capita*). The model also included regional fixed effects, with postcommunist countries as the reference category. Although the negative sign of the estimated coefficient relating major election boycotts and turnout indicates as association of major boycotts with lower turnout, the relationship does not attain conventional levels of statistical significance. By contrast, higher previous turnout, the competition for the executive branch of government, and higher levels of economic development are all associated with higher turnout, with estimated coefficients that attain conventional levels of statistical significance. As such, we should reject

[17] See, for example, Dahl (1971).
[18] See Schmitter and Karl (1991) for an example of those critical of the fallacy of "electoralism."
[19] Turnout figures come from International IDEA's available information on the proportion of registered voters who cast ballots in the election. Figures on turnout of the voting age population (VAP) were used, if available, when figures on registered voters turnout were missing.

TABLE 4.1. *Linear Regression: Voter Turnout*

	Voter Turnout
Major Boycott	−0.047
	(0.039)
Executive Election	0.051**
	(0.013)
Previous Turnout	0.579**
	(0.060)
GDP per capita	$2.85e^{-06}$**
	($9.31e^{-07}$)
Sub-Saharan Africa	0.017
	(0.019)
Asia	0.041**
	(0.017)
Latin America	0.021
	(0.018)
Middle East/North Africa	0.021
	(0.023)
Constant	0.201**
	(0.042)
N	505
(Pseudo) R^2	.4386

* Significant at the level $p > .05$, two-tailed.
** Significant at the level $p > .05$, one-tailed.
Note: Robust standard errors clustered by country.

H_1, which claims that major election boycotts are associated with reduced voter turnout.

However, there are some notable cases in which major election boycotts were associated with a marked decrease in election turnout. Low turnout followed the major boycott of the 1992 presidential election in Burkina Faso, the Comoros legislative election in 1996, and the Gambia's 2002 election.[20] In 1996 the major election boycott in Bangladesh also succeeded in suppressing turnout, and official estimates put turnout at 36% in Zimbabwe's 1996 presidential election, which was boycotted by both major opposition candidates.[21] It is worth noting, however, that in some cases the opposition claimed low turnout and the government disagreed with this assessment. In Cameroon's 1997 major election boycott, for example, the government claimed relatively

[20] Burkina Faso election victory hollow. *The Globe and Mail* (Canada). December 2, 1991; Low turnout of voters in Comoros Islands Poll. Reuters, December 2 1996; Gambia: Low voter turn out. *Africa News*, January 18, 2002.

[21] John F. Burns. Voters are few in Bangladesh as a dozen die in clashes. *New York Times*, February 16, 1996; Zimbabwe: Mugabe wins Presidential Elections. *Africa News*, Panafrican News Agency.

high turnout while the opposition declared their boycott a success and claimed that turnout was actually much lower than government reports suggested.[22]

This instance of disagreement points to a more general concern we must consider when assessing the impact of boycott on voter turnout: relying on official government statistics, as is the convention in political science. We should not ignore the possibility that when major election boycotts occur, the government turns some of its manipulation efforts to falsifying reports of voter turnout. It would stand to reason that governments that want to discredit an opposition boycott would prefer to report higher levels of turnout – though if such manipulations were occurring in any systematic fashion we would expect to see a positive estimated coefficient obtaining statistical significance for the relationship of a major boycott to voter turnout.

Even if we accept official government statistics on turnout at face value, the idea that boycotts should motivate lower turnout is based on the assumption that opposition parties are targeting their pre-election protest efforts at a domestic audience. In the post–Cold War era of international pressure for democracy, however, the opposition can anticipate support for their boycott either from domestic or international audiences. An opposition that is focused on gaining international support for its protest may not put much effort into bringing about a reduction in voter turnout as part of the boycott. These opposition protesters may be content with drawing international attention to incumbent manipulation – particularly if they suspect that the incumbent is likely to manipulate turnout statistics anyway. The importance of the international audience is explored in more detail in the next chapter.

Finally, when we consider H_1 in relation to what we know about incumbent victory in boycotted elections, we should revisit the importance of participation in the face of little to no competition. If voters do not perceive a meaningful choice when they go to the polls, their ability to select representatives or enforce accountability is extremely restricted. As such, the question of whether or not voters turn out may be moot. This is not to say that participation is irrelevant to democracy, but where competition is lacking, participation becomes little more than political theater.

Violence

Clearly, one of the perceived advantages of democratic elections, in addition to providing citizens with accountable, representative government, is the reduction in the violence associated with the competition for political power. In its ideal form, campaigns and voting should be conducted without fear of physical harm, and an election's loser is expected to accept the outcome of the election without recourse to violence. In reality, however, many elections today are

---

[22] Observer group leader says no major problems in elections. BBC Summary of World Broadcasts, October 16, 1997; Voter turnout in presidential poll estimated at 62 per cent BBC Summary of World Broadcasts, October 16, 1997.

accompanied by violence (Zakaria 1997, Collier 2009, Hafner-Burton, Hyde, and Jablonski 2013). In Bangladesh, in 2001, for example, it was estimated that only 5 people died on Election Day itself, but more than 150 were killed and nearly 2,500 wounded in political violence during the campaign period.[23] Thus, it is important to assess whether major election boycotts contribute to election violence. Although we know from the theory in Chapter 2 that the incumbent may choose to use violence as a manipulation tactic, it is not clear whether a major election boycott should increase or decrease overall election violence.

On one hand, several works have suggested that electoral competition increases the chances of election violence (Snyder 2000, Wilkinson 2004, Reif 2009). Although most of these works have argued that increased competitiveness motivates political elites to encourage violence so as to shore up their bases of support, others have suggested that the relationship between competition and violence may simply be a byproduct of increased interaction between opposing forces (Dion 1997).[24] Given how dramatically election boycotts reduce competitiveness, then, we might expect less violence in boycotted elections. In particular, if the government has signaled a willingness to use violent repression, an election boycott might be a way for the opposition to keep supporters out of harm's way by encouraging them to stay home on Election Day. On the other hand, because election boycotts are not systematically related to lower turnout, an election boycott may not reduce the interactions between opposing forces in the streets. Furthermore, as a sign of bargaining failure, election boycotts are indicative of elites' inability to avoid conflict. As such, boycotts reveal a contentious election environment, where the key political elites are unable to agree on terms of peaceful electoral participation, which may incline actors on both sides to violence. However, even though boycotts are not associated with a systematic reduction in turnout, the fact that they dramatically reduce electoral competition should mean that they also reduce elite incentives to encourage violence among supporters and, as such, should reduce the probability of electoral violence.

H₂: Major Election Boycotts Should Be Associated with a Lower Probability of Electoral Violence

Table 4.2 shows the results of a logit regression in which the dependent variable is *Election Violence*, a dichotomous variable that takes on a value equal to 1 for any election where incidents that resulted in physical harm or the destruction of property during the campaign period or on Election Day itself were reported. Here again we have a dichotomous coding that condenses much more

---

[23] Thousands of protesters call for fresh polls in Bangladesh. Deutsche Presse-Agentur, October 28, 2001.

[24] It should be noted that, although much of the research exploring questions of competitiveness and violence emphasizes the context of "ethnic politics," work such as by Reif (2009) demonstrates a more general logic of violence and competitiveness of which ethnic political violence might be considered a subset.

TABLE 4.2. *Logistic Regression: Election Violence*

	Election Violence
Major Boycott	0.562
	(0.387)
Voter Turnout	−1.324
	(0.895)
Opposition Vote Share	0.003
	(0.004)
GDP per capita	−0.000**
	(0.000)
Sub-Saharan Africa	−0.283
	(0.385)
Asia	1.346**
	(0.452)
Latin America	0.791*
	(0.406)
Middle East/North Africa	0.433
	(0.502)
Constant	0.628
	(0.694)
N	622
(Pseudo) R^2	.1032

* Significant at the level $p > .05$, two-tailed.
** Significant at the level $p > .05$, one-tailed.
Note: Robust standard errors clustered by country.

fine-grained information on particular acts of violence. As the next section on post-election demonstrations and violence discusses, probably the most important distinction among cases of violence during an election or its aftermath has to do with the source of the violence: Was it perpetrated by the opposition or the incumbent? The examples in the section that follows show that sometimes the source of violence can be clearly identified, but in many cases the perpetrator is more ambiguous and often violence is characterized as "clashes" between protesters and police.

In Table 4.2 the coefficient estimating the relationship between a major election boycott and election violence is positive, but fails to attain conventional levels of statistical significance, suggesting that major election boycotts are not associated with a lower probability that election violence will occur and, as such, we should reject H_2. In some exceptional cases election boycotts have been associated with violence. For example, the 1996 election boycott in Bangladesh was characterized by low turnout and high violence (Burns 1996), and two election boycotts in Mali in 1997 – presidential in May and legislative in July – were associated with violence. Although most of the violence in the boycott of the presidential contest in May appeared to be initiated by the incumbent, much of the violence around the legislative elections in July was attributed by impartial observers in the global media to opposition supporters.[25]

Thus, boycotts do not appear to produce dramatic consequences for the democratic quality of the elections in which they occur, at least in terms of participation and violence. To the extent that they guarantee incumbent victory, they reduce the level of competitiveness in the elections, but given that boycotts are a response to circumstances where the incumbent is expected to manipulate the elections to a degree the opposition finds unacceptable, the extent to which the elections would have been competitive had the opposition participated remains an open question.

PROTEST AFTER THE ELECTION

Just as violence is a concern during election campaigns and on Election Day, we should also be concerned about violence after the election – during the time when opposition parties can initiate post-election mass demonstrations. At Decision Point 4 in the theoretical model presented in Chapter 2, the election has occurred, supporters have been mobilized, and the opposition must decide whether to accept the results of the election or mount a challenge in the form of mass demonstrations. Recall from Chapter 3 that the opposition will be more likely to protest (1) when the incumbent wins and (2) when the opposition is stronger. If the opposition chooses to engage in protest at this time, what does it mean for political stability – both in terms of violence and the incumbent's ability to stay in office?

Violence

In the period immediately following the election, the democratic norm is that all parties to the election will accept the outcome peacefully. Violence after the election is only likely to occur if some party or parties to the electoral contest reject the outcome of the election. If there are no challenges after the election and it appears that all participants accept the outcome, we should not be concerned about post-election violence. In cases of post-election mass demonstration, however, where the incumbent likely has won and the opposition tends to be more competitive, we might be concerned about the possibility for violence. Violence took the form of rioting by opposition supporters after the 2001 elections in Zambia when Levy Mwanawasa came out of retirement to run as a candidate for the incumbent Movement for Multiparty Democracy and became president amidst accusations of widespread manipulation.[26]

---

[25] Mali; Pre-poll violence forces schools' closure. All Africa Press Service. Africa News. May 12, 1997; NEWS IN BRIEF: Mali voters fear for safety. *The Guardian* (London), July 21, 1997; Mali; Malian Police Arrest More Opposition Politicians. *Africa News*, August 12, 1997.

[26] Vanguard (Nigeria): Protests as Mwanawassa becomes third president. AAGM, January 3, 2002.

Violent protest followed Kyrgyzstan's parliamentary elections in February 2005, both in the districts where opposition candidates lost and in the capital. In what eventually came to be known as the "Tulip Revolution," opposition supporters picketed and, in some cases, stormed administrative buildings, demanding that the election results be reviewed.[27] During these protests, opposition parties and their supporters managed to seize control of the state television, and by March 24, the Supreme Court had declared the elections invalid.[28] As these events unfolded, U.S. reaction was measured, validating the right of the opposition to question the March runoff elections that had left the opposition virtually powerless in parliament, while condemning the violence and destruction of government property that accompanied the protests.[29]

Although in the preceding examples opposition protesters engaged in violence, the violence associated with protest can, and often does, come from government repression. After the ruling Cambodian People's Party was declared the winner of Cambodia's 1998 parliamentary elections, opposition parties began to launch protests.[30] The violence associated with these protests seemed largely to be the result of government retaliation, with soldiers and riot squad members using machine guns, water cannons, and tear gas to disperse the crowds.[31] Still other instances of post-election violence can come from protests that are not initiated by the opposition, and it is unclear whether the violence is being perpetrated by the government or by the protesters. For example, protesters stormed the grounds of the Armenian parliament following a 1996 presidential election that they claimed was rigged.[32] The protests turned into riots as protesters clashed with the police and broke into the parliament building.[33] The leading opposition candidate, former prime minister Vazgen Manukyan, did not publicly incite the protests, but representatives of the president accused him and his supporters of trying to stage a coup.[34]

To explore whether the opposition's choice to engage in protest after the election is likely to spark violence, from either protesters or the incumbent

[27] RusData Dialine–Assault from south to north. Russian Press Digest, March 18, 2005.
[28] Associated Press Worldstream. Report: Supreme Court invalidates Kyrgyz parliamentary elections. March 24, 2005.
[29] US urges halt to post-election violence in Kyrgyzstan; Agence France Presse – English, March 22, 2005; Unrest grows in Kyrgyzstan as president warns of civil war. Agence France Presse – English, March 22, 2005.
[30] Hun Sen foes launch poll vigil. *Courier Mail* (Queensland, Australia), August 25, 1998.
[31] Thousands attend Cambodia's largest-ever protest. Deutsche Presse-Agentur. August 30, 1998; Seth Mydans. Troops shoot at mobs and beat protesters again in Phnom Penh. *New York Times*, September 10, 1998; Police use tear gas as fresh riots break out in Cambodian capital. Deutsche Presse-Agentur, September 8, 1998.
[32] Armenian protests. *Maclean's*, October 7, 1996.
[33] Vanora Bennett. Rioters break into Armenian parliament. *Los Angeles Times, Calgary Herald* (Alberta, Canada), September 26, 1996.
[34] Protesters storm Armenian parliament Police fire over chanting crowd. *The Globe and Mail* (Canada). September 26, 1996.

government, it makes sense to compare instances of opposition-initiated protest to other instances of post-election protests not initiated by the opposition. Of the 145 cases of mass demonstrations following the elections found in the data, 68 were initiated by the opposition, and 31 cases had some opposition involvement but without a clear initiating role. In the remaining 46 cases, other actors in civil society – citizen groups, women's groups, or student groups – launched demonstrations after the election. If any reports of violence accompanied the description of protest, the *Protest Violence* variable was coded as equal to 1.

A comparison of rates of violence across instances of opposition-initiated mass demonstrations and other post-election protests reveals that approximately 61% of demonstrations initiated by the opposition were accompanied by violence, compared to 58% of other post-election demonstrations . A chi-square test indicates that this 3% difference is not statistically significant. Thus, although all post-election demonstrations are slightly more likely to be associated with violence, opposition-initiated protests after the election are no more likely to result in violence than are any post-election demonstrations. Yet if such elections are not producing more violence, are they having any other destabilizing effects?

Instability

This chapter's description of post-election demonstrations in the Cote d'Ivoire clearly shows the potential of electoral protest to launch countries into chaos, completely subverting the ability of elections to offer a peaceful means for citizens to determine who rules. In addition to the violence of specific instances of electoral protest, those concerned about regime stability, particularly in countries with a history of conflict, are often also concerned about the potential destabilizing effects of contested elections.[35] Kelly (2012) has argued that observers may be hesitant to criticize elections if they worry that criticism might inspire destabilizing protest and/or violence. Whether electoral protests have such a destabilizing impact, however, is not clear. The anecdotal record finds very few cases of electoral protest leading to regime collapse, but this chapter provides a more systematic investigation of the question of electoral protest's immediate consequences for regime stability.

H₄: Post-Election Demonstrations Should Be Unrelated to Rates of Political Instability

I used two measures from the Archigos data set (Gleditsch and Chiozza 2009) to investigate the destabilizing potential of electoral protests. *Leadership Change* indicates all country-years where power was transferred (in any manner) from one leader to another. *Irregular Exit* indicates country-years where power was transferred from one leader to another in a manner not in keeping with current

[35] See, for example, Flores and Nooruddin (2012).

TABLE 4.3. *Regular and Irregular Changes in Leadership*

	Opposition-Initiated Demonstration	No Opposition-Initiated Demonstration	Chi-Square
Leadership Change	28%	16%	$p = .006$
Irregular Exit from Power	4%	3%	$p = .823$

institutional dictates. In particular, this coding indicates instances where leaders took their own lives or were forced out of office by domestic powers, or where leadership was determined by international powers.

Table 4.3 compares the information from the Archigos data set and my own information on post-election demonstrations. Here we see that years in which post-election mass demonstrations occur are associated with a higher rate of leadership change (28%) compared to years where no post-election mass demonstrations occur (16%). This difference is statistically significant. When we look at rates of irregular exit, however, we find that post-election-demonstration years are associated with only a slightly higher proportion of irregular exits (4% rather than 3%), but this difference is not statistically significant. As such, we find support for H_4: Electoral protest is not associated with higher rates of political instability.

How is it, then, that post-election protests are associated with higher rates of regular, formal turnover in office, particularly if they tend to be motivated by incumbent victory? First, recall from Chapter 3 that some instances of opposition-initiated demonstrations occur either when there is initial confusion about who won and the opposition is ultimately declared the winner, or where a main opposition party wins and smaller opposition parties protest. Post-election protests in El Salvador in 1988, for example, ultimately saw the opposition party ARENA win control of government. The extent to which these protests would be considered destabilizing, however, is debatable, because the country was already in the midst of a civil war that lasted from 1979 to 1992. Opposition parties also led protests following Mongolia's June 2004 elections. Demonstrators amassed for rallies and took over state broadcast media to accuse the government of fraud.[36] In this case, the government's Mongolian People's Revolutionary Party ultimately ended up sharing power with the opposition Democratic Party in a coalition government.

Opposition protests also have occurred in the wake of opposition victories. Supporters of two small right-wing parties protested after the 2005 elections in Poland that they had not been granted equal media access.[37] In Macedonia's

[36] Friday. Re-vote in Mongolian elections postponed as opposition protests escalate. Agence France Presse – English, July 2, 2004; MPs protest at TV station. *The Times* (London), July 2, 2004.
[37] BBC Monitoring Europe – Political. Supplied by BBC Worldwide Monitoring. Poland: Right-wing groups protest against "total media blockade." September 21, 2005.

2006 parliamentary elections, the opposition VMRO-DPMNE won the largest proportion of seats, sparking a wave of protest by supporters of two political parties that had formed an electoral coalition to represent ethnic Albanians in Macedonia.[38]

Another possibility is that opposition demonstrations after the election may lead to a review of the incumbent's victory and a subsequent removal of the incumbent from office through regular institutional processes, such as judicial review, a recount, or a rerun of the election. This was the case with the Kyrgyzstan's "Tulip Revolution" of 2005 and the Ukrainian election of 2004. Losing opposition parties and candidates had long complained publicly about electoral conduct in the Ukraine, but after opposition candidate Viktor Yushenko lost the 2004 presidential election, his supporters staged mass demonstrations in protest.[39] The accusations of fraud that Yushenko leveled at the government came on the heels of an election campaign where, it is believed, he was poisoned in an attempt to eliminate him from the presidential competition.[40] These protests eventually forced a repeat runoff, which international actors such as the United States and the EU hailed as a triumph for democracy.[41] Yushenko won that runoff, which was deemed free and fair by observers.[42]

Thus, although post-election demonstrations are associated with an increased probability of incumbent turnover through legitimate institutional means, opposition-initiated post-election demonstrations do not increase the level of violence and do not frequently lead to violent overthrow or regime collapse. Given that these targeted regimes could benefit from democratic improvement, the normative implications of regime stability may not be seen as desirable for all. From the perspective of those who are concerned about the destabilizing effects of protest and elections, however, electoral protest does not seem to be a major force of destabilization.

BOYCOTTS AND DEMONSTRATIONS

Consideration of the immediate consequences of major election boycotts and post-election mass demonstrations naturally raises the question of the

---

[38] BBC Monitoring International Reports. Macedonian Albanian parties warn of more protests against cabinet exclusion. August 13, 2006.

[39] BBC Monitoring Kiev Unit. Supplied by BBC Worldwide Monitoring. Ukraine opposition leader says 3.5m votes stolen, November 22, 2004; BBC Monitoring Kiev Unit. Supplied by BBC Worldwide Monitoring. Rival rallies held across Ukraine. November 26, 2004.

[40] Xinhua General News Service. Poisoning Ukrainian opposition leader angers EU. December 13, 2004 .

[41] AFX European Focus. EU's Barroso welcomes Ukraine election result; sees "strengthened cooperation." December 27, 2004; State Department. Powell hails Ukraine election as "historic moment for democracy." United States has supported "democratic process, not a particular candidate." December 27, 2004.

[42] BBC Monitoring Kiev Unit. Supplied by BBC Worldwide Monitoring. CIS observers say Ukraine election legitimate. November 22, 2004.

relationship between the two. This book argues that both major boycotts before the election and opposition-initiated demonstrations after the election can be understood as instances of electoral protest. Both before and after the election the opposition must decide whether to indicate acceptance of electoral events or publicly reject them. But are these two choices related in any meaningful way? A simple bivariate comparison of major boycotts and post-election demonstrations reveals that 20% of boycotted elections are followed by protest, compared to only 8% of those elections in which the opposition participates. Although this difference is statistically significant, recall from Chapter 3 that, once we control for incumbent victory and opposition strength (Table 3.2), the relationship between major boycotts and subsequent opposition demonstrations no longer attains statistical significance.

It is worth noting here that a single country – Bangladesh – is responsible for more than one-third of the cases where boycott is followed by opposition-initiated demonstrations. From the mid-1980s to the mid-1990s, electoral politics in Bangladesh followed a fairly predictable pattern of boycott and opposition-initiated protest. The majority of leftist and centrist opposition parties boycotted the May 1986 parliamentary elections in Bangladesh, with the leftist Awami League advocating mass demonstrations in the form of a general strike to protest election fraud by the incumbent Jatiya Party; this protest turned violent (Ahmed 2001, 517). Then all the opposition candidates boycotted the presidential election in October 1986 (517). As with the May elections, strikes followed the boycott, this time advocated by the National Party, and as with the previous strikes these too turned violent.[43] In 1987 President Hussain Muhammed Ershad dissolved parliament and called for fresh elections. Opposition parties boycotted these elections and demanded that Ershad hand power over to a caretaker government. Although he initially dismissed these demands, the boycott and subsequent protests following the elections persuaded him to agree to them (Ahmed 2001, 517). Violence surrounding the election was intense, leaving 13 dead.[44] Opposition supporters were reported to have set fire to a fire station after they had cornered police there (the police fled before the station was set ablaze).[45] In the wake of this violence, the opposition called for four days of demonstrations to complement the general strike scheduled to coincide with the opening of parliament.[46] This pattern repeated itself in 1996 when the opposition Awami League again initiated a major election boycott and followed it with post-election mass demonstrations against the victorious Bangladesh Nationalist Party (BNP).

---

[43] Richard M. Weintraub. Martial law ends in Bangladesh; Opposition protests reflect continued political discontent. *Washington Post*, November 11, 1986.

[44] Ruling party is declared the winner in Bangladesh. *New York Times*, March 6, 1988; 13 are reported killed In Bangladesh voting. *New York Times*, March 4, 1988.

[45] 13 are reported killed In Bangladesh voting. *New York Times*, March 4, 1988.

[46] Alamgir Mohiuddin. BC cycle Bangladesh's opposition announces protest plans. United Press International, April 20, 1988.

CONCLUSION

Bangladesh provides an instructive counter to this chapter's opening example taken from Ivoirian politics. Like Cote d'Ivoire, Bangladesh has a long track record of frequently violent electoral protest. Unlike in Cote d'Ivoire, however, these protests have not led to major breakdowns in government or to prolonged civil conflict.

Major election boycotts are not systematically related to lower voter turnout or electoral violence. Therefore election boycotts do not appear to have either immediate negative consequences for democratic participation or a decidedly destabilizing effect on the political system. However, major election boycotts do practically guarantee incumbent victory, depriving voters of any meaningful choice of candidates. Furthermore, such limited choice at the polls would seem to trivialize the question of whether election boycotts suppress voter turnout. Of course, in systems where the incumbent is engaged in relatively high levels of manipulation, victory may well be a foregone conclusion, regardless of an opposition boycott. In such cases, the boycotting opposition may not be handing victory to the incumbent so much as rejecting the illusory idea that its participation would have provided voters with a democratic choice.

Opposition protests after the election do not appear to have any significant destabilizing effects, either in terms of violence or broader instability. Protest of Cote d'Ivoire's electoral politics in the past decade gives cause for concern, but the events surrounding electoral protest there appear to be more the exception than the rule. Furthermore, following Teorell, Torcal, and Montero (2007), we might consider post-election demonstrations to be another form of political participation – evidence that, like their counterparts in developed democracies, individuals are embracing channels of democratic influence beyond voting.[47]

For those concerned about regime stability, electoral protests do not appear to be a particularly detrimental force. For those more concerned with democratization, however, the minimal impact of electoral protest depicted in this chapter should provide cause for concern. If electoral protests are not causing problems for the regimes where they occur, where there is clearly room for democratic improvement, then how are they improving prospects for democracy? If these protests are not systematically related to electoral upheaval, can we find other – incremental – evidence of their impact?

The next chapter addresses the democratic consequences of electoral protest, focusing on subsequent electoral reform. Electoral protests do not affect regime stability, but they do have conditional consequences for election-related reforms. Furthermore, the lack of impact on voter turnout demonstrated in this chapter may actually be suggestive of where boycotts need to draw support if they are going to be effective – from international, rather than domestic actors.

---

[47] For more on protest and participation, see Blais (2010).

5

Democratic Consequences of Electoral Protest

Haiti has experienced a string of contentious elections since the late 1980s. Parliamentary elections in May 2000 were marked by violence and administrative irregularities, most typically the late opening of polling stations.[1] Chaotic delivery of the ballot boxes to the electoral commission after the elections (some poll workers simply left ballot boxes outside the commission's building, unguarded overnight, because they could not find room inside) also raised the specter of electoral malfeasance.[2] Despite these problems, observers described the elections, in which incumbent Aristide's Lavalas Party candidates were expected to win, as "generally credible."[3] However, even before the official results were announced, the Lavalas Party declared victory, and opposition parties called for the election results to be annulled.[4] International donors reacted to these events by threatening to suspend aid to Haiti.[5] Opposition parties objected to the preliminary results that showed Lavalas winning most of the available senate seats and withdrew their candidates from the runoff elections.[6] But it was Lavalas supporters who protested, demanding that the final results be released

[1] Willis Witter. Haiti's elections declared free, but fairness in doubt; Democracy seeks toehold in nation. *Washington Times*. May 23, 2000, Tuesday; Haiti: Elections get off to a "rocky start". BBC Monitoring Latin America – Political Supplied by BBC Worldwide Monitoring, May 21, 2000.

[2] David Gonzalez. Dumped ballots raise worries in Haiti vote. *New York Times*, May 23, 2000.

[3] Michael Dobbs. Aristide's Party Leading in Haitian Vote; Monitors Say Elections Generally Credible. *Washington Post*, Washington Post Foreign Service, May 23, 2000.

[4] Haitian parties urge election annulment. *New York Times*, May 25, 2000.

[5] International sponsors freeze aid pending election results. BBC Summary of World Broadcasts, May 27, 2000, Saturday, Part 5 Africa, Latin America, and the Caribbean; Latin America and the Caribbean; Venezuela; AL/W0642/S1.

[6] Owen Bowcott. Haiti poll row fuels international alarm. *The Guardian* (London), June 15, 2000.

and that the OAS recognize the Lavalas victory as legitimate.[7] The resulting conflict caused the head of Haiti's election commission to flee to the Dominican Republic and then to the United States.[8]

Opposition parties in Haiti boycotted the November presidential election that year on the grounds that the government had cheated in the May parliamentary elections to pave the way for Aristide's reelection.[9] Although the November election appeared to be less violent than some previous contests, bombings still occurred, and the OAS criticized it as being held without attention to "critical deficiencies" of the current system.[10] Aristide won the election, but international aid remained suspended on the grounds that the opposition complaints needed to be resolved.[11] The opposition refused to meet with Aristide in a standoff that persisted for nearly two years, at which point the United States suggested unblocking aid to Haiti in September 2002, with certain conditions, which included the creation of a new election management body.[12] The OAS eventually succeeded in receiving agreement from both the incumbent and the opposition on the terms proposed by the United States.[13] This agreement, however, did not alleviate political tensions in Haiti, and by 2004, Aristide had been forced out of office. UN peacekeepers then occupied Haiti for two years and fresh elections were held in 2006.

Former president and Aristide protégé, Rene Preval, was declared the winner of the February 2006 election, but not before his supporters had rioted at the initial claim that he had not won enough votes in the first round to avoid a runoff. Approximately one week after the February 7 election, Haiti's electoral management body declared Preval the first-round winner of the election, obviating the need for a second round of voting; this decision drew praise from the head of the OAS.[14] Although both the 2006 election and the protests that followed were marred with violence, from that period until the 2009 earthquake, assessments of Haiti's political situation had a cautiously optimistic tone.[15] Since then, Haiti has survived an election in which serious concerns over first-round voting led to violent post-election demonstrations. A UN-sponsored

---

[7] Michael Norton. Supporters of Aristide riot in Haiti. Toronto Star. June 20, 2000.

[8] Haiti's top election official flees nation for US. *New York Times*, June 19, 2000.

[9] Aristide says he won't step down. Deutsche Presse-Agentur, November 29, 2002.

[10] OAS says elections held without solving earlier "critical deficiencies." BBC Summary of World Broadcasts, November 30, 2000; Canute James. The Americas: Haiti bomb blasts raise tension. *Financial Times* (London), November 24, 2000.

[11] David Gonzalez. Western hemisphere's states support unblocking of aid to haiti. New *York Times*, September 5, 2002.

[12] Ibid.

[13] Felix Ulloa. Haiti. *Elections in the Americas*, p. 377.

[14] BBC Monitoring Latin America – Political. Supplied by BBC Worldwide Monitoring. February 18, 2006 Saturday. OAS's Insulza hails decision to declare Preval Haitian president.

[15] Violence mars long-awaited Haiti election. *The Australian*, February 9, 2006; Haiti's troubled elections take bad turn with protest in capital. *Wall Street Journal Abstracts*. February 14, 2006. A step backward; Rebuilding Haiti. *The Economist*, November 7, 2009.

recount resolved the electoral conflict; it showed that the candidate originally declared to have come in third (behind one opposition candidate and the candidate favored by the incumbent) actually deserved the second-place spot on the runoff ballot, edging out the incumbent's favored candidate. That candidate who rose from third to second place in the first round, Michel Martelly, ultimately won the presidency in the second round of voting in March 2011. The reaction to the runoff election was a peaceful contrast to the aftermath of the first round (Dougherty 2011).

CONTINGENT CONSEQUENCES

With respect to the democratic consequences of electoral protest, this book's central argument is that, where the incumbent is motivated to enhance the credibility of future agreements and does not feel too threatened domestically, democratic reform should be more likely to occur. This chapter brings us to the fifth and final decision point of the theory outlined in Figure 2.1. Whether electoral protest occurs before the election in the form of a major boycott or takes the form of mass demonstrations after the election, the period after the election is the point at which the incumbent must decide whether to respond to electoral protest and, if so, what form the response will take. It is the incumbent's strategic choice at this stage of the negotiation process that has the potential to produce positive consequences for democracy in the future – but only under certain circumstances.

Chapter 3 illustrated that the decision to institute a major election boycott is closely related to problems of information and incumbent credibility. Where low-information environments present more opportunities for the incumbent or opposition to misrepresent private information, the probability of those actors successfully negotiating an agreement to avoid a boycott decreases. Problems of incumbent credibility can also cause pre-election bargaining to break down and produce a boycott. Boycotted elections generate information – possibly about the ways in which the incumbent's promises were not credible, but definitely about the extent to which the protesting opposition enjoys domestic and/or international support and the extent to which that support will translate into action. The incumbent will take all this information into account when making her decision how to respond. The questions of most concern to the incumbent in the wake of electoral protest are the following: Who is paying attention to the protest? Are international actors pressuring the incumbent to democratize further? Is domestic pressure endangering the incumbent's chances of staying in power?

We know from the theoretical expectations generated in Chapter 2 that the occurrence of boycotts is not likely to be related to the strength of the opposition, because of the conflicting incentives produced by that strength for both actors. Furthermore, evidence from Chapter 4 provides empirical support for the idea that boycotts are not related to voter turnout or to post-election protests in any systematic way. As such, international support is likely to have a greater influence on the incumbent's response to boycotts. In a situation where the incumbent is confronted with a major opposition boycott that received international support, we would expect democratic reforms to result so that the incumbent can demonstrate her commitment to democracy. But when boycotts are accompanied by domestic support, the incumbent may feel her future grip on power to be too threatened to enact truly democratic reform and may instead attempt to respond with election-related reform that is actually more authoritarian in nature.

Post-election mass demonstrations initiated by the opposition further enhance the information-generation function of elections. When they are most informative, these protests can publicize the extent to which the incumbent is engaging in fraud, as they did in the Dominican Republic in 1994. Protest by the two main opposition parties after that election publicized how the incumbent president Joaquin Balaguer had used election administration procedures and a computerized voter register to systematically disenfranchise opposition supporters. According to Hatuey De Camps, long-time activist for the Dominican Revolutionary Party (PRD) – one of the parties in opposition to Balaguer's Social Christian Reformist Party (PRSC) – when the voter register was transferred to the computerized system, information for approximately 20 supporters was deleted and reassigned to the incumbent party for each of "10,000 or more" polling stations.[16] It was only in the aftermath of election protest that the opposition was able to bring this manipulation to light.

Although post-election protests increase available information, what we learned from Chapter 3 is that these protests stem not so much from problems of information but rather from credibility problems – though which actor is lacking credibility is often not clear. Was the incumbent unable to adhere to an agreed-on level of manipulation, or was the opposition unable to resist the temptation of challenging the results, even though the incumbent held up her end of the agreement? If post-election demonstrations are the result of credibility problems, then the incumbent might be motivated to reform to enhance future credibility.

Here again, though, the incumbent's willingness to enact reforms that will improve her credibility in response to post-election demonstrations depends on the kind of information that the protests reveal. By definition, mass demonstrations communicate some domestic support for the opposition, but the extent of that support will vary and likely shape incumbent response. Furthermore, because of the ambiguity that surrounds these protests, it is not clear what the impact of international attention should be on encouraging subsequent reform.

As with the paradox presented by opposition strength in Chapter 3, the issue of how domestic support might shape the incumbent's response is complex. If

---

[16] Interview conducted by the author, February 18, 2005.

opposition support of protest is so strong that an incumbent fears for her life, then reform (or even the incumbent's exit from office) is likely to result. At the same time, however, higher levels of opposition support among the domestic electorate clearly signal to the incumbent that her chances of winning free and fair elections in the future are compromised. As such, if the incumbent sees a way to reform that will provide room to maneuver, enabling her to either maintain or increase her current hold on power, then protest that receives strong domestic support might motivate reforms with less positive consequences for democracy.

Finally, if the incumbent responds to opposition pressure with reforms that increase electoral fairness (and the credibility of the incumbent's future claims to fairness), then we should see evidence of democratic improvement. But what about the possibility that the incumbent enacts reforms that only appear to make future commitments to electoral fairness more credible? Is it reasonable to expect that incumbents who have been attempting to manipulate elections to their advantage would suddenly, on being confronted with electoral protest, see the error of their ways and become repentant democrats? Even if incumbents feel pressure to respond to reform, one should be skeptical of the extent to which these reforms represent real democratic improvements as opposed to another attempt to shape political institutions to their benefit. Thus, it is important for this chapter to consider reform in different ways and to look beyond the question of whether or not protest motivates reform to see if those reforms have any further observable consequences for democratization.

The chapter begins by considering patterns of incumbent response following electoral protest. From these general observations about reform, we move to a more nuanced consideration of the incumbent's reaction to protest, presenting the distinction between democratic reforms and reforms that might represent more authoritarian entrenchment. We then use this distinction for a systematic investigation of the conditional consequences of electoral protest. The chapter ends with a discussion of several cases of protest and subsequent reform. These cases highlight many of the statistical patterns described in the chapter and underscore the complexity of these ongoing negotiations between incumbent and opposition actors and their consequences for democracy.

ELECTION-RELATED REFORM

Election-related reform is the final major concept that I measured for this study. It makes sense to focus on election-related reforms, given that electoral manipulation is at the heart of the opposition–incumbent bargaining that precedes protest. It is worth noting, however, that an emphasis on election-related reform means that other kinds of reform, such as economic reforms or civil service reforms have not been accounted for here. However, the study does include some reforms beyond the narrow scope of formal electoral laws that were likely to affect the conduct of future elections. Reforms to civil liberties, such as changes on media restrictions or the lifting of a state of emergency, can reasonably be expected to have some impact on electoral fairness and, as such, are coded as election-related reforms. In 1996, for example, Nigeria's government changed a law that previously had allowed the detention of "opponents of the state" without trial; the new law provides for judicial process.[17] In 2001, the Chilean government passed legislation to reduce restrictions on journalists and print media.[18] Although the specific impact of each of these examples of reform might vary, we would expect such reforms to have an impact on the conduct of future elections.

A study of election-related reform captures incumbent responses to electoral protest and allows us to investigate further the impact of electoral protest on democracy. The focus on election-related laws follows from the argument in this book that actors are bargaining over electoral conduct. If initial bargaining has failed such that the opposition has resorted to election-related protest, it would make sense to focus on election-related reform when looking for evidence that the incumbent is responding to these protests.

Election-related reforms refer to those legally enacted changes that can reasonably be expected to affect the fairness of future elections. Encompassed in this definition, then, are reforms of the electoral system and changes in the laws governing electoral administration. Also included are laws pertaining to civil liberties such as media freedom, police powers, and public assembly. Although not explicitly electoral in scope, such laws can be understood as election-related because their provisions will undoubtedly affect the fairness and conduct of future elections. *Election-Related Reform* was coded as equal to 1 if any of the kinds of reforms described earlier were enacted in the time period after the election in question (t) but before the next election ($t+1$).[19] Reports of reform had to specify enactment of the reform (passage of laws) to be counted in this study. Reports of rhetorical calls for reform or even of proposed reform legislation were not counted as actual reform.

The criterion of "enacted legislation" sets a fairly high bar for capturing incumbents' response, but it has the distinct advantage of capturing actual change rather than rhetorical promises. Incumbents could – and often do – respond to protest by acknowledging the opposition's complaints and promising reform in the future or by taking institutional actions that would appear to be addressing opposition concerns, such as forming committees or holding summits, without necessarily enacting legislation. After the contentious elections in

---

[17] Nigeria announces anniversary reforms. Deutsche Presse-Agentur, June 12, 1996.

[18] Deputies approve press laws vote represents step forward for free expression. *Santiago Times*, April 12, 2001.

[19] Some countries that held elections in 2005 or 2006 have not yet held another one. January 2008 was the cutoff date for reform enactment in those cases.

the Philippines in 2004, where the opposition initiated post-election demonstrations, President Gloria Macapagal Arroyo appointed a former judge to propose electoral system reform, but six year later no reforms had yet been enacted.[20] Furthermore, just as incumbents often respond by paying lip service to the need for reform, they also frequently respond by denouncing and attempting to discredit opposition protest efforts. This study does not use rhetoric or gestures to measure incumbent response for the same reason that it does not focus on post-election opposition complaints: Talk is cheap. Thus, although using the criterion of actual change as opposed to mere rhetorical promises of reform sets a high standard for capturing incumbent response to protest, this standard might reasonably be expected to produce observable consequences for democracy. In particular, if those who favor a procedural definition of democracy are correct, any improvements to the fairness of future elections should have positive consequences for democracy, and any changes that decrease electoral fairness should have negative consequences for democracy.

Furthermore, by searching for reforms enacted after each of the 765 elections in the data set, for the entire time period until the subsequent election, I have effectively coded the reported history of election-related reform across each country for the period 1975–2006 broken down by each country's electoral cycle. This strategy should not give elections or election-related protest any undue importance. If election-related protests do not matter for reform, we should simply observe comparable rates of reform across all countries, regardless of whether the opposition protested in a given election.

It is important to note that this coding criterion simply records enacted legal changes that should affect elections; it makes no judgment about the democratic nature of those reforms. Thus, within the general *Reform* coding there is a great deal of variation – from a law increasing the number of signatures needed for candidate nomination in Armenia in 1995, to state-of-emergency police powers in India 1980, and to a law banning political parties from buying radio and television advertisement in Mexico in 2006. Although a second coding, used later in the chapter, tries to distinguish those reforms that should have positive consequences for democracy from those laws that represent cosmetic changes at best and authoritarian retrenchment at worst, this initial coding captures any instance where the incumbent government made changes to the law that will have an impact on future electoral competition. Based on the theory presented in Chapter 2, we should not expect either form of electoral protest on its own to motivate incumbent response. It is only after the incumbent has a sense of whether the protest has received any support and of the nature of that support that we can start to think about if and how the incumbent might respond to electoral protest.

---

[20] Philippine leader appoints judge to reform electoral system. Agence France Presse – English, January 24, 2006.

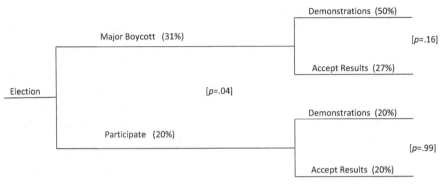

FIGURE 5.1. Rates of Election-Related Reform by Opposition Protest Choice.

Figure 5.1 compares rates of election-related reform following boycotts versus post-election demonstrations. Boycotted elections were followed by election-related reform at a higher rate than those elections where the opposition participated: Nearly one-third of boycotted elections were followed by reform versus only 20% of non-boycotted elections. In a chi-square comparison, this difference attains conventional levels of statistical significance (*p* values are reported in the figure). The statistical significance disappears, however, when we look at post-election demonstrations. Elections where protest follows boycott showed a much higher rate of subsequent reform (50%) than those elections where boycotts were not followed by protest (27%), but the difference is not statistically significant due to the small number of cases available for comparison in those categories. There is also no observable difference between rates of reform when protest follows a boycott than when it follows an election in which the opposition participated and accepted its results. Furthermore, although it may be appropriate to interpret election-related reform as the incumbent's response to opposition agitation, the fact that the initial coding does not address the extent to which reforms are democratic means the impact of such reforms on democracy remains unclear.

DEMOCRATIC REFORM VS. AUTHORITARIAN "REFORM"

The previous section considered all instances of election-related reform. Given the strategic nature of politics and the often unintended consequences of institutional change, it is difficult to assess objectively whether particular reforms are actually democratic. Some instances of reform are clearly undemocratic, meant to further cement the incumbent's own electoral advantage. For example, after an election boycott in 1999, the government of Togo enacted reforms that removed term limits from the presidency and extended the length of time that presidential candidates had to have lived in Togo, thereby disqualifying one of the main opposition candidates (*PANA* 2002). In addition, legislation enacted to ban opposition protests following the 2000 elections in Cote d'Ivoire is paradigmatic of reform that should have negative consequences for democracy.

Other reforms, such as the sweeping reforms that followed the 1997 election boycott in Indonesia, seem obviously democratic, if only because they clearly come at a cost to the incumbent. After President Suharto resigned, the following reforms were ushered in under his former vice president: release of political prisoners, press freedom laws, and the establishment of an independent election commission. Clearly press freedom and independence for the election management body were election-related reforms, and allowing imprisoned opponents of the regime to be free to participate in politics in the future was likely to make future electoral competition more difficult for the incumbent.

In most cases, however, the content of election-related reforms does not provide sufficient information to declare their democratic nature with any certainty. Following a major election boycott in Mauritania, in 1997, for example, the government instituted a series of election-related reforms of a decidedly ambiguous nature. Each of the enacted reforms – the institution of public finance for political parties, the introduction of proportional representation to elect 20% of the legislature, and the reduction of candidate registration fees – was thought to improve electoral fairness, and perceptions of Mauritania's democratic quality had improved slightly by the time of the next election in 2001.[21] In this specific context, however, the reforms might also be understood as an attempt to weaken the opposition (N'Diaye 2001). Increased public funding, reduced registration fees, and proportional representation all encourage party entry, which can lead to the fragmentation of the opposition and the cultivation of small opposition parties, thereby increasing the strength of the incumbent relative to the opposition.[22]

To address this inherent ambiguity surrounding the democratic nature of reforms, I used opposition response to reform as the criterion by which to distinguish democratic from nondemocratic reforms.[23] If there was no report of the opposition rejecting the reform, then *Democratic Reform* was coded equal to 1. If the incumbent enacted reform that the opposition rejected publicly, *Authoritarian Reform* was coded equal to 1. These two codings were mutually exclusive. This coding decision has both pluses and minuses, however. The advantage of qualifying as democratic only those reforms that passed muster with a skeptical and knowledgeable local actor – that is, one who may be most likely to find fault with policies enacted by the incumbent – is that doing so is

[21] Political Reforms in Mauritania. *Financial Times Information*, December 14, 2000.
[22] Although there are no reports of the opposition objecting to these reforms, the fact that the incumbent continued to dominate politics until a 2005 coup suggests that these reforms did not have a strong democratizing effect.
[23] International election observers have been known to use similar coding criteria when they look to opposition reaction to election results to gauge an election's legitimacy (Schedler 2002, Pastor 1999).

not likely to exaggerate the democratic nature of election-related reforms. At the same time, the coding decision lacks strict objectivity and may say as much about the strategic motivations of the opposition as it does about the nature of the reforms themselves.

In cases where reform follows protest, however, opposition incentives should bias our observations in the direction of over-counting authoritarian "reforms." It seems less likely that opposition elites who have been willing to publicly challenge the incumbent outside of standard institutional channels would be reluctant to criticize subsequent reforms enacted by the incumbent. An opposition that has previously engaged in electoral protest should feel free to criticize any reforms that it perceives to be undemocratic. In contrast, if the opposition feels that reforms are truly democratic, it may have some interest in recognizing them as such and crediting its protest activity for the reforms. This is precisely what happened in Bangladesh after the contentious 1996 election: When Prime Minister Khaleda Zia instituted provisions for a neutral caretaker government to oversee all future elections, Sheikh Hasina, the leader of the opposition Awami League party, hailed the move as a "people's victory."[24] Yet opposition leaders might reject democratic reforms in a strategic bid to push for even more concessions. The least likely possibility would seem to be a previously active opposition passively accepting undemocratic "reforms." Thus, if anything, in cases of reform following protest, this coding might run the risk of miscoding as undemocratic reforms that might actually be democratic.

As an additional check on the external validity of this coding, I compared instances of democratic reform and authoritarian reform to each country's Polity score at the time of the country's next election (Marshall, Jagers, and Gurr 2010). Table 5.1 shows the result of an ordinary least squares regression estimating the relationships of both democratic reforms and authoritarian "reforms" to changes in Polity scores, with controls for economic development and aid dependence. The sign for each of the estimated coefficients related to reform is in the expected direction: The positive estimated coefficient for democratic reform shows that democratic reforms are associated with improved Polity scores (a relationship that approaches conventional levels of statistical significance), whereas the negative sign associated with authoritarian reform suggests that authoritarian reforms should be associated with a decline in assessments of overall democratic quality. This second relationship, however, does not attain conventional levels of statistical significance.

CONDITIONAL CONSEQUENCES OF ELECTORAL PROTEST

The ultimate consequences of electoral protest for electoral reform will depend on the nature of the support that the protest receives. This section outlines a series of hypotheses derived from the theory presented in Chapter 2. The

---

[24] PM offers vote compromise to end Bangladeshi strikes. *The Gazette* (Montreal), March 27, 1996.

TABLE 5.1. *Linear Regression: Changes in Polity Score*

	Change in Polity Score
Democratic Reform	0.792[+]
	(0.477)
Authoritarian "Reform"	−0.475
	(0.923)
GDP per capita	−0.000
	(0.000)
Aid Dependent	−0.589
	(0.580)
Constant	1.295
	(0.606)
N	442
$F_{(4, 103)}$	1.49
Prob. > F	0.211
R^2	0.012

* Significant at the level $p > .05$, two-tailed z-test.
** Significant at the level $p > .01$, two-tailed z-test.
[+] Significant at the level $p > .05$, one-tailed z-test.
Note: Robust standard errors (in parentheses) clustered by country.

impacts of domestic support and international support for protest are considered separately. Although there are instances where protests receive both domestic and international support, they do not suggest clear theoretical predictions, because the ultimate effect of such protest will depend on how the incumbent perceives the import of each source of support.

Election boycotts that receive domestic support will present a dilemma for the incumbent – she should feel the need to respond, but at the same time, evidence of domestic support for the opposition is evidence of greater electoral difficulty for the incumbent in future elections, particularly if she chooses to enact democratic election-related reform. Thus, domestic support for major election boycotts should motivate the incumbent to respond with authoritarian "reforms." This section uses two indicators to assess whether a major election boycott received domestic support: (1) post-election demonstrations and (2) the opposition's support in the electorate.

H_1: Major Election Boycotts Followed by Post-Election Mass Demonstrations Should Be Associated with a Higher Probability of Authoritarian "Reform"

If a boycotted election is followed by mass demonstrations, it suggests that the opposition's protest activities are enjoying support among the domestic electorate. Though there are only 11 cases of opposition-initiated demonstrations following a major boycott, this represents a statistically significant proportion of major boycotts and a rate of post-election demonstration nearly two times that of demonstrations following elections that are not boycotted. We can think, also, of the conditions in which electoral protests occur as providing further indications of whether electoral protests receive domestic support. Where opposition parties have performed better in previous polls, their protests are likely to enjoy more support in the domestic electorate.

H_2: Major Election Boycotts Where the Opposition Enjoys More Support in the Electorate Should Be Associated with a Higher Probability of Authoritarian Reform

In theory, voter turnout might provide another indication of domestic support for boycotts, but in practice there are two reasons to be skeptical of turnout as a measure of domestic support. First, it is difficult to tell from turnout data alone whether voters support the incumbent or the opposition. As a result, it would be difficult to infer support for the opposition from reduced turnout. A relationship between a boycott and reduced turnout might indicate domestic support for the opposition, or it might indicate that incumbent supporters no longer feel the need to turn out to vote because their preferred candidate is now basically assured victory. Finally, even if we could infer increased support for the opposition from reduced turnout, such support should not inspire a response from the incumbent in the same way that mass demonstrations might. Put simply, voters who get out in the street to voice their discontent are probably much more threatening to the incumbent than those who sit silently at home.

Unlike domestic support for protest, however, international support for boycotts should motivate the incumbent to enact democratic reform, because international support does not pose problems for reelection in the same way that domestic support might. As such, an incumbent faced with international support for electoral protest should feel more motivation to enact genuine democratic reform.

H_3: Major Election Boycotts That Attract International Attention Should Be Associated with a Higher Probability of Democratic Reform

The international attention variable focuses on whether any states or intergovernmental organizations (IGOs) with a reputation for supporting democracy in developing countries, for example the UN or the EU, commented publicly on the election.[25] I coded the variable, *International Reaction*, as equal to 1 in any instance where a western democracy-promoting state or IGO was reported to have commented on the election. If no such comment was reported, I coded *International Reaction* as equal to 0. The *International Reaction* variable is an

---

[25] See coding descriptions of *International Reaction* for more information on the specific sources and searches that were performed to recover the articles used to make this determination.

indicator of international support for either the opposition or for the democratization process in general. Ideally there should be a more fine-grained coding of the actual extent to which international reactions convey this support, and in some cases international actors do communicate support for the incumbent or opposition using very direct language. Due to the delicate nature of diplomatic communication, however, it is rare to see countries or IGOs offer explicit messages of support: Instead they are more likely to communicate "hopes" or "concerns" related to a particular election without directly indicating support for either the incumbent or the opposition. For these reasons, it should be sufficient to consider instances where pro-democracy international actors signal they are paying attention to elections as supportive of electoral protest that occurs.

H_4: Post-Election Mass Demonstrations That Attract International Attention Should Not Be Associated with Higher Probabilities of Democratic Reform or Authoritarian "Reform"

Unlike election boycotts, which generate clear predictions based on whether they receive support from domestic or international actors, the expectations for post-election demonstrations are much less clear. This is because post-election demonstrations are themselves a sign of domestic support for the opposition. Thus, when the incumbent faces both domestic and international support, it is not clear which audience will take priority in any given circumstance. On the one hand, if international pressure is substantial, the incumbent might opt for democratic reform – even though it would likely mean certain defeat in future elections. On the other hand, if international attention is less intense, the incumbent might find "reforms" that offer an authoritarian advantage in the future to be more attractive. Then again, international attention might subject any reforms to more scrutiny and might cause the incumbent to shy away from further manipulation at this point. Finally, it is important to remember that because post-election demonstrations can be seen as stemming from problems of opposition credibility as much as from incumbent credibility, the incumbent who faces international attention and post-election demonstrations might prefer to challenge the legitimacy of the opposition's claims, rather than enact reform.

Multiple Regression Analyses

In testing H_1 through H_4, I constructed two indicators to capture domestic support: (1) an interaction term describing when a major election boycott turns into opposition-lead mass demonstrations after the election[26] and (2) the measure

---

[26] Mass demonstrations might be construed as domestic support for the opposition in and of themselves.

TABLE 5.2. *Logistic Regression: Election-Related Reforms*

	Model 1 Authoritarian "Reform"	Model 2 Democratic Reform
Major Boycott	−2.838* (1.361)	−0.785 (0.658)
Opposition Demonstration	−26.22** (1.507)	0.728 (0.445)
Opposition Seat Share	−2.183** (0.786)	0.072 (0.533)
Boycott*Demonstration	26.97** (2.265)	1.275 (1.078)
Boycott*Opposition Seats	10.06** (2.925)	−1.672 (2.409)
International Reaction	0.557 (0.374)	−0.026 (0.266)
Boycott *International Reaction	0.675 (1.472)	2.558** (0.770)
Demonstration* International Reaction	−12.67** (1.959)	−0.592 (0.564)
GDP per capita	−0.000 (0.000)	0.000 (0.000)
Aid Dependent	0.840 (0.626)	−0.362 (0.331)
Constant	−2.825 (0.691)	−1.585 (0.358)
N	553	553
Wald chi^2 (10)	694.78	19.94
Pseudo R^2	0.115	0.030

* Significant at the level $p > .05$, two-tailed z-test.
** Significant at the level $p > .01$, two-tailed z-test.
Note: Robust standard errors (in parentheses) clustered by country.

of opposition support used in Chapters 3 and 4 – the share of legislative seats held by the opposition before the election. I used the *International Reaction* variable described earlier to capture international support. Then I operationalized control variables for this model using a similar process as that described for the indicators of protest in Chapter 3 and the indicators of violence and reform in Chapter 4. Detailed information on data collection and coding can be found in Appendix A.

Table 5.2 presents the results from two logit regressions that use instances of reform (either authoritarian "reform" or democratic reform) to measure the probability of the incumbent enacting either type of reform. The interaction terms constructed in these models are meant to capture the conditional relationships of major election boycotts and of post-election mass demonstrations to both democratic reform and authoritarian "reforms," considering first domestic and then international factors.[27] Because of the small number of cases available to consider some of the combinations of protest, support, and reform, it is difficult to make sense of higher order interactions that might allow us to model instances of both international and domestic support for protest. As such, the most we can do with these models is consider the conditional impact of each of these sources of support separately, controlling for the presence of the other potential source of support. For the reader wishing to think more about those instances of simultaneous domestic and international support for protest, the case of Haiti that began this chapter and some of the cases that follow this regression analysis provide relevant examples.

Both models contain controls for both the level of economic development, in terms of GDP per capita, and whether the country is considered dependent on foreign aid, both of which might reasonably be thought to affect the frequency of election-related reform. The models in Table 5.2 used all election observations for which there were available data on all indicators. However, the results reported from those models are robust to alternate model specifications that focus on two subsets of observations: (1) excluding the most democratic countries in the sample or (2) including only those "late-late developing regions" of Africa, Asia, and the Middle East, following Brownlee (2011).[28] Thus, even though all developing countries are included, based on the book's theory, we can be confident that these results are not being driven by the "most democratic" countries in the sample nor by those countries with the longest electoral histories.

Model 1 provides support for H_1 and H_2: Domestic support for major election boycotts will be associated with an increased probability of authoritarian "reforms." Interaction terms are used to capture circumstances where boycotts are followed by opposition-initiated demonstrations (*Boycott*Demonstration*) and instances of boycott where the opposition enjoys more support in the electorate (*Boycott*Opposition Seats*). The positive estimated coefficient associated with the first interaction term suggests that, when boycotts are followed by post-election demonstrations, there is an increased probability of authoritarian "reform." This coefficient attains conventional levels of statistical significance. Similarly, the positive estimated coefficient for the second interaction term suggests that a boycott increases the probability of the incumbent choosing to enact authoritarian "reform" as the proportion of legislative seats controlled by the opposition increases (indicating more support for the opposition in the electorate). This estimate also attains conventional levels of statistical significance.

---

[27] Descriptive statistics for all variables used in this regression can be found in Appendix A.

[28] Countries with a previous-year Freedom House Political Freedom score of 3 or smaller were excluded in order to conduct the first robustness check. The second robustness check follows from the observations in Chapter 1 that Latin America in particular began holding elections long before many other developing regions and that both Latin America and Eastern Europe experienced decolonialization and state-building earlier than other regions (Brownlee 2011, 813). Results from both of these robustness checks can be found in Appendix A.

We should note that several of the constituent terms used to construct these conditional relationships have estimated coefficients that also obtain conventional levels of statistical significance. Because of the inclusion of the interaction terms, the coefficients associated with these variables must be interpreted as instances where the other variables used in the interaction terms are equal to zero.[29] For example, the negative coefficient associated with a major boycott in Model 1 means that, when a boycott occurs in instances where the opposition holds zero seats in the legislature and no protest follows the election; it also implies that if the election receives no international reaction, then the probability of authoritarian "reform" decreases. This relationship is entirely consistent with the theory that the incumbent needs to feel that some audience is paying attention to be motivated to respond with reform. Similarly, opposition protest and support for the opposition are associated with a reduced probability of enacting authoritarian reform. The relationship of opposition support and reform makes sense – without any protest, the incumbent is less likely to engage in reform. That election demonstrations on their own do not encourage reform is discussed further in conjunction with H_4.

Model 2 provides support for H_3: Major boycotts receiving international attention are associated with an increased probability of democratic reform. The estimated coefficient associated with the interaction term constructed to capture this conditional relationship (*Boycott*International Reaction*) is positive and attains conventional levels of statistical significance. Here then, we see that when the incumbent feels pressure to respond to protest, but does not feel an immediate domestic threat to her future electoral fortunes, democratic reform is more likely to result.

Finally, both models allow us to evaluate H_4, which claims that post-election demonstrations should not show a systematic relationship to either type of reform when the protest receives international attention. In Model 1, the interaction term capturing instances where post-election demonstrations receive international attention (*Demonstration*International Reaction*) has an estimated coefficient that is negative and statistically significant, suggesting that post-election demonstrations with international support reduce the probability that the incumbent will try to appear responsive while attempting to maintain a competitive advantage for future elections and enacting authoritarian "reform." At the same time, the estimated coefficient associated with this term in Model 2, which examines the probability of democratic reform, is also negative, but does not attain conventional levels of statistical significance. Thus, although these instances of domestic and international attention have indeterminate consequences for democratic reform predicted by the theory, they are more consistently associated with a decreased probability of authoritarian entrenchment in the guise of "reform."

---

[29] For more on interpreting the component parts of interaction terms see Brambor, Clark, and Golder (2006).

It may be that international scrutiny makes leaders more hesitant to enact reforms that are likely to be viewed as window-dressing by international actors. However, we should recall that Model 1 also reveals a negative and statistically significant estimated relationship between demonstrations and authoritarian "reform." Taken together, these two estimates suggest that, whether international actors are paying attention or not, post-election demonstrations decrease the probability that the incumbent will enact reform that further enhances her own competitive position in future elections. Thus, we are left with the following conclusions:

1. When boycotts receive support from either domestic or international actors, they can have consequences for reform. Boycotts receiving domestic support will encourage the incumbent to enact reforms that are likely to confer more advantage to the incumbent in the future, whereas boycotts receiving international support will encourage the incumbent to enact democratic reform.
2. Because of the ambiguity surrounding their causes, the consequences of post-election demonstrations for democratic reform are much less straightforward. At a minimum, post-election demonstrations appear to discourage incumbent attempts at authoritarian "reform."

CASES OF ELECTORAL PROTEST AND THEIR CONSEQUENCES

The cases presented in this section provide examples of the statistical patterns identified in the data, as well as important exceptions to those patterns. Many of the key explanatory variables used in Models 1 and 2 rely on a dichotomous coding, in which some factor is either recorded as happening (and = 1) or not (and = 0). These coding decisions were made in the interest of enhancing comparability across a wide range of cases of relatively rare events: Making more fine-grained distinctions would have reduced our ability to make systematic comparisons. What we lose with such coding decisions, however, is much of the contextual richness that is critical to understanding how electoral protests affect the long-term prospects of democracy in the countries where they occur. Another limitation of this statistical analysis is that, although we can clearly observe the conditional impact of international (or domestic) support while controlling for the other source of support, we cannot directly infer a clear pattern when both sources of support are present simultaneously. This section discusses several cases of protest in the context of different sources of support and allows us to consider their prospects for democracy, particularly in terms of the opposition's ability to compete more effectively in the future.[30] Several

---

[30] Because of the relative rarity of both electoral protest and election-related reform, probability predictions generated from the conditional relationships described in Table 5.2 tend to have overlapping confidence intervals.

of the cases presented here involve both domestic and international attention to electoral protest, demonstrating that the ultimate impact of these sources of support on reform will depend on their relative import in any given context. Furthermore, these stories of electoral protest and subsequent election-related reform may help assuage concerns about the potential spuriousness of the relationship between protest and reform discussed in Chapter 4.

Boycotts with Domestic Support

Table 5.2 shows that boycotts receiving domestic support either in terms of subsequent post-election demonstrations or more general support for the opposition in the electorate are associated with an increased probability of authoritarian "reform," but have no relationship to the probability of democratic reform. Azerbaijan provides an example of a boycott with domestic support that motivated authoritarian retrenchment – even though the boycott also received international attention. Togo's 1999 election boycott provides another example. The case of Bangladesh offers an exception to the general statistical pattern depicted in Table 5.2, in that a major election boycott was followed by protests (and even more boycotts); although the initial incumbent response suggested an attempt at authoritarian retrenchment, the ultimate consequences were arguably more positive for democracy. These three cases are now discussed in more detail.

Five prominent opposition candidates boycotted the 1998 presidential election in Azerbaijan.[31] Representatives of the government of incumbent Heydar Aliyev met with these opposition leaders before the election in an attempt to convince them to participate in the election. Ultimately, however, the government would not meet the opposition's key demand to repeal recent electoral legislation, which the opposition saw as providing an unfair advantage for the incumbent.[32] In particular, opposition parties objected to the formation of the Central Election Commission, whose 14 members were chosen by the pro-incumbent parliament and whose chair was directly selected by the president. In the end, the incumbent and opposition were not able to agree to terms of participation and a boycott ensued.

During the boycott period there were mass demonstrations and violence, as opposition supporters demanded that the elections be canceled. Much of the violence associated with these protests was instigated by the Aliyev government, as police officers beat and arrested demonstrators by the dozens.[33] Pro-democracy actors that sent election observers, such as the Organization for Security and Cooperation in Europe (OSCE) and the U.S. Democratic Party's

---

[31] "Presidential Elections." Keesings Record of World Events. October 1998 – Azerbaijan.
[32] "Pre-election Developments." Keesings Record of World Events. August 1998 – Azerbaijan.
[33] Azerbaijan arrests 300 protesters. Deutsche Presse-Agentur August 15, 1998. Keesings, September 1998 – Azerbaijan: Opposition protests during election campaign.

National Democratic Institute, criticized the election.[34] In addition, although the Clinton administration did not publicly condemn the Azerbaijani government's handling of the election, the U.S. State Department said that it was concerned about OSCE reports of irregularities and hoped that the Azerbaijani electoral commission would take complaints of fraud seriously.[35] In addition to its observers' criticisms, the OSCE issued recommendations for changes to the electoral law; President Aliyev rejected these recommendations and signed into law new measures that further enhanced his already substantial electoral advantage.[36] Opposition leaders were critical – calling into question the democratic character of the new legislation, which eventually was translated into a victory for Aliyev with 76% of the vote.

In Togo, opposition parties controlled 43% of the seats in the legislature when they boycotted the 1999 parliamentary elections, which ultimately resulted in reforms that the opposition did not consider to be democratic. To fully understand events surrounding this election, one must look back to the 1998 presidential election, in which opposition parties participated. The vote count was stopped and all regime-appointed members of the electoral commission were ordered to step down when a victory for Olympio, the opposition presidential candidate, became apparent. Two days later the Minister of the Interior announced that the incumbent president had won the election with 52% of the vote.[37] Mass demonstrations raged in the capital in the days following the election, and protesters and opposition leaders encountered harsh responses from government security forces.[38] Reaction from the United States was measured; it suggested that the government look into "irregularities" while requesting that both the government and opposition respect the law and refrain from violence.[39] The EU also expressed "concern" over the outcome of this election and held talks with Togolese representatives.[40] The United Kingdom expressed "deep concern" over the election, which, although still restrained, was the clearest statement of discontent reported from any major western powers.[41] No reforms were reported in the conduct of this election, despite the

---

[34] Azeri election called rigged. *The Gazette* (Montreal), November 15, 1995; 'Blatant violations' cloud vote in ex-Soviet republic. *The Record* (Kitchener-Waterloo, Ontario), October 13, 1998.

[35] BBC Summary of World Broadcasts. October 16, 1998, Friday. USA concerned about irregularities in Azeri presidential elections. Source: Turan news agency, Baku, in Russian.

[36] Azerbaijani opposition reacts to new elections bill. May 16, 2000. *Turkish Daily News*, May 16, 2000, retrieved February 5, 2007; President does not veto election law and signs it. *AssA-Irada*, July 8, 2000, retrieved February 7, 2007.

[37] Daniel Stroux . Togo. *Elections in Africa*, p. 894.

[38] Togo: Demonstrations continue in Togo. *Africa News*, June 25, 1998; Protests mount as challenge launched against Togo government. Associated Press Worldstream, June 26, 1998.

[39] US cites irregularities in Togo elections. Associated Press. June 25, 1998.

[40] EU holds talks with Togo on questioned elections. Associated Press Worldstream, July 30, 1998.

[41] Britain condemns Togo poll problems. Press Association. June 29, 1998.

EU's insistence on transparent elections as a condition for the resumption of assistance that had previously been frozen.[42]

Although the 1999 parliamentary elections may have been held in an attempt to normalize relations with Europe, they were boycotted by the main opposition parties, on the grounds that problems with the 1998 presidential election had not yet been resolved.[43] Reaction from western powers to the 1999 boycott was mixed. The United States delivered a stronger criticism of the government, saying that the boycott meant that the election did not reflect the will of the Togolese people.[44] The president of France, in contrast, visited Togo four months after the election and criticized the opposition for staging a boycott.[45] In April 2000, the government reformed the country's electoral law by establishing an electoral commission, which was nominally independent but was actually filled with members loyal to the president.[46]

Opposition parties boycotted the 2002 parliamentary elections on the grounds that they were not "free, transparent, nor democratic."[47] No major incidents of violence were reported during the election, but post-election protests erupted into violence.[48] The EU expressed concerns after these elections, noting that the Lome 1999 accord required both that the opposition be represented in the electoral commission and that it field candidates in the election, neither of which had happened.[49]

Some of the events around Bangladesh's 1996 election support the claim that a boycott followed by post-election protests will encourage authoritarian "reform," yet the reforms brought about as a result of these elections were arguably good for democracy in Bangladesh. The boycott of the 1996 election was, in some ways, a continuation of the parliamentary boycott that opposition parties had been undertaking since a 1994 by-election, held in the Magura district. The incumbent BNP's conduct of that by-election had spurred opposition parties, including the dominant Awami League, to accuse the BNP of fraud and to boycott parliament in protest, refusing to take their seats and participate in legislative proceedings (Ahmed 2001, 518). Further, the opposition demanded that all future elections be held under a nonpartisan caretaker government, much as the BNP and Awami League had demanded of the Ershad regime in the late 1980s.

---

[42] Daniel Stroux . Togo. *Elections in Africa*, p. 895.

[43] Opposition critical of Togo vote after low turnout. Associated Press Worldstream, March 22, 1999.

[44] Press statement: Legislative election in togo. M2 Presswire, March 23, 1999.

[45] French president stirs anger during visit to West Africa. *New York Times*, July 24, 1999.

[46] Togolese president signs new electoral law. Associated Press Worldstream, April 7, 2000.

[47] Parliamentary elections in Togo begin despite opposition boycott. Deutsche Presse Agentur, October 27, 2002.

[48] Violence erupts in Togo capital after opposition protest. Associated Press Worldstream, November 9, 2002.

[49] EU expresses concern over unchallenged Togo poll. Agence France Presse – English, November 5, 2002.

The intentions of the incumbent president, Khaleda Zia, when she dissolved parliament in November 1995 to pave the way for elections in early 1996, are not entirely clear. By some accounts, the BNP was willing to enshrine election management by a caretaker government in the constitution, but was simply unable to enact the legislation because all the opposition parliamentarians had abandoned their seats to protest the 1994 by-election (Ahmet 2001, 518). By this account, then, Zia and the BNP went ahead with the 1996 election to secure a legislative majority that would allow them to pass the caretaker legislation.[50] The massive violence and protests that accompanied the boycott of the February 1996 election, however, suggest that opposition parties and their supporters viewed Zia's claims about the unconstitutionality of appointing a caretaker government as a mere ruse to preserve the BNP's incumbency advantage.[51] Furthermore, some of Zia's own anti-boycott rhetoric in the final days of the campaign suggests an attempt at authoritarian retrenchment rather than reform. For example, in response to the boycott, she publicly threatened to purge opposition leadership and promised to "teach them a lesson."[52]

The runup to the February elections was incredibly violent; the most violent actions were committed by supporters of both the opposition and the government, rather than being directly advocated by the incumbent party leadership; for example, pro-opposition and pro-government students waged gun battles on the campus of Dhaka University that left 13 injured.[53] Opposition leaders orchestrated public demonstrations and strikes to heighten the impact of the boycott. Election Day itself was marked by low turnout and high violence, with dozens killed before the voting was completed.[54]

Before the official results were announced, Zia declared that the elections provided a new mandate for the BNP; in response the Awami League and other smaller opposition parties planned a massive three-day general strike and transportation shutdown in continued protest.[55] These protests brought more violence, and the government began to retaliate against opposition leaders, with police clashes injuring approximately 100 protesters.[56] Two weeks after the election, the Zia administration made renewed attempts to bring the opposition into a formal bargaining process and intimated a willingness to revisit the issue of a neutral caretaker government overseeing future

---

[50] John Zubrzycki. Bangladesh PM offers olive branch. *The Australian*, February 14, 1996.
[51] Ahmed Fazl. Question mark hangs over Bangla polls as clashes disrupt life. Deutsche Presse-Agentur, February 4, 1996.
[52] Mark Baker. We'll fight election boycott, Zia warns. *Sydney Morning Herald* (Australia), February 12, 1996.
[53] Ahmed Fazl. Question mark hangs over Bangla polls as clashes disrupt life. Deutsche Presse-Agentur, February 4, 1996.
[54] John F. Burns. Voters are few in Bangladesh as a dozen die in clashes. *New York Times*, February 16, 1996.
[55] Bangladeshis bracing for shutdown. Deutsche Presse-Agentur, February 23, 1996.
[56] One killed, 100 injured on first day of Bangladesh protests. Deutsche Presse-Agentur, February 24, 1996; Opposition leaders arrested, others hunted in crackdown in Dhaka Deutsche Presse-Agentur, February 25, 1996.

elections.[57] Although international pro-democracy actors did not go on record with their reactions to the violence, news reports from early March noted that western donors were pressuring both the incumbent and the opposition to resolve what, nearly a month after the election, had come to be characterized as a "crisis" by the global press.[58] On March 26, 1996, the BNP-controlled parliament passed a bill to allow for a caretaker government to oversee future elections.[59] Two days later, it was announced that Zia would step down to allow for fresh elections.[60] The Awami League won a plurality of seats in the June election and formed a government with the support of the Jatiya Party, another, smaller opposition party. Thus, after initial responses of combative rhetoric and government repression, the incumbent in this case ultimately agreed to legislation that would minimize her (or any incumbent's) ability to manipulate election administration in the future.

Boycotts with International Attention

Table 5.2 also shows that boycotts receiving international attention are associated with an increased probability of democratic reform, but not with an increased probability of authoritarian "reform." The case of Haiti that began this chapter provides one example of how boycotts with international attention can produce positive consequences for democracy. In this section, the Philippines provides another example of how a boycott receiving even weak international attention can motivate democratic reform when the incumbent does not feel domestic pressure that threatens his power. The cases of Equatorial Guinea and Chad provide further examples of boycotts in which international reaction motivated democratic reforms – but in both cases subsequent elections have seen more protest as opposition elites continue to negotiate the terms of electoral competition, challenging incumbent rulers who have been in power for more than two decades. Finally, Jamaica represents an exceptional case in which a major boycott did not generate international attention, but resulted in democratic reform – likely because the boycott did not produce a great deal of domestic pressure that would have threatened the incumbent party's sense of security.

In the Philippines, the main opposition party, the United Nationalist Democratic Organization (UNIDO), boycotted the 1981 presidential election after incumbent president Ferdinand Marcos denied its requests for more time to campaign and for equal media access (Gorvin 1989, 275). The opposition

[57] Bangladesh opposition rejects Khaleda Zia's offer of talks. Deutsche Presse-Agentur, March 3, 1996.
[58] Biswas and Hasina meet to break Bangladesh impasse. Deutsche Presse-Agentur, March 10, 1996.
[59] PM offers vote compromise to end Bangladeshi strikes. *The Gazette* (Montreal, Quebec), March 27, 1996.
[60] Anis Ahmed Reuter. Zia to step down until Bangladesh election. *The Independent* (London), March 28, 1996.

also objected to government conduct during a plebiscite, held several months earlier, on a constitutional amendment designed to restructure the system of representation.[61] About 30 people died in the violence associated with the election, which was mostly attributed to communist guerillas, not the boycotting opposition.[62] Despite the boycott the election received international praise from countries as varied as the United States and China, with Vice President George H. W. Bush saying, "We love your adherence to democratic principles and the democratic process."[63] Although some objections were voiced (particularly by the Catholic church) after the election, there were no major demonstrations. Even though the international attention in this case did not appear to support the opposition or to pressure the incumbent for reform, the lack of intense domestic pressure left Marcos feeling sufficiently comfortable to make electoral reforms within two years of the boycotted election; these reforms then paved the way for opposition participation in the 1984 parliamentary elections.[64]

Equatorial Guinea's parliamentary elections held in November 1993 were boycotted by the main opposition parties, which had banded together under the Joint Opposition Platform banner.[65] In particular, the opposition objected to particularly controversial clauses in the country's election law and the incumbent Democratic Party of Equatorial Guinea's unwillingness to allow international observers to inspect voter registration rolls.[66] The United States voiced its disapproval of these elections, with a State Department spokesman calling the government's promise to hold elections "a travesty of democracy."[67] After this election and before local elections in 1995, the incumbent government allowed the UN to help draft a new voter register and agreed to permit international observers for future elections.[68] Since then, however, President Obiang has dominated the political landscape, disregarding the UN voter registers in the 1996 presidential election – provoking another boycott from the opposition – and winning reelection in 2002 and again in 2009, marking his third decade in power.[69]

---

[61] Marcos easily wins a six-year term; vote is marked by opposition boycott. *Washington Post*, June 17, 1981.

[62] Ibid.

[63] Opposition assails Bush remarks. United Press International. July 3, 1981; Chinese leaders greet President Marcos. Xinhua General News Service, June 22, 1981.

[64] Business, labor leaders appeal to Marcos. United Press International. February 3, 1984; Philippines ruling party agrees to introduce political reforms. Xinhua General News Service, October 17, 198; BBC Summary of World Broadcasts. October 19, 1983, Philippines electoral reforms.

[65] Equatorial Guinea: Country Profile, Africa Review World of Information. Comment & Analysis; Country Profile; Statistics; Forecast; September 26, 2002, p. 1.

[66] Helga Fleischhacker . Equatorial Guinea. *Elections in Africa*, p. 353.

[67] US calls planned elections in Equatorial Guinea 'a travesty.' Associated Press, November 19, 1993.

[68] Helga Fleischhacker . Equatorial Guinea. *Elections in Africa*, p. 353.

[69] Background Note: Equatorial Guinea. 2011. U.S. State Department. http://www.state.gov/r/pa/ei/bgn/7221.htm.

Opposition parties also boycotted the May 2006 presidential elections in Chad.[70] This election, however, was praised by France, which noted the lack of violence.[71] There were no reports of favorable reaction from other international actors, but after this election the EU became involved in brokering a reconciliation between the opposition and the incumbent Idriss Deby, who had been reelected for a third term since beginning his presidency in 1990. In August 2007, the incumbent and opposition parties signed an agreement to postpone parliamentary elections and create an independent elections commission.[72] Both before and since the signing of this accord, the government of Chad has been involved in a proxy war with Sudan, supporting Sudanese rebels in their efforts to overthrow the government in Khartoum, while the Sudanese government has funded Chadian rebels with similar goals. Nevertheless, the general impression of international actors supporting the process of democratic reform in Chad is that implementation of the 2007 accord continues.[73] In 2011, legislative elections were held in February and the presidential contest occurred in April, which Deby also won with nearly 89% of the vote. Major opposition candidates boycotted the April presidential contest on the grounds that the February legislative election results had been falsified and that their demands for participating in the presidential contest had not been met.[74] The consequences of this current round of electoral protest remain to be seen; whether Chad will continue progress toward democratization or not, as Deby moves toward his third decade in power, is an open question.

The boycott in Jamaica in 1983 is an example of a major election boycott that did not receive international attention, but resulted in democratic reforms nonetheless. It should be noted, however, that such reforms may have come about because opposition supporters posed no substantial threat as a result of the boycott, which caused a dramatic reduction in voter turnout but little else in the way of public outrage. Nevertheless, two reforms occurred before the 1989 election, which increased that election's fairness: An updated voter roll was prepared for the election, and the government assumed responsibility for printing the election ballots, on special paper (Director of Elections 1989, 7). Printing ballots on special paper and allowing no one outside of the

---

[70] Chad: Low turnout threatens third multi-party election. Canwest New Service. Ottawa Citizen, May 4, 2006.

[71] France praises elections in Chad despite opposition boycott. Associated Press Worldstream, May 4, 2006.

[72] EU welcomes inter Chadian political agreement. Xinhua General News Service, August 14, 2007.

[73] Background Note: Chad. 2010. U.S. State Department. http://www.state.gov/r/pa/ei/bgn/37992.htm,

[74] Three Chadian presidential candidates suspend poll participation. BBC Monitoring-Africa, March 25, 2011; Chadian presidential candidate explains decision to boycott April 25 poll. BBC Monitoring-Africa, April 15, 2011.

government to see what the ballots looked like ostensibly reduced opportunities for ballot duplication. In addition to these concrete reforms, several interview subjects suggested that the boycott produced more subtle changes in the electoral process in Jamaica. Peter Phillips, Member of Parliament and Jamaica's current Minister of Finance and Planning, was best able to articulate this sentiment, saying that it galvanized the Election Management Committee to serve as an independent source of authority in election proceedings.[75]

Post-Election Demonstrations

Table 5.2 shows that, if not preceded by boycotts, post-election protests reduce the probability of authoritarian "reform" and have no impact on the probability of democratic reform, whether they receive international attention or not. In the case of Gabon, the combination of domestic pressure and international attention left the incumbent with little room to maneuver, forcing explicit, internationally brokered negotiations with the opposition. Returning to the case of Togo, the 2005 election provides another example in which demonstrations receiving international attention reduced the probability of clear, authoritarian retrenchment, but where the consequences for democracy were not clear. Madagascar is a case where some demonstrations have received international attention and others have not. Finally, in an exception to the general statistical pattern in Model 1, demonstrations in Panama brought about authoritarian retrenchment. Let us now consider these cases in detail.

In Gabon, the opposition, led by National Woodcutters Rally candidate and Roman Catholic priest Paul Mba Abessole, protested the outcome of the 1993 presidential elections.[76] Mass demonstrations were accompanied by an explicit rejection of the results by Abessole, who accused the incumbent president Omar Bongo of staging an "electoral coup," appointed a rival prime minister, and called on the armed forces to support him as the rightful winner of the election.[77] Abessole called for the boycott of state institutions and in February encouraged further civil disobedience, including the refusal to pay taxes.[78] These protests resulted in a constitutional deadlock that was only resolved with OAU intervention in 1994. Bongo and Abessole negotiated a series of constitutional amendments including a revised electoral code and the establishment of an independent electoral commission, which were ratified in 1995. Incumbent president Bongo – who first came to power in 1967 – continued to dominate electoral politics for the rest of the 1990s and into the first decade of the 21st

---

[75] Interview with Phillips, April 14, 2005.

[76] Helga Fleischhacker. Equatorial Guinea. *Elections in Africa*, p. 390.

[77] Protest at Gabon vote. *The Independent* (London), December 11, 1993.

[78] Helga Fleischhacker. Equatorial Guinea. *Elections in Africa*, p. 390; Opposition leader Fr Mba Abessole calls for civil disobedience. BBC Summary of World Broadcasts, February 18, 1994, Part 5 Africa and Latin America; AFRICA; WEST AFRICA; AL/1925/A.

century. Even so, international observers looked more favourably on elections during this time period, and there was less violence.[79]

Gradually, the opposition appears to be becoming more competitive. After the death of Bongo in 2009, his son Ali won a contentious presidential election, with the backing of the incumbent Gabonese Democratic Party (PDG). Since then, however, a number of opposition parties have formed a coalition (the Union Nationale) and won two of the five seats in play in the 2010 legislative by-elections. Electoral protests in the 1990s may not have been directly responsible for the birth of democracy in Gabon, but combined with international attention, they appear to have stalled authoritarian retrenchment; more recent electoral protest appears to be contributing to an incremental process that may be moving the country in a more democratic direction.

Violent protests followed Togo's 2005 presidential election when the son of the late president Gnassingbe Eyadema – who had ruled the country for more than 30 years – was declared the winner. The United States publicly denounced the election as "disturbingly flawed" and advocated a unity government to resolve the political crisis.[80] Meanwhile, someone leaked to journalists a confidential report from the EU acknowledging "presumptive evidence of massive fraud."[81] By August 2006, the government and opposition groups had come together to sign a reform agreement under the watchful eye of the United Nations, an act that elicited praise from then-UN Secretary-General Kofi Annan.[82] Legislative elections in 2007 were declared free and fair and gave the opposition control of just under 40% of seats in the legislature, and although President Faure Gnassingbe won reelection in the 2010 presidential election, the process was deemed free and fair by international observers.[83] That election had been administered by a new independent body with members representing both the incumbent party and opposition parties, and despite post-election demonstrations staged by the opposition after the results of the 2010 election were announced, it appears as though Togo is making gradual progress toward more democratic electoral processes.

Madagascar is a case that exemplifies how demonstrations, on their own even without international attention, reduce the probability of authoritarian retrenchment. Major opposition-initiated protests in 1989 brought about a series of alternations in power, even if contentious elections followed. After the 1989 presidential elections, opposition parties publicly criticized the

---

[79] Background Note: Gabon. 2010. U.S. Department of State. http://www.state.gov/r/pa/ei/bgn/2826.htm.

[80] US criticizes Togo elections. Agence France Presse – English. April 27, 2005.

[81] EU confidential report finds 'massive fraud' in Togo presidential election. Agence France Presse – English, May 6, 2005.

[82] Togo. Secretary-General welcomes signing of political reform agreement. *Africa News*, August 21, 2006.

[83] Background Note: Togo. 2011. U.S. State Department http://www.state.gov/r/pa/ei/bgn/5430.htm.

conduct of the election, accusing the incumbent of fraud, and riots broke out in the capital city of Antananarivo.[84] These actions did not, however, evoke an international reaction nor cause the government to undertake any subsequent reforms, though a new, more democratic constitution was ratified before the presidential election of 1992 (which actually concluded in February, 1993). That election resulted in a peaceful transfer of power and marked the beginning of a relatively peaceful decade of electoral activity, despite the return to power of the former dictator Ratsiraka in the 1996 presidential election. However, although his AREMA party performed well in the 1998 parliamentary elections, it did not gain an absolute majority.[85] The relative calm of the 1990s was shattered during the 2001 presidential elections, which were extremely contentious, with opposition candidate Marc Ravalomanana declaring himself president and spurring his supporters to protest and mount a general strike, as described in Chapter 3. The 2002 parliamentary elections proceeded peacefully and received positive recognition from the EU, and by the next year, the U.S. government was pledging support for Madagascar.[86] Opposition candidates (one of whom was Ratsiraka) publicly rejected the results of the 2006 presidential election in which Ravalomanana won reelection, but did not initiate mass demonstrations.[87] Furthermore, observer reports of the election were generally positive, with independent monitors declaring the election "acceptable."[88] As of 2008, the United States was characterizing Madagascar as making more change "for the better" than any other African country.[89] In 2009, however, protests in the capital caused President Ravalomanana to resign; the military took control of the country and appointed opposition leader Andry Rajoelina president, throwing the country into a political crisis that did not show any hope of being resolved until December 2012 with the intervention of the Southern African Developing Community (SADC). Ultimately, the SADC was able to convince Ravalomanana (living in exile in South Africa) to agree not to run for the presidency in 2013.

Contrary to the statistical pattern presented in Model 1, Panama provides an example of domestic support producing authoritarian "reform." The election

[84] Riot follows meeting of opposition parties. Associated Press, April 17, 1989; Three deaths reported in clashes between opposition, authorities. Associated Press, April 20, 1989.
[85] Bernard Thibaut . Madagasgar. *Elections in Africa*, p. 533.
[86] Madagascar: EU poll observers hail government efforts, note "some shortcomings." Television Malagasy. BBC Monitoring Africa. December 18, 2002; US State Department official visits Madagascar, holds talks with premier. Television Malagasy. BBC Monitoring Africa. March 10, 2003.
[87] Opposition candidates to challenge results of Madagascar's presidential poll. Associated Press Worldstream, December 11, 2006; Madagascar opposition candidate to contest poll results, cites irregularities. BBC Monitoring International Reports, December 11, 2006.
[88] Madagascar president holds strong lead as montors say vote 'acceptable.'Agence France Presse – English, December 5, 2006; Observers say Madagascar polls held in "transparency ." BBC Monitoring International Reports, December 5, 2006.
[89] Route to democracy needs revision. *Africa News*, March 28, 2011.

of Nicholas Barletta to the presidency in May 1984 sparked a wave of violent protest from supporters of his defeated opponent, Arnulfo Arias, who maintained that he lost the presidency because of fraud; violent clashes continued to erupt between his supporters and individuals associated with the government even as Barletta was sworn in.[90] Barletta was the military-backed candidate in this first presidential election in 14 years, whereas Arias was a popular candidate who had been reelected to the presidency twice and deposed twice by the military.[91] This pattern of reelection/being deposed and the violent protests sparked by his defeat both suggested high levels of domestic support for Arias. Protest over the elections was renewed in June 1987, when a former aide to "Maximum Leader of National Liberation" Manuel Noriega accused him of electoral fraud. In November 1987, in response to these protests, the military-backed government enacted a series of repressive measures, banning protest demonstrations and closing opposition newspapers.[92]

CONCLUSION

One way to gauge the prospects for democracy in the countries described in the preceding vignettes is to consider the overall political health of the opposition. In the cases of domestic support for protest where authoritarian "reform" followed, the opposition seems to have been weakened – as in Azerbaijan and Togo. The exceptional case of Bangladesh provides an example where domestic support for electoral protest resulted in democratic reform; this is a country that has seen alternations in power and yet maintained a strong opposition, even if electoral contests are still fraught with violence and conflict. Jamaica provides another example of electoral protest producing democratic reform and allowing for a strong political opposition. Haiti might also be seen as such a case, though the fragmented nature of the Haitian political party system makes it difficult to be certain. Yet democratic reforms do not always leave the opposition stronger. The cases of Equatorial Guinea and Chad are instances of democratic reform in which we might characterize the opposition as enfeebled and incumbent rulers have continued in power for multiple decades. More recent events in Gabon and Togo, however, provide some reason for modest optimism, even for these toughest cases of incumbent domination. Though in both countries, incumbent leaders have enjoyed similarly long tenures, the opposition in each appears to be gaining ground.

Democratization is clearly a complex, nonlinear process. What electoral protest is going to mean for democracy in any individual case will depend on a number of factors, both domestic and international. In this chapter, I argued

[90] Panama: Incidents occur as Barletta's election victory certified. IPS-Inter Press Service, May 31, 1984; 50 injured in Panama protest. *The Globe and Mail* (Canada), May 31, 1984.
[91] One dead, 41 injured in Panama election riots. United Press International, May 8, 1984.
[92] Panama's opposition in disarray after crackdown. *Herald*, November 25, 1987.

that how the incumbent chooses to respond to protest will matter for the future of democracy and that those incumbent responses are likely to depend on how much support the protest receives and from what source. Several illustrative cases of elections at the end of the chapter show the variety of incumbent responses that can follow electoral protest. In some examples incumbents responded to opposition protest by implementing reforms that appear to have positive consequences for democracy. The Dominican Republic after 1994, Indonesia after 1997, Lesotho post-1998, and Peru after 2000 are additional examples where electoral protests were followed by democratic reforms and opposition electoral performance has since improved.

At the risk of concluding the chapter on an overly sanguine note, however, it is important to acknowledge cases such as Azerbaijan or Equatorial Guinea, where oppositions are protesting and incumbents are responding with reforms that may be doing more to cement their own power than furthering democracy; or cases such as Chad, Madagascar, or Bangladesh, where incremental democratic improvements have been followed by instability. Clearly, the nature of support for the opposition and subsequent pressure on the incumbent have a significant influence on whether electoral protests are to have positive consequences for democracy. This chapter's findings have suggested that international support for democracy is crucial in helping translate election boycotts into democratic reform. However, in cases of post-election demonstrations, although international attention may be able to prevent authoritarian backsliding, it is not clear that it can help promote genuine democratic reform.

6

Conclusion

A glance back at some of the cases in each chapter shows the various trajectories of countries experiencing electoral protest. From its history of electoral protest, international involvement, and incumbent response, Haiti appears to be making incremental progress toward democracy; the dynamics surrounding electoral protest in Cote d'Ivoire and Bangladesh seem to have produced chronic instability in the case of the former and more stable, arguably more democratic, political competition in the case of the latter; and electoral protest in Cameroon seems only to have led to authoritarian retrenchment. Consistent with my statistical analysis, then, these cases show how major election boycotts produce the clearest consequences for democracy – whether these consequences are positive or negative is contingent on the sources of support the boycott receives. In this way, then, boycotts are high-risk protest undertakings: They may push the incumbent to engage in democratic reforms or more authoritarian "reforms," depending on forces such as domestic or international support that are largely outside of the opposition's control.

The case of Guyana presented in Chapter 2 illustrates both the book's key theoretical dynamics and the indeterminate character of the consequences of post-election demonstrations for democracy. Although Guyanese electoral politics have continued to be contentious, recent incremental improvements have been made. The PPP's domination shows signs of erosion; even though the 2011 election was the fifth in which the PPP secured more parliamentary seats than any other party, the party is currently heading a minority government, with the PNC in the Partnership for National Unity (controlling 26 of the 65 seats in the legislature) and the Alliance for Change (controlling another 7 seats) constituting a majority opposition.[1]

---

[1] Guyana governing party's Donald Ramotar wins presidency. BBC, December 2, 2011. http://www.bbc.co.uk/news/world-latin-america-15980149.

This concluding chapter addresses questions about how this book's intellectual contributions might help advance future studies of protest and democratization. First, with respect to studies of protest, does my theory of protest-as-bargaining-failure only make sense in the context of electoral protest, or does it offer insights that could be applied more broadly to the study of protest in general? Second, where the study of democratization is concerned, what can the theory presented here help us understand about particularly "tough" cases for democratization, those cases in which multiparty elections seem the least likely to lead to meaningful democratic change? For example, in the cases of Iran and Afghanistan, to what extent do we need to reconsider the fundamental assumptions about actors' motivations and available actions that guide the theory? Furthermore, what are the limits of international democracy promotion of democratic reform? Before taking on any of these questions, I provide a brief review of my main argument and findings.

MAIN ARGUMENT AND FINDINGS: SUMMARY

Within the context of multiparty elections, the theory in this book conceptualizes electoral protest as resulting from the failure of elites to strike a bargain that would successfully avoid conflict. Bowing to international pressure to hold elections, incumbent and opposition elites in the developing world must agree on the conditions for conducting multiparty elections. The most pressing issue of these negotiations is the extent to which the incumbent will engage in manipulation of the electoral process. If incumbent and opposition elites can successfully agree on an acceptable level of manipulation, multiparty elections should proceed with relatively few problems. But when incumbent and opposition elites are not able to agree on an acceptable level of manipulation, when the incumbent manipulates more than the opposition is willing to tolerate, or when the opposition simply cannot accept the election outcome, protest is likely to result. This protest can happen either before the election in the form of a major election boycott or after the election as post-election demonstrations.

This book has also highlighted the theoretical importance of the developing-world context. International pressure for democracy (the first of three developing-world scope conditions) helps us understand why incumbent elites are holding and attempting to manipulate elections and why opposition parties might feel empowered to object to incumbent manipulation. In other words, international pressure for democracy helps us understand why elites are bargaining over the terms of electoral conduct. Two other scope conditions in the developing-world context – an imbalance of resources between incumbent and opposition and low-information environments – further shape the dynamics associated with electoral protest and democratization. In addition, these two conditions help us understand the two reasons why elite negotiations break down in my theory: problems of credible commitment and information problems.

Low levels of economic development create an imbalance between the resources available to the incumbent, who controls the state, and the resources available to opposition elites, who must rely on the private sector. This resource imbalance helps us understand why incumbent elites have the option to manipulate, whereas opposition actors' options are limited to either participation or protest – not that opposition parties never engage in manipulation, but that incumbent elites can always manipulate to a greater degree. Furthermore, this imbalance helps us understand why the credibility of either actor's commitments might be called into question by the other. For the incumbent, a loss at the polls would signal an end to the stream of resources she currently enjoys through her control of the state. As such, even if the incumbent commits to a particular level of manipulation, the prospect of lost resources might make it difficult for her to adhere faithfully to the terms of that commitment. For the opposition, the prospect of gaining access to this stream of resources might make it difficult to resist the opportunity to challenge the state by engaging in protest, in instances when he loses to the incumbent.

Problems of incumbent credibility are likely to cause election boycotts, whereas post-election demonstrations can result from a lack of credibility on the part of either the incumbent or the opposition. Before the election, the incumbent's promise to curb manipulation may not be plausible to the opposition, who may decide to boycott. By contrast, opposition promises to participate in the election are easily verifiable and unlikely to influence the incumbent's plans for manipulation at this stage. After the election, it is possible that the incumbent's initial promises regarding manipulation will have been proven not to be credible, thus triggering opposition demonstrations. Alternatively, it may be the opposition actor who simply cannot keep the promise to accept the election results, particularly in circumstances where the incumbent wins but the opposition saw the potential for victory. Thus, in the post-election phase, problems of credible commitment on either the part of the incumbent or of the opposition might ultimately lead to electoral protest.

Low-information environments in the developing world create a context that is ripe for the creation and misrepresentation of private information – another reason why elites might fail to strike a successful bargain that would avoid electoral protest. In most developing countries, the media are constrained by government overreach and limited funding from the private sector, and the rate of adult literacy is low. Both media constraints and lower literacy among the general population will hinder the role of media in generating reliable public information. Media that are dependent on the government or more generally stunted by limited private sector funds will find it difficult to uncover private information that elites on both sides might be generating. Furthermore, when reporting to a less literate population, the media will not feel the same pressure to produce accurate information that they might in situations where literate individuals could more easily verify inaccuracies.

Because elections themselves produce so much information, information problems and the impact of the information environment matter for election boycotts, but not for post-election demonstrations. If the opposition misrepresents its own capacity to sanction the incumbent, the incumbent may misjudge the appropriate level of manipulation that keeps the opposition participating and may choose a level of manipulation that actually provokes protest from the opposition. Furthermore, if the opposition believes the incumbent is misrepresenting information regarding manipulation, this misunderstanding may also lead to protest. In both cases, if either side believes the other to be exaggerating, and is then forced to guess about the true nature of the other's position, there is room for error and a boycott may result.

Boycotted elections are associated with diminished democratic quality – in terms of competition – but are not systematically related to reduced rates of participation or election violence. Furthermore, the extent to which boycotts cause elections to be less competitive or are endogenous to those elections that are more likely to be uncompetitive even with opposition participation, remains an open question. Like boycotts, opposition-initiated mass demonstrations do not increase post-election violence compared to other post-election demonstrations and do not decrease regime stability. These demonstrations are associated, however, with an increased rate of incumbent exits from power via "regular" (constitutional) means.

Beyond the impact of electoral protests on the elections in which they occur and on general political stability, incumbent responses will determine whether electoral protests have positive or negative consequences for democracy. In turn, incumbent responses depend on both the type of protest and the nature of support the protest receives. Boycotts increase the probability of both democratic reforms and authoritarian "reforms," depending on the nature of support they receive. When boycotts are accompanied by domestic support, they are more likely to encourage authoritarian retrenchment in the guise of reform. When boycotts receive international support, however, the probability of democratic reform increases.

The consequences for democracy of opposition-initiated, post-election demonstrations are less clear: On the one hand, these demonstrations reduce the probability of authoritarian "reform," across several contexts; on the other hand, these demonstrations have no systematic relationship to democratic reforms under any circumstances. Thus, we see general patterns emerge with respect to boycotts but not with post-electoral demonstrations. Boycotts have more potential for democratic reform, but a higher risk of authoritarian "reform," depending on the support they receive. Although post-election demonstrations reduce the probability of authoritarian "reform" and are associated with an increased probability of a constitutional change in leadership, their consequences for democracy are even more sensitive to specific country contexts.

EXTENSIONS FOR THEORIES OF PROTEST

The theory and evidence presented in this book suggest that we should think of electoral protest as the breakdown of strategic interactions, but is this a model that we could apply to protest more generally? It may be the case that the bargaining model of protest only works in the electoral arena because of the unique coordinating quality of elections. For an incumbent regime – which we could characterize more generally as "the state" – to successfully strike a bargain with some opposition group to avoid protest, it must be able to identify the opposition group contemplating protest and it must know what this group (or groups) wants: It needs to know the nature of the "bargaining space." Elections make it easier for the incumbent to identify relevant potential protesters (opposition parties) and what it would take to keep them from protesting (less pro-incumbent manipulation). The election event, particularly in the contemporary setting of international pressure for democracy, provides a coordination point that can facilitate actual bargaining. Thus even if actors are only behaving "as if" they are bargaining, the election makes it relatively easy for the state to identify the relevant opposition and to deduce what they want.

Because multiparty elections encourage the formation of competitive political parties, they facilitate collective action on the part of the opposition that might be difficult to achieve otherwise. At the same time that these elections are facilitating collective action among individuals in the opposition, they are providing clear indications to the incumbent as to who represents the opposition. This is not to suggest that opposition parties represent the only groups in opposition to the incumbent – one need only look at the Revolutionary Armed Forces of Colombia (FARC) who claim to represent Colombia's poor and have been involved in armed conflict with the government since 1964, or the insurgencies launched by the Maoist New People's Army against the government of the Philippines since 1969, to realize that incumbents can face opposition from groups outside of the electoral arena even when they do hold elections. Yet the formation of political parties for electoral competition also provides information to the incumbent about potential sources of electoral protest. Furthermore, the nature of electoral competition gives the incumbent a pretty solid idea of what those opposition groups want: a better chance of winning the election. Armed with an understanding of who might protest and what they want, the incumbent may be in a good position to prevent electoral protest.

Thus the coordinating effects of an election for its participants may explain why we can think of electoral protest as a "bargaining failure." Given the myriad protests that occur outside of the electoral arena, however, it simply might not be realistic to think of the state as having failed to avoid protest in many instances. Acemoglu and Robinson (2006), for example, assume that protest (which they describe as any collective action that threatens elites) is likely to be a surprise to the incumbent, who is often able to discount the threat of protest because of the collective action problems that must be overcome for protest to occur (123–6). Acemoglu and Robinson's characterization suggests that the incumbent may not expect protest, but even the incumbent who actively expects protest may still be at a loss to identify the relevant opposition and their demands to avoid protest. Even so, if opposition actors and their demands can be identified, there may be instances beyond the electoral arena where the theory of protest as bargaining failure is applicable.

Examples from China provide some support for the extension beyond the electoral arena of the theory of protest as resulting from the failure of explicit bargaining. Before the student protests in Tiananmen Square in 1989, student representatives met with government officials to present their demands. Over the course of two meetings, which were conducted privately but were publicly known to be taking place, the student representatives demanded reforms addressing government corruption and the introduction of multiparty competition into Chinese electoral politics. The government countered by offering some qualified concessions with respect to corruption, but was not flexible on the question of multiparty competition. As a result, talks broke down and student groups began demonstrating in Tiananmen Square. Since the massacre that followed the 1989 demonstrations, the government has taken steps to discourage protest in major metropolitan areas, but according to Jie Chen, an expert in Chinese politics, local government officials, particularly in rural localities, are still concerned with the anticipation and prevention of local riots.[2]

China also provides examples of the difficulties that a state will encounter in attempting to anticipate and avoid protest. Even though, according to Chen, local government officials are eager to prevent riots, such prevention would require officials to identify potential instigators of riots with whom to bargain. In the wake of the Tiananmen Square massacre, potential protesters are understandably reticent to identify themselves to the government, for fear of retribution. It is not typically until riots in rural areas have occurred that government officials can piece together the nature of the protesters' grievances and work to prevent similar outbursts in the future. Thus, even governments that may attempt to identify and avoid potential protest will encounter difficulties because potential protesters are unwilling to identify themselves or their demands.

Recent research by King, Pan, and Roberts (2013) on government internet censorship in China shows that those efforts can be understood as another example of strategic attempts by the state to prevent protest when opposition actors are difficult to identify. These attempts by the Chinese government to limit internet activity are not, as is commonly assumed, aimed at quieting

[2] Chen interview, December 17, 2010. Chen is William Borah Distinguished Professor of Political Science at the University of Idaho and also holds the Changjiang Scholar Chair professorship from the Ministry of Education, PRC, and the Zhiyan Chair Professorship from Shanghai Jiaotong University.

dissidents, but rather at squelching attempts at collective action. This interpretation envisions the internet as another coordinating mechanism like elections. In this case, however, incumbent disruption of a potential coordination mechanism is an alternative strategy for protest prevention when opposition actors cannot be identified for more explicit or implicit negotiations.

The case of China and the general logic of this book's theory suggest two implications as we think about extending the theory. First, the question of incumbents responding to and hoping to avoid protest may be more of a concern for authoritarian regimes than for democratic regimes. Democracies have many more opportunities for opposition groups to voice concerns and influence policy processes, and because their hold on power is only for a fixed period of time, democratic leaders are not likely to feel as threatened by protest as their authoritarian counterparts. Second, and perhaps paradoxically, although authoritarian leaders may have more incentive to try to avoid protest because they find it more threatening to their power than do democratic leaders, fears of retribution for opposing the regime might make it even more difficult for incumbents to identify potential sources of protest and engage in strategies to avoid protest in the absence of clear coordinating mechanisms such as elections. Thus, an extension of this book's theory beyond the electoral arena will likely require renewed attention to the question of regime type.

ELECTIONS AND DEMOCRATIZATION

In part, this book represents a call to return to the democratization paradigm, which fell out of favor in the face of entirely valid criticisms from Carothers (2002) and Schedler (2002) and gave way to an emphasis on regime typologies. This book revives important aspects of the concept of democratization and its connection to elections, so as not to throw the proverbial baby out with the bathwater. Elections are not the only important features of democracy and they do not always occur in democracies, but they are important for two reasons: (1) They provide elites with bargaining opportunities that may otherwise be absent – as the preceding discussion of protest in China shows, and (2) they offer the possibility for incremental changes allowing more or less input from citizens. Any time we see changes that increase the fairness of competition and expand opportunities for citizens to offer input, we might consider those changes to be democratization. According to the perspective offered by Tilly (2004), democratization can be seen as "a gradual deposit from long-term social processes or . . . a set of political changes that might occur piecemeal, in different orders through different paths." (10) and need not be tied to some linear notion of "progress."

This book has tried to sort out some of those "piecemeal" political changes and to identify some general patterns that might help us understand the circumstances under which electoral protest should lead to democratic improvement. At the same time, this book began with two examples of electoral protest in countries where the prospects for democracy seem especially bleak. The remaining section of this conclusion addresses this question: How can my theory of electoral protest help us understand these particularly tough cases? To answer that question we might consider whether the foundational assumptions that underlie actor preferences in my theory are realistic in all cases and examine the limits of international actors to provide positive support for democratic reform.

Iran and Afghanistan Revisited

Iran is considered part of the Middle East, a region that has been notable since the end of the Cold War for its resistance to democratization (McFoul 2002, Bellin 2004, Volpi 2004, Jamal 2008, Diamond 2010). Though it borders Iran, Afghanistan is more frequently considered part of Central Asia, yet shares many of the features of Middle Eastern countries that are thought to present challenges for democracy: Both Afghanistan and Iran are majority Muslim and have a history of tribal politics (Tapper 1983; Khoury and Kostiner 1990), and both are located outside of the geographic sphere of influence for major democracy promoters such as the United States and the EU. Iran shares another feature with other countries in the Middle East thought to make it resistant to democratization: an abundance of oil (Ross 2001). Afghanistan, although not similarly afflicted with the "Dutch Disease," has nevertheless suffered through centuries of conflict and foreign occupation, which present their own challenges for democratization. These cases shed light on two issues that may arise as we consider the applicability of my theory to particularly difficult cases for democratization: the motivations of the opposition and the limits of international influence.

Clientelism is a central component of contemporary politics in Iran and Afghanistan (Shahrani 1998; Alamdari 2005; Saikal 2005; Lust 2009), and as such, we might return to the question raised in the introduction: Are electoral protests in these countries actually intended to push for fairer electoral competition, or are they just the opposition's attempt to maintain a veneer of independence while seeking patronage from the regime? It is not clear whether opposition actors in Iran are genuinely interested in improving electoral fairness or are simply hoping for enhanced access to patronage. In Afghanistan, the fact that elections were imposed via U.S. invasion may give us real reason to suspect that opposition actors are not yet convinced that elections are a means to obtaining power. In such cases, it might be tempting to conclude that, if the opposition is not protesting out of a desire for democratic reform, then we should not expect the incumbent to reform. Yet, the finding that election boycotts receiving international attention are associated with democratic reform means that incumbent governments might be motivated to respond to electoral protest with democratic reform simply to appease international actors, even if those protests only came about because the opposition was hoping to extract more patronage from the incumbent regime.

The notion that international support for electoral protests could render the "real" motives of the opposition irrelevant offers some hope for those interested in democracy promotion in cases where domestic opposition elites do not necessarily care whether elections become fairer. At the same time, the international support that appears to motivate democratic reform in many cases also presents challenges for democratization in the cases of Afghanistan and Iran. For Afghanistan, U.S, involvement shows how occupation by a country with a history of promoting democracy does not have the same effect as international support for democracy, and both cases show how international democracy promotion may provide an opportunity to cast the domestic opposition as colluding with foreign influences.

The events surrounding the second-round presidential boycott in 2009 highlight the ambiguity of international "support" for democracy in Afghanistan provided by the United States. Whereas Iran can reject western calls for democracy, U.S. occupation presents a challenge for the incumbent regime in Afghanistan, which must cooperate with the U.S. government while also cultivating the impression among Afghan citizens that it is relatively independent of the United States. Furthermore, the United States faces a delicate situation in which it must balance any desires for democratization against a fundamental need for regional stability.

By most accounts, fraud was the primary issue at stake in the negotiations that preceded the 2009 election boycott. A general consensus has emerged that incumbent-initiated fraud was rampant in the first round of the election. Afghan officials had neglected to update the electronic voter register before the first round of voting, claiming a lack of time and resources, but presumably because such an updated database would not have benefited the incumbent. Furthermore, by some accounts as many as three million fake voter identification cards had been printed in advance of Election Day.[3] During the first round of voting, there was also a problem of "ghost" polling stations – they never actually opened, but nonetheless returned large numbers of votes for the incumbent (Galbraith 2009). Even though fraud was generally anticipated for the second round as well, the Afghan electoral commission declined to heed UN advice to close those "ghost" polling stations and actually decided to open additional stations for the runoff (Starkey 2009). In addition, the head of the Independent Election Commission (IEC) was quoted by the *New York Times* as saying that a second-round victory for Karzai was assured (Galloway 2009).

All the conditions for continued electoral participation that opposition candidate Abdollah Abdollah outlined centered on fraud. In particular, he demanded the dismissal of the head of the IEC, as well as the Ministers of the Interior, Education, and Tribal Affairs – all of whom were seen as instrumental in orchestrating the first-round electoral fraud. Additionally, Abdollah wanted those ghost polling stations closed, and 20,000 observer cards distributed to

---

[3] Abdollah may pull out of runoff vote. *Boston Globe*. October 31, 2009.

his supporters to facilitate opposition monitoring of the second round of the elections (Page 2009).

Karzai rejected these conditions on the grounds that the demands had no legal basis and were aimed at disenfranchising Karzai's Pashtun supporters.[4] Administration officials and pro-government media outlets also cast doubt on claims of first-round fraud and made much of rumors about a potential power-sharing agreement between the incumbent and opposition.[5] According to all public accounts, a possible power-sharing agreement was also suggested by some anonymous "western" sources, but never demanded by Abdollah during pre-election bargaining. By bringing such questions and rumors into the public discourse, however, Karzai was able to depict his opponent as motivated by patronage, not democracy, and could frame his refusals of Abdollah's demands as a rejection of western interference, rather than an endorsement of fraud.[6]

Although the United States reportedly "urged" Karzai to reform in the wake of this boycott, such urgings came only after U.S. congratulations for Karzai's reelection (Muskal 2009; Colvin 2009). White House advisor David Axelrod justified U.S. support for Karzai in the wake of the boycott on the grounds that all available polls showed Karzai to be the likely winner of the runoff. Although Axelrod's claims about what "polls" were telling U.S. officials may indicate private information, it is also possible that the mention of polls was merely a rhetorical device meant to justify the United States' continued support of Karzai despite serious concerns over the democratic quality of the elections.

Just as Karzai did in Afghanistan, Iran has been in a position to cast international democracy promotion as foreign interference. Iran's geographic location – surrounded by other Islamic republics – and rich oil reserves have allowed it to remain isolated from and openly hostile toward western democracy-promoting nations. Thus, Iran is a case in which international pressure for democracy is not likely to turn electoral protest into democratic reform; indeed, recent research has suggested that the regime has actually used international democracy promotion against the domestic opposition – characterizing the opposition as part of a foreign "conspiracy" to destabilize the regime (Tezcür 2012).

This book began with the premise that the circumstances accompanying low levels of economic development create the conditions that encourage electoral protest, but that the dynamics of electoral protest in the developing world actually reflect more universal truths about electoral competition. From this perspective I have attempted to enrich our understanding of the dynamics

---

[4] Karzai aid says Abdollah's conditions for election runoff "dangerous." *Elections 88.* Tolo TV. BBC Monitoring South Asia, October 29, 2009.
[5] Afghan private TV discusses possibility of runoff boycott by Karzai's rival. *Debate.* Ariana TV. BBC Monitoring South Asia, October 28, 2009.
[6] Is Abdollah fueling crisis or looking for way of escape? *Weesa.* BBC Monitoring South Asia, October 27, 2009.

of electoral competition, protest, and democratization in the third wave and beyond. Electoral protest is one strategy that opposition parties in developing countries can use to try to force incumbents to make electoral competition fairer.

Because incumbents are likely to respond to such pressure with their own strategic decision making, the ultimate consequences of protest for democracy are highly contingent on the options the incumbents perceive. In circumstances where incumbents feel their future electoral fortunes are threatened by domestic support for the opposition, they are likely to try to continue to avoid meaningful democratization; in circumstances where international actors can support electoral protest, however, incumbents may be motivated to enact meaningful democratic reform. The cases of Iran and Afghanistan remind us to consider these general insights carefully, because particular circumstances such as oil wealth or the fragility of a post-conflict society may compromise the efficacy of international democracy promotion. The dynamics of protest and contingent reform may not produce dramatic democratic transformations in the span of one electoral cycle, nor do they even guarantee a country's linear progress toward full-fledged democracy or democratic consolidation. However, by understanding these dynamics better, we gain a greater understanding of how contentious electoral politics can contribute to the complex and contingent process of democratization in the developing world today.

APPENDIX A

Data Description and Robustness Checks

This project required the collection and coding of data for 765 elections in 118 countries from 1975 to 2006. The following two tables describe key variables for the project. The first table describes those variables collected and coded based on journalistic reports from major world news sources. The second table describes variables constructed from existing data sources. The discussion that follows these tables describes the process of collecting and coding data from news sources and elaborates on some of the challenges I encountered during this process.

Original Data Collection and Coding							
Variable	Description	#	Mean	S.D.	Min	Max
Electoral Protest	Dichotomous; =1 if either major boycott or post-election demonstrations occurred	765	0.15	0.357	0	1
Major Boycott	Dichotomous; =1 if majority of opposition parties/candidates boycott	765	0.074	0.262	0	1
Opposition Demonstrations	Dichotomous; =1 if opposition parties initiate post-election demonstrations	765	0.09	0.286	0	1
Election-Related Reform	Dichotomous; =1 if election-related reform reported enacted before next election	759	0.212	0.409	0	1

(continued)

(continued)

Original Data Collection and Coding

Variable	Description	#	Mean	S.D.	Min	Max
Democratic Reform	Dichotomous; =1 if opposition reported accepting election-related reforms	759	0.146	0.353	0	1
Authoritarian "Reform"	Dichotomous; =1 if opposition reported rejecting election-related reforms	759	0.064	0.245	0	1
International Reaction	Dichotomous; =1 if pro-democracy country or IGO reported commenting on election	759	0.546	0.498	0	1
Violence	Dichotomous; =1 if physical harm or property damage reported during campaign and/or on Election Day	758	0.366	0.482	0	1
Protest Violence	Dichotomous; =1 if violence reported in post-election demonstrations	741	0.136	0.343	0	1
Incumbent Victory	=1 if incumbent party retains power after the election	758	0.616	0.486	0	1

Data Collected from Other Sources

Variable	Description	#	Mean	S.D.	Min	Max
Literacy	Most recent literacy rate reported in World Bank *World Development Indicators*	540	72.54	25.79	8.69	99.77
Executive Constraint	*Polity IV XCONST variable* Higher values = more constraint on executive	726	4.76	1.94	1	7
Opposition Support	*Database of Political Institutions* (DPI) % legislative seats controlled by the opposition in year prior to election	632	0.322	0.216	0	0.926

Data Collected from Other Sources						
Variable	Description	#	Mean	S.D.	Min	Max
Opposition Cohesion	Dichotomous; =1 if at least 50% of opposition seats controlled by a single party (DPI)	539	0.775	0.417	0	1
Cold War	=1 if election year before 1989	757	0.227	0.419	0	1
Observed	Hyde (2011), Hyde and Marinov (2012); =1 if international election observers present	746	0.567	0.495	0	1
GDP per capita	Penn World Tables $US (2005) Laspeyres index	746	6130	6130	163	47,249
Executive Election	=1 if election determines control of the executive office; =1 for all presidential elections and legislative elections in parliamentary systems. Nohlen Volumes; electionguide.org	765	0.704	0.456	0	1
Turnout	International IDEA; http://www.idea.int Government-reported % registered voters that turned out (% voting-aged population where registered voter info not available)	638	0.668	0.165	0.027	0.989
Previous Turnout (unmatched)	International IDEA Turnout in previous election, regardless of type of election	556	0.676	0.165	0.027	0.989
Opposition Vote Share	DPI (OPPVOTE) Opposition total vote share Supplemented with Nohlen volumes or electionguide.org where necessary	741	17.91	21.30	0	68.18
Aid Dependent?	Dichotomous: Is country thought to be heavily dependent on foreign aid? (N19) NELDA (Hyde and Marinov 2012)	679	0.795	0.403	0	1
Polity Change	= (Polity score at next election) – (Polity score in current election)	510	0.692	3.68	−15	16

DATA COLLECTION AND CODING

Measures of election boycotts, post-election mass demonstrations, and election-related reform, as well as violence and international reactions, were all derived from journalistic accounts. Accounts were culled from Lexis Nexis's "major world news" papers and newswires, using, most commonly, a search of "[country] election" for various time periods both before and after the election. Data collection and coding were performed by hand to ensure that every coding of election-related mass demonstration, for example, reflected an instance of protest that was, in fact, election-related. Furthermore, searching for reform after each of the 765 elections in the data set for the entire time period until the subsequent election has effectively coded the reported history of election-related reform across each country for the period 1975–2006.

Boycott

Boycotts are a coordinated, public refusal, meant to challenge the status quo. Famous boycotts include African Americans' refusal to ride public transportation in the Jim Crow South; Denver housewives' refusal to shop at major supermarkets in 1966 in response to high food prices; the refusal of 61 countries, led by the United States, to participate in the 1980 Summer Olympics in Moscow after the Soviet invasion of Afghanistan; and the Soviet Union's subsequent boycott of the 1984 Summer Olympics in Los Angeles.

In this study, an election boycott is a coordinated, public refusal to participate in an election. Boycotts can be organized by citizens' groups and are sometimes undertaken by groups engaged in armed resistance to the state. These groups encourage voters to stay away from the polls in protest, sometimes with the added inducement of violence if rebel groups are involved. In most instances of election boycott, opposition leaders refuse to participate themselves and call for voters to do the same.[1]

The boycotts under study here are those organized by a political opposition that has the legal right to compete in the election. Whether or not a boycott is considered to have occurred in this study depends only on whether any eligible political actors publicly refused to compete in the election and followed through with that refusal come Election Day. Encouraging voters to stay away from the polls is typically another component of an opposition-initiated election boycott, but evidence of such activity is not an essential element of the boycotts in this study. First and foremost, the election boycotts studied here involve the public refusal to participate on the part of opposition parties or candidates.

All but one opposition candidate publicly refused to participate in Mali's presidential elections in May, 1997, for example. They objected to the government's annulment of legislative elections in the month before the

---

[1] On occasion leaders in exile will call for a boycott from abroad. Juan Peron, for example, called on his supporters to spoil their ballots in Argentinean elections while he himself was living in exile in Spain.

election.[2] Major opposition parties also boycotted the rerun of those legislative elections in July 1997, although some smaller opposition parties did compete.[3] More recently, opposition parties boycotted the parliamentary elections in Venezuela in December 2005. The opposition accused President Chavez of attempting to rig the elections, claiming that new electronic voting technology violated the secrecy of the ballot and noting that four of the country's five election judges had close ties to the president.[4]

Once a preliminary *Boycott* coding was established, I then further reviewd information from each boycott case to determine whether the boycott in question was a "major" or "minor" boycott, codings that are mutually exclusive.[5] Although previous work on boycotts characterizes them as either "total" or "partial," I have found unified boycotts to be exceedingly rare.[6] The boycott of the 2003 presidential election in Guinea was a near-universal boycott on the part of the opposition, with the leader of only one small opposition party standing in the election. General speculation held that the incumbent bankrolled this particular party to give an illusion of competition.[7] This example typifies near-unified boycotts, and the general suspicion is that when minor parties or candidates remain in the race it is because they receiving some incentive from the incumbent, typically financial, to do so. In the Dominican Republic in the early 1990s, President Balaguer was notorious for using import tax exemptions as a common side payment to support small political parties. Such support, again, was understood as a way to fragment the opposition and guarantee that some small portion of the opposition would remain "friendly" to the regime.

Major Boycott is a dichotomous variable, equal to 1 in those instances where a party or parties representing 50% or more of the opposition take part in the boycott. Major election boycotts can be undertaken by a single main opposition party, or they can be a coordinated effort among several prominent opposition parties. Five prominent opposition candidates boycotted the 1998 presidential election in Azerbaijan.[8] This boycott constituted an emblematic example of a major boycott: The bulk of the opposition publicly refused to participate in the election well in advance of Election Day, citing specific issues that they felt gave the incumbent an unfair advantage in the election, and bargaining with the incumbent had broken down. In instances of *Minor Boycott* one or more small parties (representing less than 50% of the opposition) boycott. For example, some small right-wing Christian opposition parties called for a boycott of Lebanon's parliamentary elections in August 2000, objecting to Syrian

---

[2] Keesings Record of World Events, April 1997: Mali, Presidential Election.

[3] Keesings Record of World Events, August 1997: Mali, Re-run Legislative Elections.

[4] Two injured in blasts as boycott overshadows Venezuelan election. Deutsche Presse-Agentur, December 4, 2005.

[5] See Appendix B for detailed information about each boycott.

[6] See Bratton (1998) and Lindberg (2006a) for examples of this approach to election boycotts.

[7] Rory Caroll. 2003. News roundup: Africa: Guinea's ill ruler clings to power. *The Guardian* (London). December 22.

[8] Keesings Record of World Events, October 1998: "Presidential Elections" – Azerbaijan.

occupation. Maronite Christian parties, however, did not support the boycott as they had in 1992 and urged participation in the election.[9] Whereas the 1992 boycott involving Maronite Christian parties is considered major because it involved large opposition parties, the 2000 boycott by smaller Christian parties is classified as a minor boycott. This instance is typical of minor boycotts, which are often undertaken by small opposition parties representing some minority religious or ethnic group in the population and do not primarily address the general conduct of the incumbent, so much as the treatment their party or group has received.

Post-Election Mass Demonstrations

Because this project asks why actors who have achieved legitimacy under existing institutions turn to costly, extra-institutional means of protest, it focuses on mass demonstrations when considering post-election protest. After an election, opposition parties have several tactics at their disposal to express a public rejection of it. Sometimes opposition leaders engage in a rhetorical rejection of the election, as in Kazakhstan after the 2004 elections, when opposition party leaders announced at a news conference that the second round of voting "exceeded any thinkable boundaries as far as vote-rigging, falsifications, and voter bribing are concerned."[10] Other times opposition leaders file legal challenges to protest elections. In January 2000, for example, Sri Lanka's main opposition party appealed to that country's Supreme Court to cancel the country's 1999 elections.[11] A third option for opposition parties is to call their supporters out into the streets in protest.

Rhetorical rejections are common and relatively cheap compared to acts of protest. Legal challenges, by contrast, can be costly and time consuming, but basically demonstrate a willingness to work within existing institutions. Like the boycotts that precede them, post-election mass demonstrations initiated by opposition parties indicate circumstances where the political opposition is engaging in contentious politics beyond the bounds of political institutions. When citizens take to the streets after an election to protest some aspect of its results and/or conduct, I consider post-election mass demonstrations to have occurred. In contrast to boycotts, the involvement of citizens is an essential element of opposition-initiated, post-election protest.[12]

Opposition party candidates and their supporters staged rallies following the February 2003 presidential elections in Armenia. The incumbent won a

---

[9] Weeda Hamza. PREVIEW: Lebanese head for polls after violent election campaign. Deutsche Presse-Agentur, August 24, 2000.

[10] Kazakh opposition party claims violations in runoff elections. BBC Monitoring Central Asia Unit. Supplied by BBC Worldwide Monitoring. October 4, 2004.

[11] Sri Lanka's opposition seeks dismissal of presidential election. Associated Press, January 12, 2000.

[12] See Appendix C for detailed descriptions of opposition-initiated, post-election mass demonstrations.

narrow victory in the first round of the election and ended up defeating the opposition candidate in the second round. The opposition frontrunner, Stepan Demirchyan, encouraged his supporters to turn out for the protests, stating that he was the actual winner of the presidential election and that they should go to the president's residency and "take power by force."[13] This contentious tone of protest carried over into the demonstrations near the Central Election Commission of Armenia, where protesters clashed with police.[14]

The *Demonstration* measure is a dichotomous variable, equal to 1 if any post-election mass demonstrations were reported for reasons related to the election. Beyond a basic coding for whether mass demonstrations occurred after a given election, I made a ruling regarding opposition initiation of mass demonstrations. *Opposition Initiation* refers to cases where news reports indicated that the opposition was instrumental in coordinating the mass demonstrations. Most often, opposition initiation was signaled by reports of a public call to protest, or public announcements of plans for protest, from opposition leaders, followed by mass demonstrations that news reports linked to the original pronouncements. Such linkages were established if the news reports described the protesters as "opposition supporters" while referencing calls for protest by opposition leadership. In other cases, reports that placed major opposition candidates or leaders at the site of the demonstrations (often addressing the crowd), even if initial calls to protest were not reported, were also coded as opposition initiation of protest.

Election-Related Reform

I conducted a preliminary search of *Keesing's Record of World Events* for elections from 1990 to 2002 using the following search terms: [country] & election & reform, for a period of the day after each election, up to the next election day. I read systematically the articles returned from this search to determine whether election-related reform was enacted. I then conducted a secondary search of major world newspapers and newswires in *Lexis Nexis* using the search term "[country] election reform" for 1975–2008. As with the *Keesing's* search, I read the articles returned from this search to determine whether election-related reform was enacted.

I also used the Nohlen volumes on elections around the world to search for election-related reforms.[15] To check for election-related reforms that might not have appeared in journalistic accounts, I reviewed Section 1.2 (Evolution of Electoral Provisions) for every country chapter. Using these volumes has the

---

[13] Armenian president threatens tough action over opposition unrest. BBC Monitoring Trans Caucasus Unit Supplied by BBC Worldwide Monitoring, February 22, 2003.

[14] Armenian opposition protesters want Demirchyan declared poll winner. BBC Monitoring Trans Caucasus Unit Supplied by BBC Worldwide Monitoring, February 20, 2003; Partakers in opposition rally clash with police in Yerevan. News Bulletin, February 20, 2003.

[15] Dieter Nohlen has edited volumes on elections in Africa, Asia, and the Americas that provide a country-by-country description of elections, electoral laws, and election statistics.

advantage of providing additional detailed information on most developing countries. The disadvantages of incorporating information from these volumes is that they typically only provide information on elections into the late 1990s and do not provide information on any former Soviet states, except for those in Central Asia.[16] Furthermore, these descriptions focus narrowly on what I could call electoral system or administration reform and do not tend to encompass changes to civil liberties that I consider to be election-related.

I also consulted Frederic Schaffer's book on clean election reform (2008, 203–4) for additional information on reforms from 1991 to 2006[17] and added three of the reforms cataloged by Schaffer to my initial data collection efforts.[18] The *Reform* variable, then is a dichotomous measure, equal to 1 in cases where it was determined that some laws affecting elections were changed after the election in question, but before the subsequent election. For all other cases *Reform* equals zero. In my data set there are 179 instances of election-related reform.[19]

For each reported case of election-related reform, if the opposition expressed no objection to the measures, *Democratic Reform* is coded as equal to 1. If the opposition is reported to object to the reform in question, *Democratic Reform* is coded as equal to zero.

Systematic work on the democratic consequences of electoral reform is fairly uncommon, but Schaffer's (2008) book on clean election reform provides a welcome point of comparison to assess the robustness of this coding effort. Schaffer studied what he describes as "clean election reforms." Yet, even these cases of reform where the intention is ostensibly clear – to improve the democratic quality of elections – can have negative consequences for democracy, according to Schaffer. Schaffer focuses on three potentially negative consequences of clean election reform: depression of the number of eligible voters, proliferation of cheating, and alienation of voters. He acknowledges that lawmakers sometimes intentionally use the election-related reform process to undemocratic ends (21), but he also points out that the detrimental effects of election-related reform can be unintentional as well and can come from other actors such as party leaders and poll workers. Thus, although Schaffer's study may not tell us as much about whether such detrimental consequences can be interpreted as the intentional

---

[16] Countries included in this study but not covered by Nohlen include Belarus, Yugoslavia and the former Yugoslavia, Bulgaria, Croatia, Cyprus, Czechoslovakia/The Czech Republic/Slovakia, Estonia, Hungary, Latvia, Lithuania, Macedonia, Moldova, Poland, Romania, Russia, and Ukraine.

[17] For more on Schaffer's data collection and coding, see the Methods and Evidence section of chapter 1 in his book, pp. 15–20.

[18] Four additional reforms documented by Schaffer (BRA 1998, LBR 1997, TAJ 2000, UKR 2002) seem as if they should qualify by my definition of election-related reform, However, I did not find evidence of these reforms in my own data collection, and I did not add them because the information in Schaffer (2008) was insufficient to determine that these reforms came about via legislation.

[19] Appendix D provides detailed information on all of the election-related reforms.

work of the incumbent, his assessments of the impact of these reforms provide a useful comparison to my own data coding based on opposition reaction to the reforms.

The cases of clean-election reform coded by Schaffer that are not counted as reform in my coding are instances where changes were made to electoral procedures through means other than legislation. Schaffer is interested in every effort and initiative "designed to reduce fraud and error in the casting and counting of votes" (Schaffer 2008, 3). Such initiatives need not necessarily come about through legislation, but could be within the purview of existing agencies to implement without any input from lawmakers. The decision to use indelible ink on voters' fingers, the adoption of a civic education campaign, and the use of transparent ballot boxes could all be administrative decisions that might reflect an incumbent's response to domestic or international pressure, but might just as easily reflect a technocrat's apolitical decision making. Essentially, then, although Schaffer's work represents the only other systematic account of election-related reform, the focus is sufficiently different such that comparisons to my work may not prove terribly useful.

Violence

Election violence is understood as any incidents that resulted in physical harm or the destruction of property during the campaign period or on Election Day itself. The elections in Bangladesh in 2001 provide an extreme example of election violence. Although it was estimated that only 5 people died on Election Day, more than 150 were killed and nearly 2,500 wounded in political violence during the campaign period.[20]

Protest Violence

If any reports of violence accompanied the description of post-election mass demonstrations, the *Protest Violence* variable was coded as equal to 1. Once the ruling party was declared the winner of Cambodia's 1998 elections, opposition parties began to launch protests.[21] The violence associated with these protests seemed largely to be the result of government retaliation.[22] Violence took the form of opposition supporters rioting after the 2001 elections in Zambia.[23]

---

[20] Thousands of protesters call for fresh polls in Bangladesh. Deutsche Presse-Agentur, October 28, 2001.

[21] Hun Sen foes launch poll vigil. *Courier Mail* (Queensland, Australia), August 25, 1998.

[22] Thousands attend Cambodia's largest-ever protest. Deutsche Presse-Agentur, August 30, 1998; Seth Mydans. Troops shoot at mobs and beat protesters again in Phnom Penh. *New York Times*, September 10, 1998; Police use tear gas as fresh riots break out in Cambodian capital. Deutsche Presse-Agentur, September 8, 1998.

[23] Protests as Mwanawassa becomes third president. Vanguard (Nigeria), AAGM, January 3, 2002.

After Kyrgyzstan's 2005 elections, opposition supporters stormed administrative buildings demanding that election results be reviewed.[24] In the violence that accompanied these protests, opposition parties and their supporters managed to seize control of the state television network.[25]

International Reaction

While collecting data on protest events and election-related reforms, I also coded indications of reaction from western democracy promoters. Specifically, the international reaction variable focuses on whether any states who tend to support democracy in developing countries, or intergovernmental organizations such as the UN or the EU, made public comments on the election. I coded one variable, *International Reaction*, as equal to 1 in any instance where a western democracy-promoting state or IGO was reported to have commented on the election. If no such reaction was reported, *International Reaction* was coded as equal to zero.

Incumbent Victory

For this project, I also coded incumbent victory to provide systematic evidence for several common-sense claims about opposition-initiated, election-related protest. The first claim is that, when the opposition boycotts, the incumbent wins. The second claim is that opposition parties will only protest after the election if they lose. These claims are investigated in Chapters 4 and 3, respectively. To avoid the complications that can arise given variation in term limits across countries, for incumbent victory, I focused on whether the incumbent party retains power in the election. For presidential elections, then, cases where the incumbent party retains the presidency are coded as *Incumbent Victory* = 1. For parliamentary elections, Incumbent Victory is coded as 1 if the party that controlled government before the election forms the government after the election. Cases where a party that previously controlled the government is forced into a coalition after the election are not counted as an incumbent victory (*Incumbent Victory* = 0). If presidential and legislative elections are held simultaneously and incumbent control is returned for the presidency but not the legislature (or vice versa), my coding rule privileges the presidency in determining the value for *Incumbent Victory*. There are several cases of extremely unstable party systems where judgments had to be made based on available information about the candidates and parties and their relationships to previous party organizations. It bears noting that cases where the incumbent was initially declared the winner, and then stepped down under pressure from

---

[24] Assault from south to north. RusData Dialine – Russian Press Digest, March 18, 2005.
[25] Report: Supreme Court invalidates Kyrgyz parliamentary elections. Associated Press Worldstream. March 24, 2005.

post-election protest, such as in the Philippines in 1986 or the Ukraine in 2004, are still coded as incumbent victories, because the original results determined them to be the winner, even if those results were subsequently overturned.

Two cases presented challenges for incumbent victory coding: Philippines and Haiti. In the Philippines, in 1984, direct election of the vice president was reinstated, and it was possible for vice presidents to be elected from a different party from that of the president. As such, it is not immediately clear whether the election of an individual from the incumbent president's same party or an election of a former vice president to the position of president is the better representation of the incumbent retaining power. This became an issue for the 1998 presidential election, where former vice president Joseph Estrada (elected independently to that post in 1992) beat Jose C. de Venicia Jr., who represented incumbent president Ramos's party Lakas-NUCD, and again in 2001, when vice president Gloria Macapagal-Arroyo won the presidency. Macpagal-Arroyo was the Lakas-NUCD vice presidential candidate in 1998, when de Vencia Jr. lost to Estrada, and represented the same party when she was elected president. Neither Estrada's nor Macpagal-Arroyo's wins are coded as incumbent victory, because the party of the executive was not returned to the office of president. Given Estrada's status as an outsider and the instability of his party affiliations, this coding seems appropriate for the 1998 election that he won. In the cases of Arroyo's 2001 victory, however, the fact that Lakas-NUCD had controlled the executive before 1998. and then controlled the vice presidency from 1998 to 2001, makes Arroyo's Lakas-NUCD victory look more like an incumbent victory than the case of Estrada in 1998. Nonetheless, the 2001 circumstances are technically equivalent to 1998, and as such the coding for 2001 is incumbent victory = 0.

The challenges of coding incumbent victory in Haiti stem from Haiti's constitutional prohibition on consecutive reelection of the president. In addition, the frequency with which political candidates change or create new parties make it difficult to identify Haiti's opposition and their relationship to the incumbent. Preval was Aristide's protégé, and it was widely understood that Aristide selected Preval to succeed him after his (Aristide's) first term as president.[26] Furthermore, most observers agree that Preval worked to ease Aristide's reelection after his own (Preval's) first term, even though by that time Aristide had split from the party he had formed when Preval was his prime minister.[27] The only time the closeness of their relationship has been in doubt was during Preval's most recent reelection in 2006. Given, however, that most of Aristide's supporters voted for Preval, in part on the hopes that it might aid Aristide's return to Haiti, it would appear as though voters still see them as interchangeable.

---

[26] Aristide's choice winner in Haitian vote, say observers. Deutsche Presse-Agentur, December 18, 1995.
[27] Speculation builds on how Haiti's Preval will rule. NPR Morning Edition Broadcast, February 24, 2006, Amelia Shaw reporting.

For this reason, Preval's initial election (1995), Aristides reelection (2000), and Preval's reelection (2006) are all treated as incumbent victories in this study.

CHAPTER 5 ROBUSTNESS CHECKS

Additional tests were conducted to ensure that the results presented in Chapter 5 were not being driven by the most democratic countries in the sample, nor by specific regions that have had the most success with democratic reform. The first table below replicates the models in Table 5.2 on a sub-set of the full sample, excluding the most democratic countries in the full sample (those with a FH political freedom score of 3 or lower). The second table replicates Table 5.2 but excludes those countries in Latin America and Eastern Europe.

Electoral Protest and Election-Related Reform: Conditional Relationships (FH Political Freedom Score > 3)

	Model 1 Authoritarian "Reform"	Model 2 Democratic Reform
Major Boycott	−2.936*	−14.85**
	(1.486)	(0.515)
Opposition Demonstration	−24.61**	0.091
	(1.593)	(0.717)
Opposition Seat Share	−0.558	0.286
	(0.908)	(0.768)
*Boycott*Demonstration*	28.09**	−0.192
	(2.158)	(1.253)
*Boycott*Opposition Seats*	9.455**	−6.050
	(3.110)	(3.726)
International Reaction	0.504	0.050
	(0.491)	(0.338)
*Boycott**	0.668	17.72**
International Reaction	(1.526)	(0.985)
*Demonstration**	−13.86**	0.660
International Reaction	(2.183)	(0.836)
GDP per capita	0.000	0.000
	(0.000)	(0.000)
Aid Dependent	1.105	−0.464
	(0.603)	(0.429)
Constant	−3.319**	−1.589**
	(0.676)	(0.446)
N	328	328
Wald chi² (10)	476.6	1869
Pseudo R²	0.123	0.073

* Significant at the level $p > .05$, two-tailed z-test.
** Significant at the level $p > .01$, two-tailed z-test.
Note: Robust standard errors (in parentheses) clustered by country.

Electoral Protest and Election-Related Reform: Conditional Relationships (Latin America and Eastern Europe Excluded)

	Model 1 Authoritarian "Reform"	Model 2 Democratic Reform
Major Boycott	−3.955*	−1.544*
	(1.647)	(0.669)
Opposition Demonstration	−27.39	0.781
	(1.615)	(0.453)
Opposition Seat Share	−2.709	−0.376
	(1.163)	(0.673)
Boycott*Demonstration	27.92**	0.753
	(2.369)	(1.129)
Boycott*Opposition Seats	12.82**	0.074
	(3.494)	(3.035)
International Reaction	0.279	0.060
	(0.425)	(0.329)
Boycott*	1.671	2.952**
International Reaction	(1.535)	(0.895)
Demonstration*	−13.65**	−0.690
International Reaction	(1.932)	(0.732)
GDP per capita	−0.000	0.000
	(0.000)	(0.000)
Aid Dependent	0.432	−0.205
	(0.653)	(0.378)
Constant	−2.160**	−1.695**
	(0.687)	(0.387)
N	337	337
Wald chi^2 (10)	867.5	23.92
Pseudo R^2	0.135	0.041

* Significant at the level $p > .05$, two-tailed z-test.
** Significant at the level $p > .01$, two-tailed z-test.
Note: Robust standard errors (in parentheses) clustered by country.

APPENDIX B. Boycotts

Country	Date	Election Type	Major/Minor?	Description
Afghanistan	October 9, 2004	Presidential	Major	Fifteen candidates (a majority of the opposition members) called for a boycott on Election Day when it was discovered that the indelible ink meant to prevent repeat voting could be wiped off easily.
Algeria	November 16, 1995	Presidential	Major	Three main opposition candidates refused to participate, but the boycott did not appear to be supported by a majority of the electorate.
Algeria	May 30, 2002	Legislative	Minor	Boycott was held in the Berber-dominated Kabylie region by five opposition parties, including the Socialist Forces Front (FFS) and the Rally for Culture and Democracy (RCD).
Azerbaijan	October 11, 1998	Presidential	Major	Five opposition candidates boycotted. Their key demand was reform of recent electoral legislation, deemed "undemocratic," particularly with respect to registration requirements and composition of the Chief Election Commission.
Azerbaijan	November 5, 2000	Legislative	Minor	Twelve major opposition parties warned of a boycott if election laws were not amended and candidates were not allowed to participate, but most ended up participating in the election.
Bangladesh	May 7, 1986	Legislative	Major	Majority of leftist and centrist opposition parties boycotted elections to protest election fraud.
Bangladesh	October 15, 1986	Presidential	Major	Following the boycotted parliamentary election in May 1986, all opposition parties boycotted the presidential election.
Bangladesh	March 3, 1988	Legislative	Major	Two main opposition parties boycotted after demanding that President Ershad of the ruling Jatiya Party hand over power to a caretaker government prior to the elections.

Country	Date	Type	Severity	Description
Bangladesh	February 15, 1996	Legislative	Major	Boycott called for by three opposition parties – the Awami League (main), the Muslim Jamat-e-Islam Party, and the Jatiya Party – on the grounds that elections be held under a nonpartisan caretaker government.
Belarus	October 15, 2000	Legislative	Major	Main opposition parties called for a boycott on the grounds that elections were "undemocratic." There was explicit support from the OSCE, but there did not appear to be widespread domestic support for the boycott.
Benin	March 4, 2001	Presidential & Legislative	Minor	The Benin Communist Party (PCB) called for a "peaceful boycott" at the fourth ordinary congress.
Burkina Faso	December 1, 1991	Presidential	Major	Opposition parties boycotted on the grounds that the incumbent, who had taken power in a military coup in 1987, was misusing state resources to ensure his victory in the election. Only 25% of the electorate turned out to vote.
Burkina Faso	November 15, 1998	Presidential	Major	Opposition parties boycotted, claiming that the election commission was biased and the voter register was rigged. Fifty-eight percent of the electorate turned out to vote.
Cameroon	March 1, 1992	Legislative	Minor	The first multiparty elections were boycotted by 16 of 48 registered political parties, but only 2 of 4 main opposition parties – the Social Democratic Front (SDF) and the Cameroon Democratic Union (CDU).
Cameroon	October 12, 1997	Presidential	Major	All major opposition parties boycotted based on concerns of incumbent bias, particularly the president's refusal to create an independent election management board.
Central African Republic	July 31, 1987	Legislative	Major	The main opposition leaders called for a boycott. These parliamentary elections were considered semi-competitive because they allowed the participation of candidates outside of the one legal party in the country, the RDC.
Chad	May 3, 2006	Presidential	Major	The boycott was called by an alliance of 19 opposition parties.

(*continued*)

(continued)

Country	Date	Election Type	Major/Minor?	Description
Comoros	November 22, 1992	Legislative	Major	Two of the three main opposition parties boycotted to protest the government's failure to update voter registers as well as the detention of several opposition activists.
Comoros	December 1, 1996	Legislative	Major	The opposition boycotted the election in reaction to constitutional reform adopted via referendum in October 1996; it also complained about outdated voter lists that favored the incumbent and raised demands for an independent election commission.
Congo	March 10, 2002	Presidential	Major	The candidate for the main opposition coalition declared a boycott on the grounds that "massive" vote rigging in favor of the incumbent was already underway.
Cote d'Ivoire	October 22, 1995	Presidential	Major	The election was boycotted by opposition parties after government harassment.
Cote d'Ivoire	October 22, 2000	Presidential	Major	Two major opposition parties boycotted after their candidates were disqualified from the election.
Cote d'Ivoire	December 10, 2000	Legislative	Minor	One major opposition party (RDR) boycotted the elections because its candidate was disqualified by the government (subsequently upheld by the supreme court).
Democratic Republic of Congo	July 30, 2006	Presidential & Legislative	Major	Many major opposition parties boycotted the first multiparty election in 46 years.
Egypt	November 29, 1990	Legislative	Major	Three historically dominant opposition parties (the NWP, SLP, and LSP) all boycotted November legislative elections in Egypt.
Equatorial Guinea	November 21, 1993	Legislative	Major	Main opposition parties objected to particularly controversial clauses in the country's election law and the incumbent's unwillingness to allow international observers to inspect voter registration.

Country	Date			Description
Equatorial Guinea	February 25, 1996	Presidential	Major	Opposition parties boycotted because the government threw out the voter registers that had been drawn up with the UN and produced their own registers to be used in the election.
Equatorial Guinea	March 7, 1999	Legislative	Minor	Only 1 of 14 main political parties boycotted.
Ethiopia	May 7, 1995	Legislative	Major	The election was boycotted by major opposition parties on the grounds of questionable monitoring practices.
Gabon	December 15, 1996	Legislative	Major	The boycott occurred after the incumbent ignored a written agreement with the opposition and a constitutional court ruling that elections be held before June 1996. The incumbent also reappointed a prime minister whose term was up, and he appeared poised to place family members in government.
Gabon	December 9, 2001	Legislative	Minor	Eight minor opposition parties boycotted the elections on claims of a flawed electoral register.
Gambia	January 17, 2002	Legislative	Major	The main opposition party (UDP) cited rumors of the falsification of Gambian national identity cards so that nonresidents could register to vote. Further, in the runup to the election, the government revoked the independent election commission's ability to scrutinize the credentials of those attempting to register to vote.
Ghana	December 29, 1992	Legislative	Major	Opposition parties boycotted to protest fraud that they alleged was committed during the presidential elections in November 1992.
Georgia	October 11, 1992	Legislative	Minor	Minor opposition parties in some electoral districts called for a boycott.
Guinea	June 30, 2002	Legislative	Major	This was a near-universal boycott on the part of the opposition, with the leader of only one small, opposition party standing in the election. The general suspicion is that this particular party was bankrolled by the incumbent to give an illusion of competition.

(continued)

153

(continued)

Country	Date	Election Type	Major/Minor?	Description
Guinea	December 21, 2003	Presidential	Major	The opposition accused the incumbent president of fraud and intimidation.
Haiti	June 25, 1995	Legislative	Major	Major opposition parties, including former allies of President Aristide, boycotted.
Haiti	November 26, 2000	Presidential	Major	Major opposition parties accused the incumbent of cheating.
India	April 27, 1996	Legislative	Minor	Communist parties and the National Conference party in Kashmir boycotted.
India	September 5, 1999	Presidential	Minor	The main political opposition in Kashmir boycotted.
India	April 20, 2004	Legislative	Minor	United National Liberation Front called for a boycott in Kashmir.
Indonesia	May 29, 1997	Legislative	Major	The PPP, the main opposition party, boycotted after the leader of another opposition party (Megawati Sukarnoputri of the PRD) was barred from competition.
Iran	June 11, 1993	Presidential	Minor	Both the Iranian National Party and Freedom Movement of Iran (FMI) called for a boycott of elections.
Iran	March 8, 1996	Legislative	Minor	Groups including FMI boycotted the elections. Four members of FMI had been permitted to run as independents, but had declined in protest at restrictions on campaigning.
Iran	February 20, 2004	Legislative	Major	Pro-reform candidates boycotted Iran's February parliamentary elections in 2004 after more than 2,000 reform candidates were barred from competition. The remaining 1,100 reformers boycotted in protest. Boycotters used text messages and mass e-mails to publicize their boycott.
Israel	February 6, 2001	Presidential & Legislative	Minor	The boycott, endorsed by two main Arab parties, was part of a strategy to gain political leverage.

154

Jamaica	December 15, 1983	Legislative	Major	The major opposition party (PNP) boycotted on the grounds that the government was using outdated voter registers, resulting in the election of a one-party legislature.
Jordan	November 4, 1997	Legislative	Major	The Muslim Brotherhood Organization, the Islamic Labor Front, and eight other left-wing and national parties boycotted.
Kuwait	June 10, 1990	Legislative	Major	Thirty two opposition leaders, who had been members of the dissolved 1986 parliament, led a boycott of the elections on grounds of tampering with electoral rolls, voter intimidation, and media censorship.
Kazakhstan	January 10, 1999	Presidential	Minor	Opposition movement Azamat boycotted.
Kazakhstan	October 10, 1999	Legislative	Minor	Republican People's Party of Kazakhstan (RPPK) declared a boycott after CEC refused to register their party leader (former PM Akezhan Kazhegeldin).
Lebanon	August 23, 1992	Legislative	Major	Maronite political parties boycotted the 1992 parliamentary elections with the stated objection that continued Syrian occupation of the country made fair elections impossible.
Lebanon	August 18, 1996	Legislative	Minor	Maronite leaders threatened boycott, but few parties and candidates actually did so.
Lebanon	August 27, 2000	Legislative	Minor	Three small, right-wing, Christian opposition parties boycotted in protest of Syrian occupation, but Maronite Christian parties urged participation.
Mauritania	March 6, 1992	Legislative	Major	Opposition parties in Mauritania boycotted elections to protest the alleged rigging of the presidential elections that had taken place two months earlier.
Mauritania	December 12, 1997	Presidential	Major	The formerly fragmented opposition united under the banner of the FPO (Opposition Front) and boycotted the December 1997 presidential election.

(*continued*)

Country	Date	Election Type	Major/Minor?	Description
Macedonia	October 16, 1994	Presidential & Legislative	Minor	The Democratic Alliance of Serbs in Macedonia boycotted the election.
Mali	May 11, 1997	Presidential	Major	All but one opposition candidate boycotted. They objected to the government's annulment of legislative elections in the previous month.
Mali	July 20, 1997	Legislative	Major	The rerun of those legislative elections in July 1997 was also boycotted by major opposition parties, though some smaller opposition parties did compete.
Morocco	June 25, 1993	Legislative	Minor	The main opposition parties, USFP and Istiqlal, presented shared candidates; the Party of the Democratic Socialist Avant-Garde (PADS) boycotted.
Nigeria	April 25, 1998	Legislative	Major	Opposition groups, under the banner of the "United Action for Democracy," boycotted, after the two parties supporting President Abacha dominated state legislature elections in 1997.
Niger	November 23, 1996	Legislative	Major	Opposition parties formed an alliance, the Front for the Restoration and Defense of Democracy (FRDD), and boycotted.
Pakistan	February 25, 1985	Legislative	Major	All major parties boycotted because candidates were not allowed to compete under their party labels.
Pakistan	October 6, 1993	Legislative	Minor	The Urdu-speaking migrant party, the Mohajir Quami Mahaz, Altaf-Group (MQM-A), boycotted in protest of alleged army discrimination against its candidates.
Philippines	June 16, 1981	Presidential	Major	The major opposition party UNIDO boycotted after Marcos refused requests for more time to campaign and equal access to the media.
Russia	March 26, 2000	Presidential & Legislative	Minor	Small political movements such as Union 2000 (Soyuz 2000) boycotted

Country	Date	Election	Severity	Description
South Africa	April 26, 1994	Presidential	Minor	The Conservative Party and Azanian People's Organization (AZAPO) – small parties representing white voters – boycotted.
Sudan	December 11, 2000	Presidential	Major	The government denied the opposition's request to lift the state of emergency that had been in place for nearly a year. With the state of emergency in place, the opposition complained that the elections could not be fair.
Tajikistan	February 25, 1995	Legislative	Major	PPUJ and the umbrella organization UTO (United Tajik Opposition) boycotted after the leader of PPUJ was disqualified from competing.
Thailand	April 2, 2006	Legislative	Major	The opposition boycott came after weeks of public demonstrations protesting Thaskin's alleged corruption and abuses of power.
Togo	August 25, 2003	Presidential	Major	Opposition parties boycotted after a key opposition candidate, Gilchrist Olympio, was disqualified from the race.
Togo	March 21, 1999	Legislative	Major	Main opposition parties boycotted on the grounds that issues from the 1998 presidential election, which had received a great deal of criticism from the EU and the UK, had not been resolved.
Togo	October 27, 2002	Legislative	Major	Opposition parties boycotted the elections on the grounds that they were not "free, transparent, nor democratic."
Tunisia	November 2, 1986	Legislative	Major	All opposition parties boycotted the elections to protest unfair electoral practices. Specifically, the opposition parties (which had only begun to gain official recognition as of 1981) objected to the government's rejection of a number of their candidate lists.
Venezuela	December 4, 2005	Legislative	Major	All opposition parties boycotted the elections, accusing President Chavez of attempting to rig the elections, claiming that new electronic voting technology violated the secrecy of the ballot and noting that four of the country's five election judges had close ties to the president.
Yemen	April 27, 1997	Legislative	Major	The Yemeni Socialist Party, the country's largest opposition party in parliament, and several other small opposition parties boycotted.

(continued)

(continued)

Country	Date	Election Type	Major/Minor?	Description
Yugoslavia	September 24, 2000	Presidential & Legislative	Minor	Opposition parties in Montenegro – the Democratic Party of Socialists (DPS) and Socialdemocratic Party – boycotted in a push for independence.
Zambia	November 18, 1996	Presidential & Legislative	Major	UNIP, the major opposition party, and five minor opposition parties boycotted to protest the disqualification of key opposition candidates, including former president Kenneth Kaunda.
Zimbabwe	April 8, 1995	Presidential	Major	Five opposition parties boycotted the election. At issue for the opposition were a constitution and electoral laws that, they argued, created an uneven electoral playing field.
Zimbabwe	March 16, 1996	Presidential & Legislative	Major	Both of the major opposition presidential candidates, Rev. Ndabaningi Sithole, of the ZANU party and retired bishop Abel Muzorewa of the UP Party, boycotted, citing interference from the government's central intelligence agency in opposition party operations and unfair electoral laws.
Zimbabwe	March 9, 2002	Presidential & Legislative	Minor	A small opposition party (Liberty Party) boycotted on the ground that the elections would not be free and fair.

APPENDIX C. Post-Election Mass Demonstrations

Country	Date	Election Type	Opposition Initiated or Supported?	Violence?	Description
Afghanistan	September 18, 2005	Legislative	Initiated	Yes	In the North, protestors closed the election office, accusing the incumbent of vote rigging and corruption. In one instance opposition candidates and their supporters ransacked and occupied an election administration office in the northern city of Konduz, demanding a vote recount.
Albania	March 31, 1991	Legislative	Supported	Yes	Up to five protesters were reportedly shot by Albanian Security Forces. Local party leader Arben Broci was presumed one of the slain.
Albania	May 26, 1996	Presidential	Initiated	Yes	Socialist Party protested against allegedly rigged elections. Police intervened with violence.
Algeria	April 8, 2004	Presidential	Initiated	Yes	Supporters of the main opposition candidate (Ali Benflis, of the FLN) protested in the streets of Algiers, Algeria's capital. Clashes were reported between security forces and Benflis supporters.
Angola	September 29, 1992	Pres/Leg	Initiated	Yes	UNITA, Angola's main opposition party, publicly rejected the results of the election, sparking a wave of violent protests. These elections were the first after 16 years of civil war in which UNITA had represented the armed resistance to the MPLA government.

(continued)

(continued)

Country	Date	Election Type	Opposition Initiated or Supported?	Violence?	Description
Armenia	September 22, 1996	Presidential	Initiated	Yes	Manukyan supporters charged vote fraud. Protestors stormed the parliament building before being turned away by police.
Armenia	February 19, 2003	Presidential	Initiated	Yes	An opposition rally in support of Peoples' Party of Armenia was organized by opposition candidate Stepan Demirchyan.
Armenia	May 25, 2003	Legislative	Initiated	No	Opposition parties publicly rejected results, sparking demonstrations that seemed to be specific to particular opposition candidates.
Azerbaijan	November 5, 2000	Legislative	Supported	Yes	Opposition supporters rallied to demand the president's resignation. Fifteen police were reported injured in the violence that broke out at this demonstration.
Azerbaijan	October 15, 2003	Presidential	Supported	Yes	Supporters of the leading opposition party staged mass demonstrations after their candidate's defeat. The protest violence left two people dead.
Azerbaijan	November 6, 2005	Legislative	Initiated	Yes	Opposition parties organized mass demonstrations, claiming the elections were rigged. The only reported violence came as police turned water cannons on protesters to disperse them.
Belarus	September 9, 2001	Presidential	Supported	No	Mass demonstrations occurred after the elections. Although there was no indication that opposition leaders had called for the protest, the demonstrations were opposing the president's reelection, suggesting that they were instigated by opposition supporters.

Country	Date	Election type	Initiated/Supported	Mass protest	Description
Belarus	October 17, 2004	Legislative	Supported	Yes	Student supporters of the opposition as well as opposition leaders engaged in mass demonstrations almost as soon as the election began. Demonstrations turned violent as protesters reportedly clashed with police.
Belarus	March 19, 2006	Presidential	Initiated	Yes	Demonstrations protested a third term victory for the incumbent. Demonstrators occupied central Minsk, erecting a tent city. Government police crushed the demonstrations with harsh repression and arrests, which were widely condemned by international actors.
Bangladesh	November 15, 1981	Presidential	Initiated	No	Nearly 4,000 supporters of the opposition Awami League marched to protest the reelection of acting incumbent Abdus Sattar for a full term.
Bangladesh	May 07, 1986	Presidential	Initiated	Yes	Opposition Awami League called for a national strike to protest fraud and voter intimidation. At least 15 were wounded in clashes either between protesters and police or with individuals whom police called "strike opponents."
Bangladesh	October 15, 1986	Presidential	Initiated	Yes	Opposition National Party called for a half-day general strike, which was supported by student protesters. At least one student was killed and others injured when police opened fire on demonstrators at Dhaka University.
Bangladesh	March 3, 1988	Legislative	Initiated	Yes	Both opposition parties called for four days of demonstrations and a general strike to protest rigged elections. Protesters cornered police in a fire station and set it on fire after police fled.

(*continued*)

(*continued*)

Country	Date	Election Type	Opposition Initiated or Supported?	Violence?	Description
Bangladesh	February 15, 1996	Legislative	Initiated	Yes	A senior police officer was gunned down and more than 100 people were injured in street riots as police used force to break up a sit down demonstration by the opposition.
Bangladesh	October 1, 2001	Legislative	Initiated	No	Opposition Awami League organized an antigovernment rally in the capital, attended by an estimated 50,000 activists and supporters.
Bolivia	July 1, 1979	Presidential	Initiated	No	Hernan Siles Zuazo, candidate for the UDP, called for mass demonstrations, which were followed by a general strike four days later. Siles won the most votes in the election, but did not secure a majority. Therefore, according to Bolivia's constitution, the legislature chose the president, but did not select Siles
Bulgaria	June 10, 1990	Legislative	No	No	Students and anarchist groups protested the election.
Bulgaria	June 25, 2005	Legislative	No	No	Supporters of an extremist group (Ataka) protested to try to prevent formation of a post-election government.
Cambodia	July 26, 1998	Legislative	Supported	Yes	Once the ruling party was declared the winner of the elections, opposition parties began to launch protests, accusing the government of fraud.

Country	Date				
Cambodia	July 27, 2003	Legislative	Initiated	Yes	Leaders of the Khmer Front Party spearheaded mass demonstrations after their party did not win a single seat in the elections. The protest continued a pattern of violence that began on Election Day, aimed mostly at the main opposition party, the royalist FUNCINPEC; this violence led to the assassination of two FUNCINPEC supporters.
Cameroon	October 11, 1992	Legislative	Supported	Yes	Although it went on to form part of the government, young supporters of the former ruling PCT protested in the streets of the capital almost as soon as elections began in the Congo in 1992.
Central African Republic	March 15, 1981	Presidential	No	Yes	There were reports of "youths" protesting in the capital and "clashes" between protesters and police.
Cote d'Ivoire	October 22, 2000	Presidential	Supported	Yes	Supporters of a candidate who had been barred from the election, Alassane Dramane Ouattara, demanded a new vote. Angry mobs overturned cars and clashed with police. Security forces fired on unarmed demonstrators.
Congo	June 1, 1992	Presidential	Supported	No	There were street protests in Brazzaville by young militants of Congo's former ruling party.
Czech Republic	June 2, 2006	Legislative	No	No	The Society of Decent Citizens and activist Jan Sinagl staged post-election demonstrations in Prague's Wenceslas Square.
Dominican Republic	May 16, 1986	Presidential & Legislative	No	Yes	City workers protested the vote count in mayoral elections held concurrently with national-level elections.

(continued)

163

Country	Date	Election Type	Opposition Initiated or Supported?	Violence?	Description
Dominican Republic	May 16, 1990	Presidential & Legislative	Initiated	Yes	Demonstrations were part of a 48-hour period of "national mourning" organized by Juan Bosch's opposition Dominican Liberation Party to protest the incumbent's victory.
Dominican Republic	May 16, 1994	Presidential & Legislative	Initiated	Yes	Opposition supporters clashed with police and stopped traffic as protests erupted after the incumbent was declared winner. Two protesters suffered gunshot wounds in separate clashes with police.
Democratic Republic of Congo	July 30, 2006	Presidential & Legislative	Supported	No	Congo's opposition presidential candidate publicly rejected the election results; his supporters stopped traffic and threw stones in the capital.
Egypt	September 7, 2005	Presidential	Initiated	No	Leaders and supporters of Egypt's more secular opposition protested after the elections, claiming that Mubarak had stolen the election. Approximately 1,500 marched in protest.
Egypt	November 9, 2005	Legislative	Initiated	No	Opposition activists marched through downtown Cairo to protest electoral fraud.
El Salvador	February 20, 1977	Presidential	Initiated	Yes	Leaders of the opposition led mass demonstrations to criticize fraud on the part of the government.
El Salvador	March 20, 1988	Legislative	Initiated	No	Opposition ARENA claimed that it had won a majority of legislative seats and called on supporters to protest after the election.

Ethiopia	May 15, 2005	Legislative	Supported	Yes	Opposition supporters protested the government's claim of victory. Clashes between police and student demonstrators left one girl dead, seven people injured, and hundreds arrested. Ethiopian security forces killed 22 people, wounded dozens, and placed some opposition politicians under house arrest.
Fiji	April 4, 1987	Legislative	No	No	There was "civil disobedience" to protest the post-election coalition government. Neither the initiation nor support of this action was attributed to opposition political parties.
Gabon	December 5, 1993	Presidential	Initiated	No	Mass demonstrations accompanied an explicit rejection of the results by opposition leader Abessole, who accused the incumbent president of staging an "electoral coup," appointed a rival prime minister, and called on the armed forces to support him as the rightful winner of the election. Abessole called for the boycott of state institutions and in February encouraged further civil disobedience, including the refusal to pay taxes.
Gabon	November 27, 2005	Presidential	Initiated	Yes	Opposition parties publicly rejected the results, which led to violent demonstrations in the opposition stronghold of Port Gentil and in the country's capital, Libreville. The opposition then called for a general strike to protest the results of the election that they said was rigged.

(continued)

Country	Date	Election Type	Opposition Initiated or Supported?	Violence?	Description
Ghana	November 3, 1992	Presidential	No	Yes	Post-election disturbances and rioting were reported, but were not attributed to the leaders or supporters of any opposition party.
Guinea-Bissau	March 28, 2004	Legislative	No	No	Voters protested the delayed opening of voting stations.
Guinea-Bissau	June 19, 2005	Presidential	Initiated	Yes	The secretary-general of Guinea Bissau's opposition Social Renovation Party, whose candidate finished third in the first round of voting, led a public demonstration. While the first round of voting was relatively calm, the second round of voting was marked by armed attacks on the Ministry of the Interior, the presidential palace, and central election commission offices while votes were being counted.
Georgia	November 2, 2003	Legislative	Initiated	No	Georgia's opposition leaders called on their supporters to protest what they described as the "total rigging" of the elections. It was alleged that poll workers had been falsifying vote tallies to give the government party a lead in the election, while exit polling showed the opposition National Movement to be leading. Within two weeks, the movement grew 20,000 strong.
Guatemala	March 7, 1982	Presidential & Legislative	Supported	Yes	Losing opposition candidates called the election fraudulent and drew "small gatherings" of demonstrations.

Country	Date	Election Type			Description
Guinea	December 14, 1998	Presidential	No	No	21 naked women protested the detention of an opposition leader in this West African country.
Guyana	December 9, 1985	Legislative	Supported	No	Opposition supporters protested an election that was widely considered rigged.
Guyana	December 15, 1997	Presidential	Initiated	Yes	Demonstrations, led by the opposition PNC, began on December, 19, the day Janet Jagan was sworn into office as president and continued into January. Street demonstrations continued for a month on a near-daily basis, and four separate bombings marked this time period.
Guyana	March 19, 2001	Legislative	Supported	Yes	Following the election "hundreds of persons" demonstrated that they were disenfranchised, but without necessarily declaring a clear party allegiance. Once a recount resulted in no change to the distribution of seats, the opposition began to protest government appointments with demonstrations, some peaceful and some violent.
Haiti	May 21, 2000	Legislative	Supported	No	Former president Aristide supporters protested the delay in releasing official results after the election.
Haiti	February 7, 2006	Presidential & Legislative	No	Yes	Haitians reported as protesting alleged fraud, but not linked to any opposition parties.
Hungary	April 7, 2002	Legislative	Supported	No	Some small demonstrations and denouncement of the election results by the leader of two small parties on the far right followed Hungary's 2002 parliamentary election.

(continued)

(*continued*)

Country	Date	Election Type	Opposition Initiated or Supported?	Violence?	Description
India	January 3, 1980	Legislative	No	No	In West Bengal, hundreds protested what they called an anti-Bengali campaign by Assamese students to remove "foreigners" from voting rolls. Most of the protesters were thought to be part of PM Indira Gandhi's "youth wing."
India	November 22, 1989	Legislative	No	No	Protesters demonstrated in front of India's Election Commission offices to protest vote fraud and violence in elections. The demonstration was organized by a nonpartisan group called "Independent Initiative," but most of the slogans were against PM Rajiv Gandhi and his Congress Party.
India	April 27, 1996	Presidential	No	Yes	Post-election protests occurred in Kashmir.
Indonesia	June 7, 1999	Legislative	Supported	Yes	Supporters of PDI Perjuangan and the Democratic People's Party (PRD) staged a demonstration at the governor's office demanding a rerun of the election.
Indonesia	July 5, 2004	Presidential	No	No	Flawed ballots caused voters to protest, but no party affiliation was noted. Student demonstrations were also reported.
Iran	February 20, 2004	Legislative	No	Yes	Demonstrators were reported protesting manipulation of the vote count in the South and clashed with police. There was no mention of reform candidates or supporters directly involved.

Country	Date	Type			Description
Jamaica	December 15, 1983	Legislative	Initiated	No	PNP leader Michael Manley addressed a group of demonstrators before the newly elected parliament's swearing-in.
Jamaica	February 9, 1989	Legislative	No	Yes	Supporters of both major parties accused each other of fraud. Both sides protested and prepared for assaults from members of other party.
Jamaica	December 18, 1997	Legislative	No	Yes	Voters backing the losing JLP put up flaming roadblocks to protest the stabbing death of a poll worker (but party members were reported as not supporting the protests). Police responded with gunfire.
Korea	March 25, 1981	Legislative	No	No	Students staged an anti-government protest at Sung Kyun Kwan University.
Korea	March 25, 1992	Presidential & Legislative	No	Yes	Students in four Korean cities staged protests against vote rigging.
Korea	December 6, 1987	Presidential	Initiated	Yes	Opposition leaders called for protest following the elections in Korea, accusing the government of vote rigging. Their supporters responded with mass demonstrations.
Kuwait	October 5, 1992	Legislative	No	No	Kuwaiti women protested to demand the right to vote.
Kuwait	July 5, 2003	Legislative	No	No	Kuwaiti women protested for the right to vote.
Kyrgyzstan	February 20, 2000	Legislative	No	Yes	Protesters in Bishkek seized the constitutional courthouse demanding an annulment of second-round results. These demonstrations were not attributed to political parties.

(continued)

Country	Date	Election Type	Opposition Initiated or Supported?	Violence?	Description
Kyrgyzstan	February 27, 2005	Legislative	Initiated	Yes	Protests took place both in individual districts where opposition candidates lost and in the capital. Opposition supporters picketed and in some cases stormed administrative buildings demanding election results be reviewed. During these protests, opposition parties and their supporters managed to seize control of the state television.
Kazakhstan	October 10, 1999	Legislative	Initiated	No	Opposition party leaders and supporters held a "sanctioned meeting" to protest violations of election law during the elections.
Kazakhstan	September 19, 2004	Legislative	Supported	No	"Unsanctioned picketing" outside the Eurasian Industrial Association following elections was attributed to political opposition parties.
Lebanon	August 23, 1992	Legislative	Initiated	No	Lebanese Christians called a three-day general strike to protest controversial elections.
Lesotho	May 23, 1998	Legislative	Initiated	Yes	Opposition supporters in Lesotho organized two weeks of protests, which turned violent. The central business district of the capital, Maseru, was burned.
Liberia	October 11, 2005	Presidential & Legislative	Initiated	Yes	CDC filed an official protest over conduct of election; CDC youths took to the streets of Monrovia and were dispersed after they become violent.
Macedonia	October 16, 1994	Presidential & Legislative	Initiated	No	All the main opposition parties and their supporters staged a peaceful demonstration to protest what they perceived to be first-round election fraud.

Country	Date	Election	Role	Violence	Description
Macedonia	October 31, 1999	Presidential	Initiated	No	Post-election protests erupted following the presidential election, with the opposition alleging fraud. Widespread rigging was reported.
Macedonia	April 14, 2004	Presidential	Initiated	Yes	Opposition supporters demonstrated while the leader of the opposition VMRO-DPMNE, Nikola Gruevski, called on the electoral commission to annul the results of the election.
Macedonia	July 05, 2006	Legislative	Initiated	No	The VMRO-DPMNE, led by Gruevski, won the most seats, sparking a wave of protest by supporters of two political parties that formed an electoral coalition to represent ethnic Albanians in Macedonia. No protest was reported from the main opposition party that had controlled the government prior to the 2006 election.
Madagascar	October 7, 1982	Presidential	Initiated	Yes	The losing candidate in the 1982 presidential election organized mass demonstrations that turned violent, resulting in looting in the capital of Madagascar.
Madagascar	April 6, 1989	Presidential	Initiated	Yes	Opposition parties publicly criticized the conduct of the election, accusing the incumbent of fraud, and riots broke out in the capital.
Madagascar	December 16, 2001	Presidential	Initiated	Yes	Supporters of opposition candidate Ravalomanana's began weeks of demonstration when he was not declared the winner.
Malawi	June 15, 1999	Presidential & Legislative	Supported	Yes	Opposition supporters clashed with government supporters outside the country's high court. Opposition supporters were accusing the government of rigging the election.

(continued)

Country	Date	Election Type	Opposition Initiated or Supported?	Violence?	Description
Malawi	May 20, 2004	Presidential & Legislative	Initiated	Yes	Opposition parties in Malawi publicly objected to the results of the May 2004 presidential election and accused the country's election commission and state radio of fabricating results, which sparked violent demonstrations.
Mauritania	March 6, 1992	Legislative	No	No	Protests in reaction to disputed elections were reported, with no mention of party affiliations.
Mexico	July 7, 1985	Legislative	Initiated	Yes	PAN supporters in the city of Monterrey protested alleged election fraud during the elections. In particular, they believed the election of the governor in that state had been rigged.
Mexico	July 6, 1988	Presidential & Legislative	Initiated	No	Encouraged by opposition leaders, supporters held marches through Mexico City and blocked main border crossings.
Mexico	July 6, 2006	Presidential & Legislative	Initiated	Yes	Mass demonstrations were mounted in Mexico City for months by supporters of opposition candidate Lopez-Obrador, who accused the incumbent PAN of rigging the election.
Mongolia	June 27, 2004	Legislative	Initiated	No	Opposition parties organized protests. Demonstrators amassed for rallies and took over state broadcast media to accuse the government of fraud.
Morocco	June 25, 1993	Legislative	Supported	Yes	The opposition demanded the cancellation of the results of the elections concerning four ministers. Supporters took to the streets in protest and more than 600 women marched on the Royal Palace.

Niger	July 7, 1996	Presidential & Legislative	Supported	No	Post-election protest occurred as opposition parties alleged fraud. Trade unions supported the opposition claims, calling for general strikes across the country, which they claimed were well supported.
Nigeria	August 6, 1983	Presidential	Supported	Yes	Protests were reported in response to the incumbent's reelection, which the opposition complained was the result of fraud.
Nigeria	June 12, 1993	Presidential & Legislative	Supported	Yes	Protests occurred in response to the incumbent's sudden annulment of the election in the course of vote counting when it became apparent that a Southerner, named Abiola, might win.
Nigeria	April 25, 1998	Legislative	Supported	Yes	Demonstrations followed the elections and protesters clashed with the police.
Nigeria	April 12, 2003	Legislative	Initiated	No	Although most opportunities for mass demonstrations were blocked by government denial of permits, opposition supporters used other means to express their support for the opposition protest. There was a movement to wear black arm- or wristbands, and many supporters used other public events, such as the inauguration of governors, to protest Obasanjo's reelection.
Nigeria	April 19, 2003	Presidential	Initiated	No	Opposition supporters protested the election in the Niger Delta region and claimed that six people had been killed by the police or army.

(continued)

Country	Date	Election Type	Opposition Initiated or Supported?	Violence?	Description
Pakistan	February 25, 1985	Legislative	Initiated	Yes	Opposition activists from the Movement of Restoration Democracy were arrested to prevent planned protest demonstrations, but demonstrations occurred anyway; buses were set on fire.
Panama	May 6, 1984	Presidential	Initiated	Yes	Violent protest from supporters of the defeated candidate, Arnulfo Arias stemmed from accusations of fraud.
Panama	May 7, 1989	Presidential	Initiated	Yes	Marchers led by opposition presidential candidate protested the seizure of ballots by Noriega's soldiers to prevent tabulation of election results.
Paraguay	August 13, 2000	Presidential	No	Yes	Incumbent supporters rallied to protest early projections that showed the opposition candidate winning.
Peru	April 9, 2000	Presidential	Initiated	Yes	The main opposition challenger to Fujimori's presidency, Alejandro Toledo, withdrew from the runoff alleging fraud in the first round of voting, which brought on massive protests organized by his supporters. There was some violence associated with the protests.
Philippines	April 7, 1978	Legislative	Initiated	Yes	Two days after the election, opposition leaders organized marches and peaceful demonstrations to protest fraud on the part of Marcos.

Country	Date	Election type	Initiated/Supported		Description
Philippines	May 14, 1984	Legislative	Initiated	Yes	Violent protests followed the 1984 elections, when the opposition charged Marcos with vote rigging.
Philippines	February 7, 1986	Presidential	Initiated	No	Opposition candidate Aquino orchestrated a large-scale protest movement that included nonviolent demonstrations and strikes.
Philippines	May 11, 1987	Legislative	Initiated	No	Protest and fraud accusations followed this election.
Philippines	May 11, 1992	Legislative	Initiated	No	Protests erupted when only about 600,000 votes separated the first- and second-place finishers. The second-place finisher accused Ramos (the winner) of fraud and led protests in her home province.
Philippines	May 8, 1995	Presidential	Supported	Yes	Some violent protest and criticism from opposition candidates followed the election, but it was not clear that the opposition was directly responsible for organizing the protests.
Philippines	May 10, 2004	Presidential & Legislative	Initiated	No	The losing opposition candidate, a popular actor, accused the government of fraud, and mass demonstrations followed the elections.
Poland	June 4, 1989	Legislative	Supported	No	Anticommunist demonstrations by various "illegal" organizations (mostly representing students and young people) occurred three days after a Solidarity victory at the polls.
Poland	September 19, 1993	Presidential	No	No	Anarchist Federation attempted to stage an anti-election demonstration.

(continued)

Country	Date	Election Type	Opposition Initiated or Supported?	Violence?	Description
Poland	September 25, 2005	Legislative	Initiated	No	Supporters of two small right-wing parties protested after the elections that they had not been granted equal media access.
Romania	May 20, 1990	Legislative	No	Yes	Riots and protests occurred, with no clear identification of those responsible for anti-government demonstrations – though the government reported trying to find out who was behind the demonstrations. Government-supported miners with clubs were brought in to commit violence against protesters.
Romania	September 27, 1992	Legislative	No	No	Student demonstrators marched in support of Democratic National Salvation Front, which won the elections.
Romania	November 3, 1996	Presidential	No	No	A rally was held after the first round of voting to support the opposition candidate in the second round.
Romania	November 28, 2004	Presidential & Legislative	Supported	No	Young supporters of opposition presidential candidate rallied between first and second rounds of voting to protest fraud in the first round, though nuclear criticisms came from the opposition candidate.
Russia	March 14, 2004	Presidential	No	No	Three million people checked the "against all candidates" box in the Russian election.

Country	Date	Election Type		Protest Description
Senegal	February 28, 1988	Presidential	Supported	Yes	Government allegations were made that the opposition candidate incited violence after the election; young supporters protested outside of the courthouse at the candidate's subsequent trial.
Senegal	May 9, 1993	Presidential & Legislative	Supported	Yes	Protests of reported fraud in the elections included some "militants of the opposition parties."
South Africa	August 22, 1984	Legislative	No	Yes	United Democratic Front (anti-apartheid organization) and students protested elections for separate chambers for coloreds and Indians.
South Africa	May 6, 1987	Legislative	No	Yes	Workers, students and church members protested white-only elections.
South Africa	September 6, 1989	Presidential	No	Yes	Black demonstrators clashed with police as they protested for the right to vote.
Syria	November 9, 1981	Legislative	No	Yes	Anti-election demonstrators clashed with the army. No specific actors were identified as organizing or supporting protests.
Taiwan	December 21, 1992	Legislative	No	No	Supporters of several individual candidates protested their candidate's loss, but there were no coordinated efforts by opposition DPP.
Taiwan	March 18, 2000	Presidential & Legislative	No	Yes	Anti-government protests turned violent. The victorious opposition candidate urged calm.
Taiwan	March 20, 2004	Presidential	Supported	Yes	Tens of thousands of supporters for Taiwan opposition leader Lien Chan held protests across the island to condemn the unfair election.

(continued)

(*continued*)

Country	Date	Election Type	Opposition Initiated or Supported?	Violence?	Description
Thailand	January 6, 2001	Legislative	No	Yes	Voters in southeastern Thailand protested, upset over irregularities; 500 protesters repeatedly halted vote counting by occupying vote counting centers. Rioting was also reported.
Thailand	April 2, 2006	Legislative	No	Yes	Voters were arrested for publicly tearing up ballots.
Togo	June 14, 1998	Presidential	Initiated	Yes	Demonstrators, many wearing red scarfs and bandanas, shouted opposition slogans and called for the ouster of President Gnassingbe Eyadema. Security forces retaliated by burning the campaign offices of Gilchrist Olympio, the country's main opposition candidate.
Togo	October 27, 2002	Legislative	Initiated	Yes	Around 1,000 people demonstrated to protest against the party victory of President Gnassingbe. Protesters set tires ablaze in the streets, smashed car windows, and attacked shops in the capital.
Togo	June 1, 2003	Presidential	Initiated	Yes	Opposition supporters burned down the mayor's office and destroyed ballot boxes in the town of Tsevie, 35 kilometers north of Lome, after they heard a report that the boxes had been stuffed by the ruling party with votes favoring current president Gnassingbe Eyadema.

Togo	April 24, 2005	Presidential	Initiated	Yes	The announcement that Faure Gnassingbe, son of the country's long time ruler Gnassingbe Eyadema, won the presidential contest sparked off violent protests by supporters of the opposition candidate, who had alleged electoral fraud and proclaimed himself the winner on Wednesday.
Uganda	February 23, 2006	Presidential & Legislative	Supported	Yes	Some scattered protests followed Uganda's 2006 election, which the opposition claimed it had won.
Ukraine	October 31, 2004	Presidential	Initiated	No	After opposition candidate Viktor Yushenko lost the 2004 presidential election, his supporters staged mass demonstrations in protest.
Uruguay	November 27, 1994	Legislative	No	Yes	Street protests and rock throwing following the election were blamed on the leftist coalition Broad Front by both incumbent and main opposition parties.
Venezuela	July 30, 2000	Legislative	Supported	Yes	Clashes reported between supporters of incumbent Chavez and the opposition. Rocks and bottles were thrown. Troops also had to quell violent protest in southwestern Bolivia after the incumbent governor lost to a pro-Chavez candidate.
Venezuela	December 4, 2005	Legislative	Initiated	No	Massive street demonstration in Caracas, when Chavez was out of the country, called for a fair vote in the upcoming presidential elections, presumably in response to alleged fraud in the December legislative election.

(continued)

(continued)

Country	Date	Election Type	Opposition Initiated or Supported?	Violence?	Description
Zambia	November 8, 1996	Legislative	Initiated	No	Barred opposition candidate Kenneth Kaunda followed an election boycott by leading demonstrators demanding the removal of the incumbent government.
Zambia	December 27, 2001	Presidential & Legislative	Initiated	Yes	Opposition parties, divided during the election, united to stage demonstrations calling for a recount.
Zambia	September 20, 2006	Presidential & Legislative	Initiated	Yes	Violent demonstrations erupted when the incumbent, Mwanawasa, was declared the winner. These demonstrations were said to evoke a sense of déjà-vu because they so resembled the aftermath of the 2001 elections.
Zimbabwe	June 24, 2000	Presidential	No	Yes	Zimbabwe congress of trade unions organized a strike to protest political violence.
Zimbabwe	March 31, 2005	Legislative	Supported	No	Demonstrations followed the opposition's public rejection of election results.

APPENDIX D. Election-Related Reforms

Country	Previous Election Date	Opposition Accepted?	Description
Albania	March 31, 1991	Yes	Helsinki Final Act confirms a commitment to democracy and human rights.
Algeria	November 16, 1995	No	Constitutional reform consisting of a new law on political parties and a modified electoral law, seen as disadvantaging opposition parties.
Argentina	October 14, 2001	Yes	Lower house passes an amendment to limit duration of campaigns and to require parties to select candidates via open internal elections.
Armenia	July 5, 1995	Yes	Increased number of signatures required for nomination and financial deposit required from every presidential nominee, returned only if candidate receives more than 5% of the vote.
Armenia	March 16, 1998	Yes	Composition of the Central Election Commission changed.
Azerbaijan	October 3, 1993	Yes	New electoral law before 1995 election. 125-member legislature filled with a mix of single-member districts and PR. More restrictive registration requirements for candidates and parties.
Azerbaijan	October 11, 1998	No	Before the 2000 elections, Law on the Central Election Commission changed the number of CEC members and their method of selection: 18 members, 1/3 representing majority party in parliament, 1/3 representing the minority, and 1/3 nonpartisan. Seen as manipulated by incumbent.
Azerbaijan	November 5, 2000	No	Referendum on 39 constitutional amendments, including further changes to party registration laws and CEC composition.
Bangladesh	March 3, 1988	Yes	Referendum reestablishing parliamentary government after a period of military rule.

(continued)

(continued)

Country	Previous Election Date	Opposition Accepted?	Description
Bangladesh	February 15, 1996	Yes	New constitutional amendment to install neutral caretaker government before every election.
Bangladesh	June 12, 1996	Yes	Military authorized to arrest without warrant any lawbreakers during general elections.
Bolivia	May 7, 1989	Yes	Electoral law reforms in 1991: polling-station-level vote results cannot be revised; new rules for selecting members of Electoral Court.
Bolivia	June 6, 1993	Yes	Presidential and vice presidential terms extended from four years to five; dates of presidential and legislative elections separated.
Bolivia	June 30, 2002	Yes	Constitutional amendments allowing for referendums and candidates to run as independents.
Botswana	October 15, 1994	Yes	Constitutional amendments enacted in 1997, limiting presidency to aggregate period of 10 years, allowing postal votes from citizens abroad, and reducing qualifying age of candidates to 18.
Brazil	November 15, 1978	Yes	1980 legislation opened party formation beyond two legal political parties. Legislation before the 1982 elections banned electoral coalitions and required parties to stand candidates for all elected offices.
Brazil	November 15, 1986	Yes	New constitution enacted as part of transition to democracy.
Brazil	October 3, 1994	Yes	Constitutional amendment allowing incumbent governors and mayors to run for reelection.
Brazil	October 6, 2002	Yes	Senate bill revoking reelection of president, governors, and mayors; also reform to reduce campaign costs.
Bulgaria	November 11, 2001	No	Government introduces a lottery to encourage voter turnout – those who vote are eligible for prizes.

182

Country	Date		Description
Cambodia	May 23, 1993	No	National Election Commission established before the 1998 elections.
Cambodia	July 26, 1998	Yes	Election laws amended to reform composition of the National Electoral commisson, at the behest of prime minister.
Cambodia	July 27, 2003	Yes	Constitutional amendment reduces the number of seats needed to form a government from two-thirds to one-half plus one.
Cameroon	October 11, 1992	No	Constitutional reforms in 1995 established a Senate and Regional Assemblies
Cote d'Ivoire	October 28, 1990	No	New electoral laws passed in 1994 combined different laws for various types of elections into one electoral code and, perhaps most notably, did NOT produce an independent electoral commission.
Central African Republic	July 31, 1987	Yes	1991 constitutional reform ending official dominance of single party (membership in the party had been voluntary since before the 1987 election, which saw some "opposition" candidates).
Central African Republic	November 22, 1998	Yes	Establishment of an electoral commission.
Chad	May 03, 2006	No	Agreement to revise electoral lists, renew citizen voting cards, and reduce incumbent influence by changing electoral commission. Talks boycotted by two main opposition parties.
Chile	December 12, 1999	Yes	Liberalization of press laws improving free speech.
Colombia	May 31, 1998	Yes	Constitutional reform allows presidential reelection.
Colombia	May 26, 2002	Yes	Reorganization of political parties, requirement of 2% votes for legal status, punishment for political leaders considered disloyal ("Transfuga").
Comoros	March 6, 1996	No	Constitutional reform, adopted in October 1996, allows for reelection.
Costa Rica	February 6, 1994	Yes	Term for president, legislators, and municipal councilors extended from four years to five.
Costa Rica	February 03, 2002	Yes	Qualified end to ban on presidential reelection in 2003. Presidents now allowed to run for reelection eight years after their first term in office.

(*continued*)

Country	Previous Election Date	Opposition Accepted?	Description
Dominican Republic	May 16, 1990	Yes	Electoral law reformed in 1992 to increase the number of electoral commission members, to change the organization of the electoral commission, and to create a new voter roll.
Dominican Republic	May 16, 1994	Yes	Reform of 14 articles of the Dominican Constitution, including a ban on presidential reelection and the possibility of a runoff vote in the event that no one candidate obtains an absolute majority.
Dominican Republic	May 16, 2002	Yes	National Congress (senators and deputies) divided the electoral court into a chamber for disputes and another one for administrative matters.
Ecuador	May 1, 1994	Yes	Independent candidates permitted, approved in a plebiscite in August 1994.
Ecuador	May 19, 1996	Yes	Assembly members approved an increase in the number of deputies in the new Congress to be installed in 1998 to 120 members.
Egypt	June 7, 1979	No	New disciplinary codes to address "indiscipline" and permit harsh government responses to public demonstration; Electoral Law No. 114 introduces PR, outlaws independent candidates.
Egypt	May 27, 1984	Yes	Law No. 188 in 1986 abolished reservation of seats for women.
Egypt	April 6, 1987	No	Electoral system amended to accommodate some independents.
Egypt	June 8, 1989	No	1990 Law No. 201 returns to two-round, absolute majority system; PR abolished completely.
Egypt	October 18, 2000	Yes	Reforms to allow multi-candidate competition for presidency.
Equatorial Guinea	November 21, 1993	Yes	Prior to local elections in 1995, the incumbent government allowed the UN to help draft a new voter register and agreed to international observers for future elections.
Gabon	September 16, 1990	Yes	Reforms reduced presidential term to five years, put maximum age limit on presidency of 70 years, established a deposit refund, and allowed independent candidates to run.

184

Gabon	December 5, 1993	Yes	Reform package approved by 1995 referendum introduces constitutional government and does away with elements of dictatorship.
Gabon	December 15, 1996	No	1997 reforms extended presidential term to seven years, lifted the 70-year-age ban, and introduced nonelected post of vice president.
Gambia	April 04, 1977	Yes	1982, direct election of president introduced.
Gambia	April 29, 1992	No	New constitution passed in 1996, which lowered voting age from 21 to 18.
Ghana	June 18, 1979	Yes	New constitution approved by referendum in April 1992; ban on opposition parties lifted in May 1992.
Georgia	October 11, 1992	No	New constitution with a strong presidency; opposition leaders characterize it as severely slanted in favor of the president.
Georgia	November 5, 1995	Yes	1999 amendment to the constitution, introducing one nation-wide district for PR and increasing threshold to 7%.
Georgia	March 28, 2004	No	Decreased PR threshold to 5% and increased number of directly elected lawmakers. Opposition charges these reforms are aimed at weakening their electoral performance.
Guatemala	March 7, 1982	No	Draconian restrictions on political and press freedoms.
Guatemala	November 11, 1990	Yes	New congress reduced from 116 to 95 seats. Supreme Electoral Tribunal granted power to call early congressional elections as soon as August.
Guyana	December 15, 1980	Yes	1985 reforms improved provisions for overseas voting, established an independent electoral commission, updated voter lists, and gave government control of printing ballot papers.
Guyana	December 09, 1985	Yes	1990 reforms established preliminary counting of votes at polling locations, restructured electoral commission, and (once again) promised new voter registers.
Guyana	December 15, 1997	Yes	The electoral system was modified before the 2001 election, as part of the Herdmanston Accord to settle a national crisis. A regional element was added to the PR system.

(continued)

(*continued*)

Country	Previous Election Date	Opposition Accepted?	Description
Guyana	August 28, 2006	Yes	"Recall" provision supported by both incumbent and major opposition parties: Legislators who are elected on party lists can be recalled if, once elected, they declare they no longer back the party under which they won their seat.
Haiti	December 16, 1990	Yes	Establishment of a nine-member council to run national and local elections.
Haiti	November 26, 2000	Yes	Government and opposition negotiate to create a new election management body with help of OAS.
Honduras	November 29, 1981	No	1985 legislation permits more than one presidential candidate from a given party.
Honduras	November 25, 2001		Constitutional reform introducing referendums and plebiscites on the initiative of 10 legislators in the 128-seat congress, the president, or 6% of voters.
India	January 3, 1980	No	September 1980 PM Gandhi assumes wide-ranging powers of preventative detention.
Indonesia	May 29, 1997	Yes	Sweeping reforms to electoral law, political parties, and the number of seats in the next People's Consultative Assembly.
Iran	October 23, 1998	Yes	1999 law required council of guardians to account for disqualifications and accept petitions.
Israel	July 23, 1984	No	1992 legislation introduced direct election of prime minister; not applied until 1996 election.
Jamaica	December 15, 1983	Yes	Voter registers updated; government assumes responsibility for printing ballots.
Jordan	November 08, 1989	Yes	In 1991, 32-year-old martial law decree is lifted and political parties reauthorized; prior to 1993 elections electoral system changed to SNTV by government, while parliament is in recess.

Jordan	June 17, 2003	No	2007, election of mayors and municipal council members introduced, part of what king called "homegrown democratic reforms."
Kenya	December 29, 1992	Yes	KANU and opposition ally passed minor constitutional and political concessions in October 1997.
Kuwait	January 27, 1975	Yes	1980 reform increases number of constituencies from 5 to 25 to limit government influence in large constituencies.
Kuwait	October 5, 1992	Yes	1994: franchise extended to naturalized citizens.
Kuwait	July 5, 2003	Yes	2005: franchise extended to women
Kuwait	June 29, 2006	Yes	July 2006 reform reduces the number of constituencies from 25 to 5, in line with opposition demands to curb corruption.
Kyrgyzstan	July 10, 2005	Yes	New 2006 constitution designed to limit presidential powers
Kazakhstan	December 1, 1991	No	First post-soviet constitution enacted in 1993; party registration rules depress new party entry.
Kazakhstan	March 7, 1994	Yes	Second constitution enacted in 1995, before December elections.
Lebanon	August 18, 1996	Yes	Voter ID cards introduced for the 2000 election.
Lesotho	May 23, 1998	Yes	In October 1998, opposition and government agreed on the formation of an Independent Political Authority to oversee elections.
Mauritania	December 12, 1997	Yes	2000 reforms included public finance for parties (conditional on achieving a particular municipal election threshold); PR introduced for 20% of assembly seats; candidate registration fees reduced.
Malaysia	July 8, 1978	No	1981 restrictions on freedom of speech; only politicians, political parties, or registered political movements permitted to make comment on government affairs.
Malaysia	March 21, 2004	No	2007 constitutional amendment extending tenure of head of the Election Commission, whom opposition claimed is biased.
Mexico	July 4, 1976	Yes	1977 reform of method of electing members to House of Deputies; 100 of 400 seats reserved for PR.

(continued)

(continued)

Country	Previous Election Date	Opposition Accepted?	Description
Mexico	July 4, 1982	Yes	Reforms to Senate election rules to improve access for minority parties.
Mexico	July 7, 1985	Yes	1989 constitutional reforms supported by PRI and PAN to award an absolute majority in the lower house to party winning 35% of vote.
Mexico	August 18, 1991	Yes	1993 reform supported by PRI and PAN put an upper bound on number of seats a party could win.
Mexico	August 21, 1994	Yes	1996 electoral law increased threshold for representation in Multi-Member Constituencies to 2%.
Mexico	July 02, 2006	Yes	2007 law bans political parties from buying advertisement on radio and TV.
Mali	April 12, 1992	Yes	1996 electoral law created independent election management body.
Mongolia	July 22, 1990	Yes	1992 constitution introduces directly elected president and unicameral parliament; 1992 electoral law created multi-member constituencies elected by plurality rule.
Mongolia	June 6, 1993	No	January 1996 changes to electoral law create single-member districts with qualified majority rule of 25%. Opposition wanted PR.
Morocco	October 2, 1984	No	Reforms approved by referendum limit the king's right to dissolve parliament and enshrine human rights in the constitution. Opposition parties encouraged boycott of the referendum.
Morocco	June 25, 1993	No	PR electoral system approved in 1996 referendum.
Morocco	November 14, 1997	Yes	1999 reforms under new king allowed political exiles to return and increased freedom of speech.
Nicaragua	October 20, 1996	No	2000 electoral law politicized the electoral council and made the outgoing president immune from prosecution.
Nigeria	June 12, 1993	No	Suspension of constitution under Abacha after controversial elections.

Niger	February 27, 1993	No	As part of 1996 military coup, parliament dissolved and political parties banned.
Niger	October 17, 1999	No	Ban on political parties and party activities lifted.
Pakistan	February 25, 1985	Yes	1988 reforms to electoral laws meant to combat cheating and streamline the electoral process; political parties also permitted.
Pakistan	April 30, 2002	No	Constitutional amendments strengthen presidential powers at the expense of the legislature.
Panama	May 6, 1984	No	1987 ban on public protest.
Papua New Guinea	June 13, 1987	Yes	Photos of party leaders added next to party names on ballots to help illiterate voters.
Peru	April 8, 1990	No	1992 Fujimori suspends the constitution and the judiciary.
Peru	April 9, 2000	Yes	With the help of the OAS, government and opposition amend the constitution to reduce presidential and legislative terms from five years to one, so that fresh elections could be held in 2001.
Philippines	June 16, 1981	Yes	Electoral reforms included the election of assemblymen by province instead of region, the abolition of bloc voting, opposition representation on citizens' electoral committees, and coalitions among political parties. These reforms were apparently made to appease the opposition, including a promise to temporarily lift Marcos's powers to detain suspected subversives during the election and draw up new voter registration lists.
Philippines	February 7, 1986	Yes	Constitution of 1987 reinstated the basic structure of electoral politics pre-Marcos, gave all registered parties the right to appoint poll watchers, and also removed partisan representatives from the Board of Election Inspectors.
Philippines	May 8, 1995	Yes	Party list electoral system introduced for the 1998 election.
Papua New Guinea	June 13, 1987	No	Changed the length of grace period for no confidence motions from 6 months after new election to 18 months. Opposition leader and deputy voted against change.

(continued)

(*continued*)

Country	Previous Election Date	Opposition Accepted?	Description
Poland	November 5, 1995	Yes	New constitution enacted in 1997.
Korea, Republic of	February 12, 1985	Yes	1987 reforms included direct presidential elections and the release from prison of hundreds of political opposition members.
Korea, Republic of	March 25, 1992	Yes	1994–6 various reforms implemented including redrawing constituency boundaries, instituting local-level elections, and expanding freedom of expression for political opposition.
South Africa	April 29, 1981	Yes	1983 constitution creates representative body for "colored" and Asian citizens in South Africa.
South Africa	April 06, 1989	Yes	1993 formal end to apartheid.
South Africa	April 26, 1994	No	1996 new constitution adopted. 1998 law requires voter ID cards with bar codes.
El Salvador	March 19, 1989	Yes	1991 reforms included the creation of a Supreme Electoral Tribunal and gave political parties a greater role in the organization and updating of the electoral register.
Senegal	February 28, 1988	Yes	1992 new electoral rules established voter registers, voter ID cards, and the use of indelible ink to prevent repeat voting. Approved by both incumbent and opposition parties.
Senegal	February 27, 2000	Yes	A new constitution enshrined the right to form opposition parties and confirmed the status of the prime minister.
Sierra Leone	May 6, 1977	Yes	1991 constitution returns the country to multiparty rule.
Singapore	August 28, 1993	No	Electoral reforms creating more multi-seat races in future elections; criticized by opposition as favoring incumbent party.

Country	Date		Description
Sri Lanka	July 21, 1977	Yes	Constitutional reforms in 1978 changed parliamentary terms to six years and introduced PR. Presidential elections introduced in 1981.
Sri Lanka	October 20, 1982	Yes	1983 Emergency Regulations curtail political and civil rights.
Sri Lanka	October 10, 2000	Yes	Creation of independent electoral commission in 2001.
Sri Lanka	November 17, 2005	Yes	Unspecified electoral reforms agreed upon by all parties.
Sudan	March 6, 1996	No	New constitution enacted in 1998 during civil war; considered controversial for lack of opposition input.
Syria	November 30, 1998	Yes	Implementation of martial law frozen in 2000.
Tajikistan	February 26, 1995	Yes	Constitutional reforms approved by referendum in 1998 include legalization of religiously oriented parties and bicameral parliament.
Taiwan	December 6, 1986	No	1992 constitutional reforms decrease president's term from six years to four and introduce direct election of the provincial governor and mayors of two largest cities; criticized by the opposition as superficial.
Taiwan	December 21, 1992	Yes	Direct presidential election introduced in 1994 and legislator terms extended from three years to four.
Taiwan	December 2, 1995	Yes	1997 reforms suspended elections for provincial governor in a move to eliminate provincial-level bureaucracy.
Taiwan	March 20, 2004	Yes	2005 reforms required referendum for future constitutional amendments and reduced the number of seats in parliament from 225 to 113.
Thailand	April 4, 1976	Yes	1978 constitution prohibits independent candidates.
Thailand	July 24, 1988	Yes	1992 end of state of emergency; further constitutional reforms to reduce power of military-appointed Senate and to require PM is a member of parliament.
Thailand	September 13, 1992	Yes	1995 reforms lower voting age to 18 and reduce number of Senate seats to 2/3 number of elected MPs.
Thailand	November 17, 1996	Yes	1997 reforms require direct election of senators and minimum of a bachelor's degree for candidates to be eligible to run for parliament, compulsory voting, and an independent electoral commission.

(continued)

(continued)

Country	Previous Election Date	Opposition Accepted?	Description
Togo	February 6, 1994	No	1997 modifications to the electoral law changed composition of electoral commission and weakened its position. Opposition boycotted the vote that ratified these changes.
Togo	March 21, 1999	No	New electoral code that for the first time sets up an independent commission to oversee future ballots in 2000. Various amendments to electoral law in 2002 such as residency requirements for presidential candidates seen as move to disqualify opposition candidate.
Togo	October 27, 2002	Yes	December 2002: elimination of term limits for presidency.
Togo	April 24, 2005	Yes	2006 political reform agreement between incumbent and opposition.
Tunisia	April 2, 1989	Yes	1993 reforms to the electoral system established 25 multi-member constituencies.
Tunisia	October 24, 1999	Yes	2002 constitutional reform bill approved by referendum.
Turkey	October 14, 1979	Yes	1983 Political Parties Bill bans those in government or main opposition as of September, 1980, from political competition for 10 years.
Turkey	November 6, 1983	No	1987 referendum restores political rights of those banned in 1983. The day after the referendum, PM Ozal declares party leadership eligible to nominate candidates (rather than being selected through primaries under previous law); main opposition party challenged this change.
Turkey	October 20, 1991	Yes	1995 constitutional reforms allow university professors and students to join political parties, lowers voting age to 18, and increases parliamentary seats from 450 to 550.
Turkey	April 18, 1999	Yes	2001 constitutional reforms increase freedom of expression.
Turkey	November 3, 2002	Yes	2003 reforms make it more difficult for courts to ban political parties.

Uruguay	November 27, 1994	Yes	Electoral reforms limiting parties to one presidential candidate, chosen through primary elections; presidential runoff also instituted.
Uzbekistan	December 26, 2004	Yes	2006 reforms meant to strengthen the role of political parties.
Venezuela	December 4, 1988	No	1992 constitutional reforms impose harsh restrictions on press freedoms; widely criticized by opposition.
Venezuela	December 5, 1993	Yes	1997 electoral reforms automate the electoral process, update voter registries, and establish an independent electoral commission
Venezuela	December 6, 1998	No	New constitution approved by referendum in 2000.
Yemen	July 5, 1988	Yes	1992 election law in place for 1993 elections, first to allow official party registration; plurality electoral formula.
Yemen	April 27, 1993	Yes	Reform to include candidate symbols on the ballot for the 1997 election.
Yemen	April 27, 1997	Yes	1999 reform of electoral list system provides more openness in the nomination procedures elections and allows candidates to receive financial aid from Yemeni citizens.
Yemen	September 23, 1999	Yes	2001 constitutional reform extending terms of president and legislature approved by referendum.
Zambia	October 31, 1991	No	1996 constitutional amendment changes eligibility requirement for presidential candidates; seen as move to disqualify opposition candidate.
Zimbabwe	June 24, 2000	No	2001 reforms allowed police to ban political gatherings and prosecute anyone who attended a meeting where the government is criticized. They effectively banned opposition political parties and ended freedoms of association, speech, and movement.
Zimbabwe	March 9, 2002	Yes	Wide-ranging electoral reforms were adopted in 2004, including establishment of an independent election commission, a single day of voting instead of two, and counting of votes at polling centers.

References

Abazov, Rafis. 2003. The Parliamentary Elections in Kyrgyzstan, February 2000. *Electoral Studies* 22: 545–52.

Acemoglu, Daron and James A. Robinson. 2006. *Economic Origins of Dictatorship and Democracy*. Cambridge: Cambridge University Press.

Ahmed, Nizam. 2001. Bangladesh. In *Elections in Asia and the Pacific: A Data Handbook*. Dieter Nohlen, Florian Grotz and Christof Hartmann, eds. Oxford: Oxford University Press: 515–52.

Alamdari, Kazem. 2005. The Power Structure of the Islamic Republic of Iran: Transition from Populism to Clientelism and Militarization of the Government. *Third World Quarterly* 26(8): 1285–1301.

Barkan, Joel D. 2000. Protracted Transitions among Africa's New Democracies. *Democratization* 7(3): 227–43.

Beaulieu, Emily and Susan D. Hyde. 2009. In the Shadow of Democracy Promotion: Strategic Manipulation, International Observers, and Election Boycotts. *Comparative Political Studies* 42(3): 392–415.

Beber, Bernd and Alexandra Scacco. 2012. What the Numbers Say: A Digit-Based Test for Election Fraud. *Political Analysis* 20(2): 211–234.

Beck, Thorsten, George Clarke, Alberto Groff, Philip Keefer, and Patrick Walsh. 2001. New Tools and New Tests in Comparative Political Economy: The Database of Political Institutions. *World Bank Economic Review* 15 (September): 165–76.

Bellin, Eva, 2004. The Robustness of Authoritarianism in the Middle East – Exceptionalism in Comparative Perspective. *Comparative Politics* 36: 139–57.

Blais, André. 2010. Political Participation. In *Comparing Democracies 3*. Lawrence LeDuc, Richard G. Niemi, and Pippa Norris, eds. Los Angeles: Sage Publications: 165–83.

Blaydes, Lisa. 2010. *Elections and Distributive Politics in Mubarak's Egypt*. Cambridge: Cambridge University Press.

Boix, Carles. 1999. Setting the Rules of the Game: The Choice of Electoral Systems in Advanced Democracies. *American Political Science Review* 93(3): 609–24.

Boix, Carles. 2003. *Democracy and Redistribution*. Cambridge: Cambridge University Press.

Borger, Julian and Ian Black. 2009. National: Turmoil in Iran: Poll Victory or Coup? World leaders urged by opposition to reject result: Defeated leader vows to head protest march: Massive show of force by Ahmadinejad supporters. *The Guardian* (London), June 15.

Brambor, Thomas, William Roberts Clark, and Matt Golder. 2006. Understanding Interaction Models: Improving Empirical Analysis. *Political Analysis* 14: 63–82.

Bratton, Michael. 1998. Second Elections in Africa. *Journal of Democracy* 9(3): 51–66.

Bratton, Michael and Nicholas van de Walle. 1997. *Democratic Experiments in Africa: Regime Transitions in Comparative Perspective*. Cambridge: Cambridge University Press.

Brownlee, Jason. 2007. *Authoritarianism in an Age of Democratization*. Cambridge: Cambridge University Press.

Brownlee, Jason. 2011. Executive Elections in the Arab World: When and How Do They Matter? *Comparative Political Studies* 44(7): 807–28.

Burns, John. F. 1996. Voters are few in Bangladesh as a dozen die in clashes. *New York Times,* February 16.

Cameroon: A Transition in Crisis. 1997. *Article 19: Global Campaign for Free Expression*. October.

Campbell, Tracy. 2003. Machine Politics, Police Corruption and the Persistence of Vote Fraud: The Case of the Louisville Kentucky Election of 1905. *Journal of Policy History* 15(3): 269–300.

Carothers, Thomas. 2002. The End of the Transition Paradigm. *Journal of Democracy* 13(1): 5–21.

Chandra, Kanchan. 2004. *Why Ethnic Parties Succeed: Patronage and Ethnic Head Counts in India*. Cambridge: Cambridge University Press.

Chong, Dennis. 1991. *Collective Action and the Civil Rights Movement*. Chicago: University of Chicago Press.

Chwe, Michael Suk-Young. 2001. *Rational Ritual: Culture, Coordination, and Common Knowledge*. Princeton, NJ: Princeton University Press.

Clayton, Jonathan. 2010. Civil war looms as troops open fire on protesters who want poll loser to quit. *The Times* (London), December 17.

Collier, Paul. 2009. *Wars, Guns, and Votes*. New York: Harper.

Colvin, Ross. 2009. Obama backs Karzai, despite vote-rigging. Reuters. http://www.reuters.com/articlePrint?articleId=USTRE59J59D20091102; accessed 11/2/09.

Cooper, Andrew F. and Thomas Legler. 2006. *Intervention without Intervening? The OAS Defense and Promotion of Democracy in the Americas*. New York: Palgrave MacMillan.

Cornelius, Wayne A. 2002. La eficacia de la compra y coaccion del voto en las elecciónes mexicanas de 2000. *Perfiles Latinoamericanos* 20: 11–32.

Cox, Gary W. 1987. *The Efficient Secret: The Cabinet and the Development of Political Parties in Victorian England*. New York: Cambridge University Press.

Cox, Gary W. 1997. *Making Votes Count: Strategic Coordination in the World's Electoral Systems*. New York: Cambridge University Press.

Cox, Gary W. and Jonathan N. Katz. 2002. *Elbridge Gerry's Salamander: The Electoral Consequences of the Reapportionment Revolution*. New York: Cambridge University Press.

7e

Cox, Gary W. and J. Morgan Kousser. 1981. Turnout and Rural Corruption: New York as a Test Case. *American Journal of Political Science* 25(4): 646–63.

Dahl, Robert A. 1971. *Polyarchy*. New Haven: Yale University Press.

DeNardo, James. 1985. *Power in Numbers: The Political Strategy of Protest and Rebellion*. Princeton, NJ: Princeton University Press.

Diamond, Larry. 2002. Thinking about Hybrid Regimes. *Journal of Democracy* 13(2): 21–35.

Diamond, Larry. 2010. Why Are There No Arab Democracies? *Journal of Democracy* 21(1): 93–104.

Di Lorenzo, Amanda and Enrico Sborgi. 2001. The 1999 Presidential and Legislative Elections in Niger. *Electoral Studies* 20(3): 470–6.

Dion, Douglas. 1997. Competition and Ethnic Conflict: Artifactual? *Journal of Conflict Resolution* 41(5): 638–48.

Dixon, Robyn. 2011. Africa's other corner of strife: Ivory Coast's post-election fury is escalating, and a peaceful outcome may not be possible. *Los Angeles Times*, March 25.

Dougherty, Kevin. 2011. Haitian election 'beautiful turn of events' observer says; Quebec MNA sees Martelly's rise as positive sign for nation's future. *The Gazette* (Montreal), April 6.

Eisinger, Peter K. 1973. The Conditions of Protest Behavior in American Cities. *American Political Science Review* 67(1): 11–28.

Elkins, Zachary. 2000. Gradations of Democracy? Empirical Tests of Alternative Conceptualizations. *American Journal of Political Science* 44(2): 293–300.

Farer, Tom J. 1993. Collectively Defending Democracy in a World of Sovereign States: The Western Hemisphere's Prospect. *Human Rights Quarterly* 15: 716–50.

Fathi, Nazila. 2009. A recount offer fails to silence protests in Iran. *New York Times*, June 17.

Fearon, James D. 1995. Rationalist Explanations for War. *International Organization* 49(3): 379–414.

Filkins, Dexter and Alissa J. Rubin. 2009. Karzai rival said to be planning to quit runoff. *New York Times*, November 1.

Fleischhacker, Helga. 1999. Gabon. In *Elections in Africa: A Data Handbook*. Dieter Nohlen, Michael Krennerich, and Bernhard Thibaut, eds. Oxford: Oxford University Press: 387–410.

Flores, Thomas Edward and Irfan Nooruddin. 2012. The Effects of Elections on Post-Conflict Peace and Reconstruction. *Journal of Politics* 74(2): 558–70.

Galloway, Gloria. 2009. Tensions soar as Karzai rejects opponent's call to fire election officials. *The Globe and Mail*, October 27.

Gandhi, Jennifer and Adam Przeworski. 2007. Authoritarian Institutions and the Survival of Autocrats. *Comparative Political Studies* 40, 1297–1301.

Geddes, Barbara. 1994. *Politician's Dilemma: Building State Capacity in Latin America*. Berkeley: University of California Press.

Gleditsch, Kristian Skrede and Giacomo Chiozza. 2009. Introducing Archigos: A Dataset of Political Leaders. *Journal of Peace Research* 46(2): 183–269.

Gleditsch, Kristian Skrede and Michael D. Ward, 2006. Diffusion and the International Control of Democratization. *International Organization* 60, 911–33.

Gorvin, Ian, ed. *Elections since 1945: A Worldwide Reference Compendium*. Chicago: St. James Press.

Greene, Kenneth F. 2007. *Why Dominant Parties Lose: Mexico's Democratization in Comparative Perspective*. Cambridge: Cambridge University Press.

Grotz, Florian and Maria Rodriguez-McKey. 2001. Armenia. In *Elections in Asia and the Pacific: A Data Handbook*. Dieter Nohlen, Florian Grotz, and Christof Hartmann, eds. Oxford: Oxford University Press: 319–46.

Grotz, Florian and Maria Rodriguez-McKey. 2001. Azerbaijan. In *Elections in Asia and the Pacific: A Data Handbook*. Dieter Nohlen, Florian Grotz, and Christof Hartmann, eds. Oxford: Oxford University Press: 347–70.

Hafner-Burton, Emilie, Susan D. Hyde, and Ryan S. Jablonski. 2013. When Do Governments Resort to Election Violence? *British Journal of Political Science*. Published online February 26, 2013.

Hartlyn, Jonathan. 1998. *The Struggle for Democratic politics in the Dominican Republic*. Chapel Hill, NC: The University of North Carolina Press.

Howard, Marc Morjé and Philip G. Roessler. 2006. Liberalizing Electoral Outcomes in Competitive Authoritarian Regimes. *American Journal of Political Science* 50(2): 365–381.

Huntington, Samuel P. 1991. *The Third Wave: Democratization in the Late Twentieth Century*. Norman: University of Oklahoma Press.

Hyde, Susan D. 2011. *The Pseudo-Democrat's Dilemma: Why Election Monitoring Became an International Norm*. Ithaca: Cornell University Press.

Hyde, Susan D. and Nikolay Marinov. 2012. Which Elections can be Lost? *Political Analysis* 20(2): 191–210.

Jamal, Amaney. 2008. *Barriers to Democracy: The Other Side of Social Capital in Palestine and the Arab World*. Princeton, NJ: Princeton University Press.

Kelly, Judith. 2011. Do International Election Monitors Increase or Decrease Election Boycotts? *Comparative Political Studies* 44: 1527–56.

Kelly, Judith. 2012. *Monitoring Democracy: When International Observation Works, and Why It Often Fails*. Princeton, NJ: Princeton University Press.

Khoury, Philip S. and Joseph Kostiner. 1990. *Tribes and State Formation in the Middle East*. Berkeley: University of California Press.

King, Gary, Jennifer Pan, and Margaret E. Roberts. 2013. How Censorship in China Allows Government Criticism but Silences Collective Action. *American Political Science Review*.

Lehoucq, Fabrice. 2003. Electoral Fraud: Causes, Types, and Consequences. *Annual Review of Political Science* 6: 233–56.

Lehoucq, Fabrice. 2007. When Does a Market for Votes Emerge? In *Elections for Sale: The Causes and Consequences of Vote Buying*. Frederic Charles Schaffer, ed. Boulder: Lynner Rienner: 33–46.

Lehoucq, Fabrice and Ivan Molina. 2002. *Stuffing the Ballot Box: Fraud, Electoral Reform, and Democratization in Costa Rica*. Cambridge: Cambridge University Press.

Levitsky, Stephen and Lucan Way. 2010. *Competitive Authoritarianism: Hybrid Regimes after the Cold War*. Cambridge: Cambridge University Press.

Lindberg, Staffan I. 2005. Consequences of Electoral Systems in Africa: A Preliminary Inquiry. *Electoral Studies* 24: 41–64.

Lindberg, Staffan I. 2006a. *Democracy and Elections in Africa*. Baltimore: Johns Hopkins University Press.

Lindberg, Staffan I. 2006b. Opposition Parties and Democratisation in Sub-Saharan Africa. *Journal of Contemporary African Studies* 24(1)123–38.

Lohmann, Susanne. 1994. The Dynamics of Informational Cascades: The Monday Demonstrations in Leipzig, East Germany 1989–91. *World Politics* 47: 42–101.

Lust, Ellen. 2009. Competitive Clientelism in the Middle East. *Journal of Democracy* 20(3): 122–35.

Lust-Okar, Ellen. 2005. *Structuring Conflict in the Arab World: Incumbents, Opponents, and Institutions*. Cambridge: Cambridge University Press.

Magaloni, Beatriz. 2006. *Voting for Autocracy: Hegemonic Party Survival and its Demise in Mexico*. Cambridge: Cambridge University Press.

Magaloni, Beatriz. 2008. Credible Power-Sharing and the Longevity of Authoritarian Rule. *Comparative Political Studies* 41: 715–41.

Marcus, Richard R. and Paul Razafindrakoto. 2003. Participation and the Poverty of Electoral Democracy in Madagascar. *Afrika Spectrum* 38(1): 28.

Marinov, Nikolay. 2006. Is the Globalization of Elections Good for Democracy? Presented at the International Studies Association annual convention, March 22–25.

Marshall, Monty G., Keith Jagers, and Ted Robert Gurr. 2010. *Polity IV Project: Regime Characteristics and Transitions, 1800–2010*. Vienna, VA: Center for Systemic Peace.

McAdam, Douglas. 1982. *Political Process and the Development of Black Insurgency, 1930–1970*. Chicago: University of Chicago Press.

McCarthy, John D. and Mayer N. Zald. 1977. Resource Mobilization and Social Movements: A Partial Theory. *American Journal of Sociology* 82(6): 1212–41.

Migdal, Joel. 1974. *Peasants, Politics, and Revolution*. Princeton, NJ: Princeton University Press.

Miller, Warren E. 1999. Temporal Order and Causal Inference. *Political Analysis* 8(2): 119–46.

Muskal, Michael. 2009. US congratulates Afghan President Karzai on another term in office. *Los Angeles Times*, November 2.

Mwanasali, Musafiky. 2008. From Non-Interference to Non-Indifference: The Emerging Doctrine of Conflict Prevention in Africa. In *The African Union and its Institutions*. John Akokpari, Angela Ndinga-Muvumba and Tim Murithi, eds, *The African Union and its Institutions*. Cape Town: Fanele: 41–62.

National Democratic Institute. 1997. Parliamentary Elections in Indonesia: A Background Paper. May 23. Washington, DC: National Democratic Institute.

N'Diaye, Boubacar. 2001. Mauritania's Stalled Democratization. *Journal of Democracy* 12(3): 88–95.

Nohlen, Dieter. 2005. *Elections in the Americas: A Data Handbook*. Oxford: Oxford University Press.

Nohlen, Dieter, Michael Kennerich, and Bernhard Thibaut. 1999. *Elections in Africa: A Data Handbook*. Oxford: Oxford University Press.

Nohlen, Dieter, Florian Grotz and Christof Hartmann. 2001. *Elections in Asia and the Pacific: A Data Handbook*. Oxford: Oxford University Press.

Nooruddin, Irfan. 2002. Modeling Selection Bias in Studies of Sanction Efficacy. *International Interactions* 28(1): 57–74.

North, Douglass C. and Barry Weingast. 1989. Constitutions and Commitment: The Evolution of Institutions Governing Public Choice in Seventeenth Century England. *Journal of Economic History* (49): 803–32.

Ottoway, Marina. 2003. *Democracy Challenged: The Rise of Semi-Authoritarianism*. Washington, DC: Carnegie Endowment for International Peace.

Page, Jeremy. 2009. Election stalemate after Karzai rejects rival's plan. *The Times* (London), October 27.

Pastor, Robert. 1999. The Role of Election Administration in Democratic Transitions: Implications for Policy and Research. *Democratization* 6(4): 1–27.

Phillips, Sarah. 2008. *Yemen's Democracy Experiment in Regional Perspective*. New York: Palgrave Macmillan.

Phillips, Peter. 2005. Interviewed by Emily Beaulieu. Digital recording. April 14.

PM offers vote compromise to end Bangladeshi strikes. 1996. *The Gazette* (Montreal), March 27.

Political reforms in Mauritania. 2000. *Financial Times Information*, December 14.

Pop-Eleches, Grigore and Graeme B. Robertson. 2009. Elections, Information and Liberalization in the Post Cold War Era. Presented at the APSA annual meeting. Toronto.

Posusney, Marsha Pripstein. 2002. Multi-Party Elections in the Arab World: Institutional Engineering and Oppositional Strategies. *Studies in Comparative International Development* 36(4): 34–62.

Posusney, Marsha Pripstein. 2005. Multiparty Elections in the Arab World: Election Rules and Opposition Responses. In *Authoritarianism in the Middle East*. Marsha Pripstein Posusney and Michele Penner Angrist, eds. Boulder, CO: Lynne Reinner.

Powell, Robert. 1999. *In the Shadow of Power*. Princeton, NJ: Princeton University Press.

Przeworski, Adam. 1991. *Democracy and the Market: Political and economic reforms in Eastern Europeand Latin America*. Cambridge: Cambridge University Press.

Przeworski, Adam. 2009. Conquered or Granted? A History of Suffrage Extensions. *British Journal of Political Science* 39: 291–321.

Przeworski, Adam, Michael E. Alvarez, José Antonio Cheibub and Fernando Limongi. 2000. *Democracy and Development: Political Institutions and Well-Being in the World, 1950–1990*. Cambridge: Cambridge University Press.

Reif, Megan. 2009. Beyond the Bhutto Assassination: Competitiveness and Electoral Violence at the Constituency- and Polling-Station Levels in Pakistan's 2008 National Assembly Elections. Presented at the Midwest Political Science Association annual meeting, Chicago.

Renwick, Alan. 2010. *The Politics of Electoral Reform: Changing the Rules of Democracy*. Cambridge: Cambridge University Press.

Roberts, David. 1994. The Cambodian Elections of 1993. *Electoral Studies* 13(2): 157–62.

Robertson, Graeme B. 2011. *The Politics of Protest in Hybrid Regimes: Managing Dissent in Post-Communist Russia*. New York: Cambridge University Press.

Ross, Michael. 2001. Does Oil Hinder Democracy? *World Politics* 53(3): 325–61.

Saikal, A. 2005. Afghanistan's Weak State and Strong Society. In *Making States Work: State Failure and the Crisis of Governance*. Simon Chesterman, Michael Ignatieff, and Ramesh Thakur, eds. Washington, DC: United Nations University Press.

Schattschneider, Elmer E. 1960. *The Semi-Sovereign People*. New York: Holt, Rinehart and Winston.

Schaffer, Frederic Charles. 2008. *The Hidden Costs of Clean Election Reform*. Ithaca: Cornell University Press.

Schedler, Andreas. 2002. Elections without Democracy: The Menu of Manipulation. *Journal of Democracy* 13(2): 36–50.

Schedler, Andreas. 2006. The Logic of Electoral Authoritarianism. In *Electoral Authoritarianism: The Dynamics of Unfree Competition*. Andreas Schedler, ed. Boulder, CO: Lynne Rienner: 1–26.

Schmitter, Phillipe and Terry Karl. 1991. What Democracy Is, and Is Not. *Journal of Democracy* 2(3).

Shahrani, M. Nazif. 1998. The Future of the State and the Structure of Community Governance. In *Fundamentalism Reborn? Afghanistan and the Taliban*. W. Maley, ed. London: Hurst & Company: 212–42.

Simpser, Alberto. 2013. *Why Governments and Parties Manipulate Elections: Theory, Practice, and Implications*. New York: Cambridge University Press.

Skocpol, Theda. 1979. *States and Social Revolutions*. Cambridge: Cambridge University

Snyder, Jack. 2000. *From Voting to Violence: Democratization and Nationalist Conflict*. New York: W. W. Norton Company.

Starkey, Jerome. 2009. Vote fraud could be worse this time, say observers. *The Times* (London), October 30.

Tapper, Richard. 1983. *The Conflict of Tribe and State in Iran and Afghanistan*. New York: St. Martin's Press.

Tarrow, Sidney. 1989. *Democracy and Disorder: Protest and Politics in Italy, 1965–1975*. Oxford: Clarendon Press.

Teorell, Jan, Mariano Torcal, and José Ramón Montero. 2007. Political Participation: Mapping the Terrain. In *Citizenship and Involvement in European Democracies: A Comparative Analysis*. Jan Van Deth, José Ramón Montero, and Anders Westholm, eds. London: Routledge: 334–357

Tezcür, Güneş Murat. 2012. Democracy Promotion, Authoritarian Resiliency, and Political Unrest in Iran. *Democratization* 19(1): 120–40.

Thibaut, Bernhard. 1999. Comoros. In *Elections in Africa: A Data Handbook*. Dieter Nohlen, Michael Krennerich, and Bernhard Thibaut, eds. Oxford: Oxford University Press.

Tilly, Charles. 2004. *Contention and Democracy in Europe, 1650–2000*. Cambridge: Cambridge University Press.

Trefs, Matthias. 2005. Guyana. *Elections in the Americas: A Data Handbook, Volume 1*. Oxford: Oxford University Press: 353–72.

Tucker, Joshua A. 2007. Enough! Electoral Fraud, Collective Action Problems, and the "2nd Wave" of Post-Communist Democratic Revolutions. *Perspectives on Politics*, 5(3): 537–53.

Volpi, F. 2004. Pseudo-Democracy in the Muslim World. *Third World Quarterly* 25 (6): 1061–78.

Wang, Chin-Shou and Charles Kurzman. 2007. The Logistics: How to Buy Votes. In *Elections for Sale: The Causes and Consequences of Vote Buying*. Frederic Charles Schaffer, ed. Boulder, CO: Lynner Rienner: 61–80.

Wedeen, Lisa. 2008. *Peripheral Visions: Publics, Power, and Performance in Yemen*. Chicago: University of Chicago Press.

Wilkinson, Steven. 2004. *Votes and Violence: Electoral Competition and Ethnic Riots in India*. Cambridge: Cambridge University Press.

Wintrobe, Ronald. 1998. *The Political Economy of Dictatorship*. Cambridge: Cambridge University Press.

Worth, Robert F. and Nazila Fathi. 2009. Defiance grows as Iran's leader sets vote review. *New York Times*, June 16.

Zakaria, Fareed. 1997. The Rise of Illiberal Democracy. *Foreign Affairs* 76(6): 22–43.

Ziblatt, Daniel. 2009. Shaping Democratic Practice and the Causes of Electoral Fraud: The Case of Nineteenth-Century Germany. *American Political Science Review* 103(1): 1–21.

Index

manipulation (*cont.*)
 incumbent, and incumbent victory, 96
 incumbent, bargaining failure concerning,
  56
 incumbent's chosen level of, 28
 incumbent's previous choices, 41
 level opposition will accept, 38
 levels of, 62
 levels of pro-incumbent, 61
 lower levels of, 33
 negative perceptions of, 39
 negotiations over, 51
 opportunities for, 33
 opposition, 128
 opposition knowledge of, 39
 opposition motivation to expose, 76
 opposition tolerance for, 48
 opposition toleration of, 35, 39
 overall level of, 78
 past incumbent, 40
 pre-election by incumbent, 57
 prior, impact of, 42
 promised incumbent level of, 62
 promised level of, 44
 reduction by incumbent of, 48
 safeguards against, 50
 strategic, 68
 tolerated by opposition, 70
 total amount incumbent undertakes, 32
 unacceptable level of, 42
 verification of, 44
 vote count, 45
Manley, Michael, 169
Manukyan, Vazgen, 91, 160
Marcos, Ferdinand, 118, 174, 175, 189
Marcus, Richard R. and Razafindrakoto, Paul,
  54, 199
Marinov, Nikolay, 10, 199
Marshall, Monty G., Keith Jagers, and Ted
  Robert Gurr, 62, 106, 199
Martelly, Michel, 99
mass demonstrations, 1, 17, 58, 69, 110, 142,
  160, 161, 162, 163, 164, 169, 171, 173,
  175, 179
 and boycotted elections, 107
 and incumbent response, 108
 and opposition support, 100
 and post-election protest, 142
 as bargaining failure, 72
 causes of, 46
 causes of post-election, 23
 consequences of post-elections, 48

 in Bangladesh, 95
 launched by opposition, 56
 opposition in Ukraine, 94
 opposition-initiated, 92, 129
 opposition-led, 109
 organization and initiation of, 69
 post-election, 46, 69, 70, 72, 73, 74, 75, 76,
  78, 90, 92, 93, 94, 95, 99, 100, 109, 140,
  142, 143
 post-election in Cote d'Ivoire, 80
 post-election in Dominican Republic, 68
 post-election in Philippines, 74
 post-election opposition-initiated, 74
 post-election, probability of, 72
 pre-election in Azerbaijan, 114
 reform following post-election, 23
 relationship to elections, 72
 U.S.-funded in Guyana, 52
Massachusetts
 Australian ballot adopted by, 11
Mauritania, 105, 155, 172, 187, 199, 200
 major election boycott in 1997, 105
McAdam, Douglas, 6, 199
McCarthy, John D. and Mayer N. Zald, 5,
  199
McFoul, Michael, 133
media
 absence of reliable, 42
 coverage of incumbents, 33
 coverage of opposition in, 47
 favorable coverage, 40
 in developing countries, 128
 lack of reliable, 17
 lack of reliable and independent, 40
 laws pertaining to freedom of, 102
 monopolization of, 16
 numbers of outlets, 61
 observers in global, 90
 pressure on, 78
 restrictions, 102
 television, radio, or print, 41
Mexico, 23, 76, 172, 187, 188, 198, 199
 2006 elections in, 76
 as democratized, 21
 election law in, 103
 resource imbalance in, 16
 survey, 44
Middle East, 32, 86, 89, 111, 195, 198, 199
 elections in, 16
 incumbent manipulation in, 33
 Iran as part of, 133
Midgal, Joel, 6, 199